The
Mediation
Process

Practical Strategies
for Resolving Conflict

Christopher W. Moore

The Mediation Process

*Practical Strategies
for Resolving Conflict*

Jossey-Bass Publishers

San Francisco • London • 1987

THE MEDIATION PROCESS
Practical Strategies for Resolving Conflict
by Christopher W. Moore

Copyright © 1986 by: Jossey-Bass Inc., Publishers
433 California Street
San Francisco, California 94104

Jossey-Bass Limited
28 Banner Street
London EC1Y 8QE

Christopher W. Moore
2337 Ninth Street
Boulder, Colorado 80302

Library of Congress Cataloging-in-Publication Data
Moore, Christopher W. (date)
  The mediation process.

  (The Jossey-Bass social and behavioral science
series)
  Bibliography: p. 321
  Includes index.
  1. Mediation. 2. Conflict management. I. Title.
II. Series.
HM136.M684   1986   302.3   85-23675
ISBN 0-87589-673-1 (alk. paper)

Manufactured in the United States of America

The paper in this book meets the guidelines for
permanence and durability of the Committee on
Production Guidelines for Book Longevity of the
Council on Library Resources.

JACKET DESIGN BY WILLI BAUM
FIRST EDITION
        First printing: March 1986
        Second printing: January 1987
        Third printing: October 1987

Code 8603

The Jossey-Bass
Social and Behavioral Science Series

Preface

All societies, communities, organizations, and interpersonal relationships experience conflict at one time or another in the process of day-to-day interaction. Conflict is not necessarily bad, abnormal, or dysfunctional; it is a fact of life. Conflict and disputes exist when people are engaged in competition to meet goals that are perceived as, or actually are, incompatible. However, conflict may go beyond competitive behavior and acquire the additional goals of inflicting physical or psychological damage on or destroying an opponent. It is then that the negative and harmful dynamics of conflict take their full costs.

All disputes, however, do not have to follow the negative course described above. Conflict can lead to growth and be productive for all parties. Productive conflict resolution, however, depends on the abilities of the participants to devise efficient cooperative problem-solving procedures, the participants' capacities to lay aside distrust and animosity and work together, and the availability of solutions that will at least partially satisfy all of the participants' interests. Unfortunately, many people in conflict are unable to develop an effective process, deal with the psychological barriers to settlement, or develop integrative solutions on their own. People in conflict often need help to resolve their differences.

Mediation, the assistance of a neutral and impartial third party in helping people resolve their own differences, has a long history of application. However, until now there has not been a comprehensive work that details what mediators actually do to aid people in conflict. There are several reasons why so little has been written on the actual practice of mediation, as opposed to defining the procedure's merits or applications. First, mediators themselves disagree about whether mediation is an art or a science. Many mediators believe that their practice is closer to an art form and have been reluctant to encourage, or have actively resisted, systematic study of what they do.

Second, many mediators subscribe to what might be described as the "magic theory" of mediation. A mediator's skills or moves are considered secrets that, if revealed to the public, would render them less effective. Thus some mediators have inhibited research by protecting their "secrets."

A third argument against careful analysis of the mediation process is the confidential nature of the subject matter that the people in conflict discuss and the confidentiality of the mediation process itself. This confidentiality has often been a barrier to research. (Yet for years researchers have studied psychiatric cases, which presumably fall under the same privacy or confidentiality restriction as mediated disputes.)

A fourth inhibiting factor is the problem of inserting researchers into highly polarized, multiple-party disputes where the acceptability and presence of "neutral" third parties is in itself controversial. The mediator's presence is often tenuous. Parties are often even less likely to accept the presence of researchers who wish to study the process of mediation.

Fifth, researchers in conflict resolution have generally focused more on negotiation as a means of dispute resolution than on mediation. Negotiation has been studied by game theorists, economists, social psychologists, anthropologists, legal scholars, industrial relations researchers, and international relations scholars. Clearly more emphasis has been placed on resolution of disputes by the principal parties than on resolution through third-party intervention.

Finally, mediation has not been studied because the process encompasses a variety of skills and is practiced in so many different ways that researchers have encountered difficulties in focusing on such a comprehensive process.

During the past twelve years, I have been actively involved as a mediator of organizational, environmental, family, community, criminal, and public policy disputes. This broad experience leads me to believe that there are some common mediation principles and procedures that can be applied effectively to a wide range of conflicts. This belief has been confirmed by the literature in the field of mediation. There is a great need for a general work on mediation that details the "how-to" aspects of the process.

The Mediation Process: Practical Strategies for Resolving Conflict integrates my personal experience and research, detailing what is known about the mediation process as it has been applied in a variety of areas and types of disputes. This book outlines how mediation fits into the larger field of dispute resolution and negotiation and then presents a comprehensive stage-by-stage sequence of activities that can be used by mediators to assist participants in disputes to reach agreement.

I have written this book for several groups. First are the practicing mediators who work in a variety of arenas and who have repeatedly expressed their need for a comprehensive description of mediation process and theory. The book should be helpful to practitioners in labor, family, organizational, environmental, public policy, community, and other diverse areas of mediation practice.

Second are professionals—lawyers, managers, therapists, social workers, planners, and teachers—who handle conflicts on a daily basis. Although these professionals may choose to become full-time mediators, they are more likely to use mediation principles and procedures as additional tools to help them within their chosen fields of work. The material presented here will aid any professional who wishes to promote cooperative problem solving between his or her clients.

Third are people who have to negotiate solutions to complex problems. Since mediation is an extension of the negotiation process and, in fact, a collection of techniques to promote more efficient negotiations, an understanding of the mediation process can be tremendously helpful for people directly involved in bargaining. Mediation can teach negotiators how to be cooperative rather than competitive problem solvers and how to achieve win-win rather than win-lose outcomes. An understanding of mediation can also aid negotiators in deciding when to call in a third party and what the intervenor should do for them.

Fourth are trainees and students in both mediation training programs and academic seminars in alternative dispute resolution. This book is suitable for use in law, business, social work, counseling, management, education, sociology, and psychology seminars. Undergraduates as well as graduates will find it useful in learning mediation skills.

Overview of the Contents

Part One provides an overview of the entire process of mediation and dispute resolution. Chapter One describes the broad field of dispute resolution and details how mediation fits in as an important means of handling conflicts. In this chapter I present a spectrum of conflict management approaches and identify when mediation is appropriate and when it has a high probability of success. Chapter Two examines the mediation process in more depth. After defining mediation, I explore some of the types of disputes to which the procedure has been applied, introduce the twelve stages of the mediation process, and survey several variables that determine how directive the mediator should be in his or her interventions.

Part Two discusses mediator activities that occur *prior* to joint negotiations between the disputing parties. Chapter Three covers procedures for mediator entry and explores both how an intervenor becomes involved in a dispute and what impact being invited by a sole party, all parties, or an uninvolved secondary party has on the final settlement. Chapter Four describes the process of searching for a dispute resolution approach and arena with the parties. Procedures that can assist disputants in evaluating the various methods of resolving their conflicts are covered, and the means of deciding which approach to use are explored.

Chapter Five presents data collection techniques that mediators can use to gather information about the parties' negotiation procedures and the substantive issues in dispute. Special emphasis is placed on the skills used to intervene in conflict situations. Chapter Six explores procedures for designing a mediation plan. Who should be involved, the physical setup of the session, and strategies for the first session are detailed. Chapter Seven examines procedures for conciliation, the process of emotionally preparing the parties for negotiation over substantive issues. Techniques for responding to strong emotions, perceptual problems, and communication difficulties are discussed.

Part Three explores mediation procedures in joint session with all disputants present. Chapter Eight focuses on beginning a joint session with the disputing parties. Strategies and opening statements for both the intervenor and the parties are described and analyzed. Chapters Nine and Ten examine the steps by which the issues in dispute can be identified; an agenda can be developed; and the substantive, procedural, and psychological interests of the parties can be explored. The useful technique of reframing, or defining, issues and interests is presented. Chapter Eleven presents procedures and strategies for generating settlement options. The technique of proposal-counterproposal as well as more cooperative problem-solving methods is described.

Part Four covers the conclusion of mediation and the various steps involved in reaching a settlement. Chapters Twelve and Thirteen present procedures for assessing settlement options and preparing final agreement packages. In these chapters I explore acceptable bargaining ranges, incremental convergence, leaps to agreement, procedures for building bargaining formulas, and the usefulness of deadlines. Chapter Fourteen discusses how agreements can be finalized. Procedures for drafting, increasing compliance, and monitoring agreements are examined. Chapter Fifteen addresses specific techniques and problems that are encountered in some but not all disputes. Both the caucus and mediator power are examined, as are procedures for working with multiparty disputes and for funding mediation. A brief conclusion rounds out the text.

The resources contain a code of professional conduct that

has served as a model for several states and mediation programs, a sample contact letter, a form that explains the confidential nature of the mediation process, and two sample agreements.

Acknowledgments

All knowledge is socially produced. Although I bear responsibility for the identification, elaboration, and development of the ideas presented in this book, I have clearly drawn on the experiences and advice of others engaged in the practice of mediation.

The first group of people to whom I am indebted are my fellow mediators. Since 1973 when I first became involved in mediating an intense interracial community dispute, I have worked with four active groups of mediators and conflict resolvers. Each group has contributed significant insights and pushed me to develop my thinking.

First and foremost are the mediators at the Center for Dispute Resolution in Denver, Colorado: Susan Wildau, Mary Margaret Golten, Bernard Mayer, and our associates and interns. They have been my colleagues in developing and practicing many of the ideas contained in this book. Susan Carpenter and W. J. D. Kennedy of ACCORD Associates also provided insights and support in researching and refining mediation theory and practice while I worked as a mediator and director of training for that organization. The members of the Training Action Affinity Group of the Movement for a New Society—Suzanne Terry, Stephen Parker, Peter Woodrow, and Berit Lakey—and the authors of the *Resource Manual for a Living Revolution*—Virginia Coover, Charles Esser, and Ellen Deacon—worked with me to develop intervention skills for multiparty disputes and effective conflict resolution training techniques. Work with academic colleagues was also important. Norman Wilson, Paul Wehr, and Martin Oppenhimer encouraged and supported my research.

Mentioned above are the theoretical and experiential contributors. Just as important are the people who type the drafts and edit them. First and foremost of my "technical advisers" is

Nancy Wigington. Nancy worked with me from the beginning; without her assistance, this project would not have been possible. I acknowledge the editorial assistance and encouragement of my parents, Benjamin and Bess Moore, who helped assemble the final draft, and the emotional support of the Juniper Street Collective, Tom, Sara, Joan, and Peter Mayer, Reggie Grey, Ethan Green, Chet Tchozewski, and Bernard Mayer. A final word of thanks to Susan Wildau and Stephanie Jusdon for their faith in me as a scholar and reflective practitioner and for emotional support during graduate school.

Boulder, Colorado   Christopher W. Moore
January 1986

Contents

Preface   ix

The Author   xxi

Part One: Understanding Dispute Resolution and Mediation

1. Approaches to Managing and Resolving Conflict   1

   The Singson-Whittamore Dispute • Conflict Management and Resolution Approaches

2. How Mediation Works   13

   A Definition of Mediation • Arenas of Mediation • Mediation Activities: Moves and Interventions • Hypothesis Building and Mediation Interventions • The Stages of Mediation • Variables That Influence Mediation Strategies and Moves

Part Two: Laying the Groundwork for Effective Mediation

3. Initial Contacts with the Disputing Parties   44

   Tasks of the Mediator in the Entry Stage • Implementing Entry • Timing of Entry

4. Selecting a Strategy to Guide Mediation   61

Mediator-Disputant Relationship for Making Decisions • Ap-
proach and Arena Decision: General Move Categories •
Identification of Interests • Dispute Outcomes • Criteria for
Selecting an Approach and Arena • Conflict Strategies and
Approaches • Selecting and Making a Commitment to an
Approach and Arena • Coordination of Approaches and
Arenas

5. Collecting and Analyzing Background Information   78

Framework for Analysis • Selecting an Appropriate Data
Collection Method • Selecting the Appropriate Data Col-
lector • Data Collection Strategy Selection • The Appro-
priate Interviewing Approach • Interviewing: Appropriate
Questions and the Listening Process • Conflict Analysis •
Data Reporting • Integrating the Information • Verifying
Data • Interpreting Data

6. Designing a Detailed Plan for Mediation   103

Participants in Negotiations • Location of Negotiations •
Physical Arrangement of the Setting • Negotiation Procedures • Issues, Interests, and Settlement Options • Psychological Conditions of the Parties • Establishing Ground
Rules or Behavioral Guidelines • Establishing a Tentative
Agenda • Educating the Parties and Gaining a Commitment
to Begin • Identifying Special Problems

7. Building Trust and Cooperation   124

Strong Emotions • Misperceptions or Stereotypes • Special
Perceptual Problems • Perception of Trust • Communication
and Conciliation • Nonverbal Communication

Part Three: Conducting Productive Mediation

8. Beginning the Mediation Session   153

Opening Statements • How Parties Begin Negotiating •
Choosing an Opening to Negotiations • Turning the Negotiation Session Over to Disputants • Facilitating Communication and Information Exchange • Establishing a Positive
Emotional Climate

9. Defining Issues and Setting an Agenda   172

Topic Areas and Issues • Identifying and Framing Issues •
Variables in Framing and Reframing Issues • Explicit-

Implicit Reframing and Timing • Appropriate Language or Syntax • Determining an Agenda • Procedural Assistance from the Mediator

10. Uncovering Hidden Interests of the
Disputing Parties   187

Difficulties in Identifying Interests • Procedures for Identifying Interests • Productive Attitudes • Indirect Moves for Discovering Interests • Direct Moves for Discovering Interests • Positions, Interests, and Bluffs • Interest Identification, Acceptance, and Agreement

11. Generating Options for Settlement   199

Developing an Awareness of the Need for Options • Strategies for Option Generation • Procedures for Generating Options • Option Generation Procedures • Types of Settlement Options

Part Four: Reaching a Settlement

12. Assessing Options for Settlement   218

The Settlement Range • Recognizing the Settlement Range • Negative Settlement Range

13. Final Bargaining   227

Incremental Convergence • Leap to Agreement • Formulas and Agreements in Principle • Procedural Means of Reaching Substantive Decisions • Deadlines • Mediators and Deadline Management • Enhancing the Usefulness of Deadlines

14. Achieving Formal Settlement   248

Implementing the Settlement • Criteria for Compliance and Implementation Steps • Monitoring the Performance of Agreements • Formalizing Settlement

15. Strategies for Dealing with Special Situations   262

Caucuses • Mediator Power and Influence • Multiperson Negotiating Teams • Teams with Constituents • Mediation Services Funding • Funding the Parties Themselves

Conclusion   297

Resource A
Code of Professional Conduct   299

Resource B
Sample Contact Letter   308

Resource C
Sample Waiver and Consent Form   310

Resource D
Sample Agreements   312

References   321

Index   337

The Author

Christopher W. Moore is a partner in the Center for Dispute Resolution in Denver, Colorado. He received his B.A. degree (1969) from Juniata College in history, his M.A. degree (1972) from Antioch-Putney Graduate School in teaching social studies, and his Ph.D. degree (1983) from Rutgers, The State University of New Jersey, in political sociology and development.

Since the early 1970s, Moore's major work has been in the field of dispute resolution. He has mediated community, domestic, housing, criminal, business, organizational, and environmental disputes, and he has served as a trainer of conflict managers for a variety of conflicts. Moore has developed and conducted training programs on general and domestic mediation and negotiation; these programs are also presented nationwide by the staff of the Center for Dispute Resolution. He has also pioneered seminars on natural resource conflict management that have been sponsored by the U.S. Geological Survey, U.S. Forest Service, Minerals Management Service, Bureau of Land Management, and the U.S. Army Corps of Engineers.

Moore's books include *Natural Resources Conflict Management* (1982), *Building Social Change Communities* (1978,

xxi

with others) and *Resource Manual for a Living Revolution* (1976, with others). He is a member of the Society of Professionals in Dispute Resolution, a mediator and arbitrator for the American Arbitration Association, and a member of the Association of Family and Conciliation Courts.

The
Mediation
Process

Practical Strategies
for Resolving Conflict

ONE

Approaches to Managing and Resolving Conflict

Conflict seems to be present in all human relationships and in all societies. From the beginning of recorded history, we have evidence of disputes among children, spouses, parents and children, neighbors, ethnic and racial groups, fellow workers, superiors and subordinates, organizations, communities, citizens and their government, and nations. Because of the pervasive presence of conflict and because of the physical, emotional, and resource costs that often result from disputes, people have always sought to find ways of resolving their differences. The solutions they seek are those that allow them to satisfy their interests and minimize their costs.

In most disputes, the people involved have a variety of means at their disposal to respond to or resolve their conflict. An examination of a sample dispute will illustrate the possible options.

The Singson-Whittamore Dispute

Singson and Whittamore are in conflict. It all started three years ago when Dr. Richard Singson, director of the Fairview Medical Clinic, one of the few medical service providers in a small rural town, was seeking two physicians to fill open positions on his staff. After several months of extensive and difficult recruiting, he hired two doctors, Andrew and Janelle Whitta-

more, to fill the respective positions of pediatrician and gyne-
cologist. The fact that the doctors were married did not seem to
be a problem at the time they were hired.

Fairview Clinic liked to keep its doctors and generally
paid them well for their work with patients. The clinic was also
concerned about maintaining its patient load and income and
required each doctor joining the practice to sign a five-year contract detailing what he or she was to be paid and what conditions
would apply should the contract be broken by either party. One
of these conditions was a no-competition clause stating that
should a doctor choose to leave the clinic prior to the expiration of the contract, he or she could not practice medicine in
the town or county in which the Fairview Clinic was located
without paying a penalty. This clause was designed to protect
the clinic from competition and to prohibit a doctor from joining the staff, building up a practice, and then leaving with his or
her patients to start a private competitive practice before the
term of the contract had expired.

When Andrew and Janelle joined the Fairview Clinic
staff, they both signed the contract and initialed all the clauses.
Both doctors performed well in their jobs at the clinic and were
respected by their colleagues and patients. Unfortunately, their
personal life did not fare so well. The Whittamores' marriage
went into a steady decline almost as soon as they began working
at Fairview. Their arguments increased, and the amount of tension between them mounted to the point that they decided to
get a divorce. Since both parents wanted to be near their two
young children, they agreed to continue living in the same
town.

Since each physician at the clinic had a specialty, they all
relied on consultations with their colleagues. Thus, some interaction between the estranged couple was inevitable. Over time
the hostility between the couple grew to such a point that the
Whittamores decided one of them should leave the clinic, for
their own good and that of other clinic staff. Since they believed Andrew, as a pediatrician, would have an easier time finding patients, they agreed that he was the one who should go.

Andrew explained his situation to Singson and noted that

because he would be leaving for the benefit of the clinic, he expected that no penalty would be assessed for breaking the contract two-and-a-half years early and that the no-competition clause would not be applied to him.

Singson was surprised and upset that his finely tuned staff was going to lose one of its most respected members. And he was shocked by Whittamore's announcement that he planned to stay in town and open up a medical practice. Singson visualized the long-range impact of Whittamore's decision: The doctor would leave and set up a competing practice, and many of his patients would leave the clinic and follow him. The clinic would lose revenues from the doctor's fees, lose patients, incur the cost of recruiting a new doctor, and, if the no-competition clause was not enforced, establish a bad precedent for managing doctors in the clinic. Singson responded that the no-competition clause would be enforced if Whittamore wanted to practice within the county, and the clinic would have to arrive at a penalty for violating the contract. He estimated that the penalty could be as much as 100 percent of the revenues that Whittamore might earn in the two-and-a-half years remaining on his contract.

Whittamore was irate at Singson's response. He considered it unreasonable and irresponsible. If that was the way the game was to be played, he threatened, he would leave and set up a practice, and Singson could take him to court to try to get his money. Singson responded that he would get an injunction against the practice if necessary and would demand the full amount if pushed into a corner. Whittamore left Singson's office mumbling that he was going to "get that son of a gun" as he went down the hall.

This conflict has several different parts: the Whittamores' relationship with each other, the Whittamores' relationship to other staff members of the clinic, the potential conflict between Andrew Whittamore's patients and the clinic, and Andrew Whittamore's relationship with Richard Singson. For ease of analysis, we will examine only the Singson-Whittamore component of the dispute. What alternative means of conflict resolution do these two people have to handle their differences?

Conflict Management and Resolution Approaches

People in conflict in this society have a variety of means of resolving their disputes. Figure 1 illustrates some of these choices. Each of these options varies concerning the formality of the process, the privacy of the approach, the people involved, the authority of the third party (if there is one), the type of decision that will result, and the amount of coercion that is exercised by or on the disputing parties.

On the left-hand side of the continuum are informal, private procedures that involve only the disputants. On the other end, one party relies on coercion and often on public action to force the opposing party into submission. In between are a variety of approaches that we will examine in more detail.

Disagreements and problems can arise in almost any relationship. The majority of disagreements are usually handled informally. People often *avoid* each other because the issue is not that important, because they do not have the power to force a change, or because they do not believe that a change for the better is possible.

When avoidance is not possible or tensions become so strong that the parties cannot just let the disagreement ride, they usually resort to *informal problem-solving discussions* to resolve their differences. This is probably where the majority of disagreements end in daily life. Either they are resolved, more or less to the satisfaction of the people involved, or the issues are dropped for lack of interest or lack of ability to push the resolution through to a conclusion.

In the Singson-Whittamore case, the Whittamores avoided dealing with their potential conflict with the medical clinic until it was clear that Andrew was going to leave. At this point Andrew initiated informal discussions. Neither approach was either appropriate or successful in resolving their disagreement. Clearly their disagreement had escalated into a dispute. Gulliver (1979, p. 75) notes that a disagreement becomes a dispute "only when the two parties are unable and/or unwilling to resolve their disagreement; that is, when one or both are not prepared to accept the status quo (should that any longer be a possibility) or to

Figure 1. Continuum of Conflict Management and Resolution Approaches.

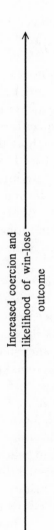

Conflict avoidance	Informal discussion and problem solving	Negotiation	Mediation	Administrative decision	Arbitration	Judicial decision	Legislative decision	Nonviolent direct action	Violence

Private decision making by parties

Private third-party decision making

Legal (public), authoritative third-party decision making

Extralegal coerced decision making

Increased coercion and likelihood of win-lose outcome

accede to the demand or denial of demand by the other. A dispute is precipitated by a crisis in the relationship." People involved in a dispute have a variety of choices concerning means of resolving their differences.

Negotiation is a bargaining relationship between parties who have a perceived or actual conflict of interest. The participants voluntarily join in a temporary relationship designed to educate each other about their needs and interests, to exchange specific resources, or to resolve one or more intangible issues such as the form their relationship will take in the future or the procedure by which problems are to be solved. Negotiation is a more intentional and structured dispute resolution process than informal discussions and problem solving. Negotiation is clearly an option for Whittamore and Singson, although the degree of emotional and substantive polarization will make the process difficult to accomplish.

Mediation is an extension and elaboration of the negotiation process. Mediation involves the intervention of an acceptable, impartial, and neutral third party who has no authoritative decision-making power to assist contending parties in voluntarily reaching their own mutually acceptable settlement of issues in dispute. As with negotiation, mediation leaves the decision-making power in the hands of the people in conflict. Mediation is a voluntary process in that the participants must be willing to accept the assistance of the intervenor if the dispute is to be resolved. Mediation is usually initiated when the parties no longer believe that they can handle the conflict on their own and when the only means of resolution appears to involve impartial third-party assistance. Whittamore and Singson might consider mediation if they cannot negotiate a settlement on their own.

Beyond negotiation and mediation, there is a continuum of techniques that decrease the personal control that the people involved have over the dispute outcome, increase the involvement of external decision makers, and rely increasingly on win/lose and either/or decision-making techniques. These approaches can be divided into public and private, and legal and extralegal approaches.

If a dispute is within an organization there is often an *administrative* or *executive dispute resolution approach.* In this process a third party, who has some distance from the dispute but is not necessarily impartial, may make a decision for the parties in dispute. The process can be private if the system within which the dispute occurs is a private company, division, or work team; or public if it is conducted in a public agency by a mayor, county commissioner, planner, or other administrator. An administrative dispute resolution generally attempts to balance the needs of the entire system and the interests of the individual.

In the Singson-Whittamore dispute, both parties might choose to appeal to the board of directors of the Fairview Clinic for a third-party decision. If both parties trust the integrity and judgment of these decision makers, the dispute might end here.

Arbitration is a generic term for a voluntary process in which people in conflict request the assistance of an impartial and neutral third party to make a decision for them regarding contested issues. The outcome of the decision may be either advisory or binding. Arbitration may be conducted by one person or a panel of third parties. The critical factor is that they are *outside* of the conflict relationship.

Arbitration is also a private process in that the proceedings and often the outcome are not open to public scrutiny. People often select arbitration because it is more informal than a judicial proceeding and frequently faster, less expensive, and private. In arbitration the parties often are able to select their own arbiter or panel, and thus have more control over the decision than if the third party were appointed by an outside authority or agency.

Whittamore and Singson have both heard of arbitration but are reluctant to turn their problem over to a third party before they are sure that they cannot solve it themselves. Neither wants to risk an unfavorable decision. In addition, Singson does not want an external decision that might erode clinic management's prerogative to control the contract process.

A *judicial approach* involves the intervention of an institutionalized and socially recognized authority into private dispute resolution. The approach shifts from a private process to a public one. In a judicial approach, the disputants usually hire lawyers to act as surrogate disputants to argue their respective cases before an impartial and neutral third party, a judge and perhaps a jury as well. These parties represent society's interests and values. The judge (or jury) usually makes a decision based on case law and legal statutes. The outcome is usually win-lose and is premised on a decision regarding who is right and who is wrong. Because the third party is socially sanctioned to make a decision, the results of the process are binding and enforceable. The disputants lose control of the outcome but may gain from forceful advocacy of their point of view and by a decision that reflects societally sanctioned norms.

Whittamore and Singson have both considered using a judicial approach to resolve their dispute. Singson is willing to go to court, if necessary, to obtain an injunction to prevent Whittamore from establishing a private practice and to enforce the no-competition clause in the contract. Whittamore is willing to go to court to test the constitutionality of such a clause.

The *legislative approach* to dispute resolution is another public and legal means of solving a conflict. It is usually used for larger disputes affecting broad populations, although it may have significant utility for individuals. In this approach, the decision regarding the outcome is made by another win-lose process—voting. The individual has only as much influence on the final outcome as he or she, and those who share his or her beliefs, can mobilize. Legislative decisions, although they usually decide negotiated compromises in the form of bills, still often result in win-lose outcomes.

Whittamore has considered using this approach to resolve his dispute. He believes there should be a law against no-competition contracts. Some of his patients agree with him. One patient has even suggested a campaign to pass a bill prohibiting this type of contract.

Finally, there is the *extralegal approach*. The approaches I have examined so far are either private procedures the parties use alone or with the assistance of a third party to negotiate a settlement, or third-party decision making that is either privately or publicly sanctioned. The last category is extralegal in that it does not rely on a socially mandated—or often socially acceptable—process and uses coercion to force an opponent into compliance or submission. There are two types of extralegal approaches: nonviolent action and violence.

Nonviolent action involves a person or group in committing or not committing acts that force an opponent to behave in a desired manner (Sharp, 1973). These acts, however, do not involve physical coercion or violence and often try to minimize psychological harm as well. Nonviolent action works best when the parties are mutually dependent on each other and must rely on each other for their well-being. When this is the case, one of the parties may force the other to make concessions by refusing to cooperate or by committing undesirable acts.

Nonviolent action often involves civil disobedience—violation of widely accepted social norms or laws—to raise an opponent's consciousness or bring into public view practices that the nonviolent activist considers unjust or unfair. Nonviolent action can be conducted on an individual level or by a group and may be either public or private in nature.

Whittamore has considered nonviolent action on personal and group levels to resolve his dispute. On the individual level, he has considered occupying Singson's office until the director will bargain in good faith and give him a fair settlement. He has also considered opening a private practice, challenging the terms of the contract, and forcing the clinic to take him to court or drop the case. If he goes to court, he can exploit the publicity, and mobilize his patients to pressure the clinic to settle.

One of his patients has suggested organizing a picket or vigil outside the clinic to embarrass Singson into a settlement. If that were to be unsuccessful, he has suggested a group sit-in. Whittamore is unsure of the effect of these approaches, as well as of the costs.

The last approach to dispute resolution is *violence* or *physical coercion*. This approach assumes that if the costs to the person or property of an opponent and the costs of maintaining his position are high enough, the adversary will be forced to make concessions. For physical coercion to work, the initiating party must possess enough power to actually damage the other party, must be able to convince the other side that it has the power, and must be willing to use it.

Although Whittamore and Singson are very angry with each other, they have not come to blows. Both are physically fit and could conceivably harm each other significantly, but neither feels he could force the issue with a private fight. Whittamore, in the heat of anger, has considered sabotaging some of the clinic's valuable equipment but has decided that such action would have adverse consequences. Singson has also considered violence and has wondered what Whittamore's reaction would be if he were to be assaulted by agents Singson could hire for that purpose. He too has decided against physical violence as too risky, costly, and unpredictable.

Figure 1 illustrates the continuum of means that are available to people in conflict to resolve their disputes. The question that remains is, Which approach will Whittamore and Singson choose?

Whittamore wants to stay in town so that he can be near his children. He also wants to practice medicine. Establishing a new practice will be expensive, so he wants to minimize his dispute resolution costs. He hopes for a quick decision so that he may leave the clinic soon to avoid more adverse contact with Janelle and to minimize any harm to his personal relationships with other staff members. He also needs to establish a private practice quickly so that he can generate income. Physical violence was a fleeting fantasy, although nonviolent action is still a possibility if the clinic does not acquiesce. Judicial and legislative approaches seem unreasonable at this time because of the cost and length of time they will take to achieve a change.

Singson is also trying to decide what action he will take. He wants to keep management control over the contract process, wants to solve the problem himself and not rely on outside agents, and wants to minimize such costs as legal fees, patient attrition, or bad publicity. He too wants to find an amicable solution but feels that his interaction with Whittamore has reached an impasse.

Whittamore and Singson's conflict illustrates a case that is ripe for negotiation. Singson and Whittamore are

- Interdependent and must rely on the cooperation of one another in order to meet their goals or satisfy their interests.
- Able to influence one another and can undertake or prevent actions that can either harm or reward.
- Pressured by deadlines and time constraints and share an impetus for early settlement.
- Aware that alternative procedures and outcomes to a negotiated settlement do not appear as viable or desirable as a bargain that they reach themselves.
- Able to identify the critical primary parties and involve them in the problem-solving process.
- Able to identify and agree on the issues in dispute.
- In a situation in which the interests of the parties are not entirely incompatible.
- Influenced by external constraints, such as unpredictability of a judicial decision, potentially angry patients or staff, costs of establishing a new practice, and expenses of recruiting a new physician, that encourage them to reach a negotiated settlement.

The above conditions are critical to successful negotiation. However, Singson and Whittamore's relationship also contains elements that will make negotiations on their own extremely difficult. To overcome these problems, they need a mediator. A mediator may be called into negotiations when

- The emotions of the parties are intense and are preventing a settlement.
- Communication between the parties is poor in either quantity or quality and the parties cannot change the situation on their own.
- Misperceptions or stereotypes are hindering productive exchanges.
- Repetitive negative behaviors are creating barriers.
- There are serious disagreements over data—what information is important, how it is to be collected, and how it will be evaluated.
- There are multiple issues in dispute and the parties disagree about the order and combination in which they should be addressed.

- There are perceived or actual incompatible interests that the parties are having difficulty reconciling.
- Perceived or unnecessary value differences divide the parties.
- The parties do not have a negotiating procedure, are using the wrong procedure, or are not using a procedure to its best advantage.
- The parties are having difficulties starting negotiations or have reached an impasse in their bargaining.

Because Whittamore and Singson's relationship has some of the characteristics listed here, they will decide to use mediated negotiations as a means of resolving their dispute. The following chapters examine in more detail the process of conflict management that they have selected.

TWO

How Mediation Works

Although mediation is widely practiced in interpersonal, organizational, community, and international disputes, and techniques have been documented in particular applications or cases, there has been little systematic study or description of specific strategies and tactics used by mediators. What analysis and description have been conducted either have been presented on the most general level or are so specific as to limit their broad application.

This book addresses the need for a systematic and practical approach to mediation practice. It has three major goals: (1) to illustrate the effects and dynamics of mediation on negotiations as a means of dispute resolution, (2) to begin developing a theoretical explanation for the current practice of mediation as it has been applied in a variety of arenas, and (3) to provide practitioners with concrete and effective techniques to assist parties in dispute resolution. With these goals in mind, I will explore mediation and how it relates to negotiated settlements.

A Definition of Mediation

When a mediator from the United Nations enters an international dispute, a labor mediator is engaged in negotiations prior to a strike, or a family mediator assists a couple in reaching a divorce settlement, what activities are they performing? What is their relationship to the parties? What are the objectives of the mediators?

13

Mediation is the intervention into a dispute or negotiation by an acceptable, impartial, and neutral third party who has no authoritative decision-making power to assist disputing parties in voluntarily reaching their own mutually acceptable settlement of issues in dispute. I will examine several components of the definition.

For mediation to occur, the parties must begin negotiating. Labor and management must be willing to hold a bargaining session, governments and public interest groups must create forums for dialogue, and families must be willing to come together for mediation to begin. *Mediation is essentially negotiation* that includes a third party who is knowledgeable in effective negotiation procedures, and can help people in conflict to coordinate their activities and to be more effective in their bargaining. Mediation is an extension of the negotiation process in that it involves extending the bargaining into a new format and using a mediator who contributes new variables and dynamics to the interaction of the disputants. Without negotiation, however, there can be no mediation.

Intervention means "to enter into an ongoing system of relationships, to come between or among persons, groups, or objects for the purpose of helping them. There is an important implicit assumption in the definition that should be made explicit: the system exists independently of the intervenor" (Argyris, 1970, p. 15). The assumption behind an outsider's intervention is that a third party will be able to alter the power and social dynamics of the conflict relationship by influencing the beliefs or behaviors of individual parties, by providing knowledge or information, or by using a more effective negotiation process and thereby helping the participants to settle contested issues. Rubin and Brown (1975) have argued that the mere presence of a party who is independent of the disputants may be a highly significant factor in the resolution of a dispute.

The third aspect of this definition is *acceptability,* the willingness of disputants to allow a third party to enter a dispute and assist them in reaching a resolution. Acceptability does not mean that disputants necessarily welcome a mediator and are willing to do exactly as he or she says. It does mean that the parties approve of the mediator's presence and are willing to listen to and seriously consider the intervenor's suggestions.

Impartiality and neutrality are critical to the process of mediation (Young, 1972). *Impartiality* refers to the attitude of the intervenor and is an unbiased opinion or lack of preference in favor of one or more negotiators. *Neutrality*, on the other hand, refers to the behavior or relationship between the intervenor and the disputants. Mediators often either have not had a previous relationship with disputing parties or have not had a relationship in which they have directly influenced the rewards or benefits for one of the parties to the detriment of the other. Neutrality also means that the mediator does not expect to directly gain benefits or special payments from one of the parties as compensation for favors in conducting the mediation.

People seek a mediator's assistance because they want procedural help in negotiations. They do not want an intervenor who is biased or who will initiate actions that are detrimental to their interests.

The need for impartiality and neutrality does not mean that a mediator may not have personal opinions about a dispute's outcome. No one can be entirely impartial. What impartiality and neutrality do signify is that the mediator can separate his or her opinions about the outcome of the dispute from the desires of the disputants and focus on ways to help the parties make their own decisions without unduly favoring one of them. The final test of the impartiality and neutrality of the mediator ultimately rests with the parties. They must perceive that the intervenor is not overtly partial or unneutral in order to accept his or her assistance.

Kraybill (1979) and Wheeler (1982) address the tensions between impartiality and neutrality and the personal biases of mediators by distinguishing between the substantive and procedural interests. Wheeler argues that mediators generally distance themselves from commitments to specific substantive outcomes—the amount of money in a settlement, the exact time of performance, and so forth—but have commitments to such procedural standards as open communication, equity and fair exchange, durability of a settlement over time, and enforceability. Mediators are advocates for a fair process and not for a particular settlement.

Conflicts involve struggles between two or more people over values, or competition for status power and scarce resources (Coser, 1967). Mediators enter a variety of levels of conflicts—latent, emerging, and manifest—according to their degree of organization and intensity. Latent conflicts are characterized by underlying tensions that have not fully developed and have not escalated into a highly polarized conflict. Often, one or more parties may not even be aware that a conflict or the potential for one even exists (Curle, 1971). Changes in personal relationships in which one party is not aware of how serious a breach has occurred, future staff cutbacks, unannounced plans for the siting of a potentially controversial facility such as a mine or waste disposal site, or potential unpopular changes in public policy are examples of latent conflicts.

Mediators (or facilitators) working with people involved in the resolution of latent disputes help participants to identify people who will be affected by a change or those who may be concerned about the future problem, assist them in developing a mutual education process about the issues and interests involved, and work with participants to design and possibly implement a problem-solving process.

Emerging conflicts are disputes in which the parties are identified, they acknowledge that there is a dispute, and most issues are clear, but no workable negotiation or problem-solving process has developed. Emerging conflicts have a potential for escalation if a resolution procedure is not implemented. Many disputes between co-workers, businesses, and governments illustrate this type of conflict. Both parties recognize that there is a dispute, and there may have been a harsh verbal exchange, but neither knows how to handle the problem. In this case the mediator helps establish the negotiation process and helps the parties begin to communicate and bargain.

Manifest conflicts are those in which parties are engaged in an ongoing dispute, may have started to negotiate, and may have reached an impasse. Mediator involvement in manifest conflicts often involves changing the negotiation procedure or intervention to break a specific deadlock. Labor mediators who intervene in negotiations before a strike deadline are working to resolve manifest conflicts. Child custody and divorce mediators also usually intervene in fully manifest disputes.

A mediator has *no authoritative decision-making power.* This characteristic distinguishes the mediator from the judge or arbiter, who is designated by law or contract to make a decision for the parties based on societal norms, laws, or contracts rather than the specific interests or personal concepts of justice held by the parties. The goal of the judicial decision is not reconciliation but a decision concerning which of the parties is right.

The judge examines the past and evaluates "agreements that the parties have entered into, violations which one has inflicted on the other," and "the norms concerning acquisition of rights, responsibilities, etc. which are connected with these events. When he has taken his standpoint on this basis, his task is finished" (Eckhoff, 1966-67, p. 161).

The mediator, on the other hand, works to reconcile the competing interests of the two parties. The mediator's goal is to assist the parties in examining the future and their interests or needs, and negotiating an exchange of promises and relationships that will be mutually satisfactory and meet their standards of fairness. The mediator does not have decision-making authority, and parties in dispute therefore often seek the services of a mediator because they can retain ultimate decision-making power.

If the mediator does not have authority to decide, does he or she have any influence at all? The mediator's authority, such as it is, resides in his or her ability to appeal to the parties to reach an agreement based on their own interests or the past performance or reputation of the mediator as a useful resource. Authority, or recognition of a right to influence the outcome of the dispute, is granted by the parties themselves rather than by an external law, contract, or agency.

So far I have identified that a mediator is a third party who is impartial in attitude and neutral in relationship toward disputing parties. I will now describe the mediator's functions. The definition states that a mediator *assists* disputing parties.

Assistance can refer to very general or to highly specific activities. I will examine here some of the more general roles and functions of the mediator, and will discuss specifics later when analyzing intervention moves made during particular phases of negotiation.

The mediator may assume a variety of roles and functions to assist parties in resolving disputes (American Arbitration Association, n.d.):

- *The opener of communications channels* who initiates communication or facilitates better communication if the parties are already talking.
- *The legitimizer* who helps all parties recognize the right of others to be involved in negotiations.
- *The process facilitator* who provides a procedure and often formally chairs the negotiation session.
- *The trainer* who educates novice, unskilled, or unprepared negotiators in the bargaining process.
- *The resource expander* who provides procedural assistance to the parties and links them to outside experts and resources, such as lawyers, technical experts, decision makers, or additional goods for exchange, that may enable them to enlarge acceptable settlement options.
- *The problem explorer* who enables people in dispute to examine a problem from a variety of viewpoints, assists in defining basic issues and interests, and looks for mutually satisfactory options.
- *The agent of reality* who helps build a reasonable and implementable settlement and questions and challenges parties who have extreme and unrealistic goals.
- *The scapegoat* who may take some of the responsibility or blame for an unpopular decision that the parties are nevertheless willing to accept. This enables them to maintain their integrity and, when appropriate, gain the support of their constituents.
- *The leader* who takes the initiative to move the negotiations forward by procedural, or on occasion, substantive suggestions.

The last component of the definition refers to mediation as a voluntary process. *Voluntary* refers to freely chosen participation and freely chosen settlement. Parties are not forced to negotiate, mediate, or settle by either an internal or external party to a dispute. Stulberg (1981b, pp. 88-89) notes that "there is no legal liability to any party refusing to participate in a mediation process. . . . Since a mediator has no authority unilaterally to impose a decision on the parties, he cannot threaten the recalcitrant party with a judgement."

Voluntary participation does not, however, mean that there may not be pressure to try mediation. Other disputants or external forces, such as judges or constituents, may put significant pressure on a party to try negotiation and mediation. Some courts in family and civil cases have even gone so far as to order that parties try mediation as a means of resolving their dispute before the court hears the case. Attempting mediation does not, however, mean that the participants are forced to settle.

Arenas of Mediation

Mediation has a long history. The Bible refers to Jesus as a mediator between God and man: "For there is one God, and one mediator between God and man, the man Christ Jesus; who gave himself as ransom for all, to be testified in due time" (I Timothy 2:5-6). Churches and clergy have often been mediators between their members or other disputants. Until the Renaissance, the Catholic church in Western Europe was probably the central mediation and conflict management organization in Western society. Clergy mediated family disputes, criminal cases, and diplomatic disputes among the nobility. Bianchi (1978), in describing one mediated case in the Middle Ages, details how the church and the clergy provided the sanctuary where the offender stayed during dispute resolution and served as intermediary between two families in a case involving rape. The families agreed to settle with monetary restitution to the woman's family and promises to help her find a husband.

Jewish rabbinical courts and rabbis in Europe were vital in mediating or adjudicating disputes among members of that faith. These courts were crucial to the protection of cultural identity and ensured that Jews had a formalized means of dispute resolution. In many locales they were barred from other means of dispute settlement because of their religion.

With the rise of nation-states, mediators took on new roles as formal secular diplomatic intermediaries. Diplomats such as ambassadors and envoys acted to "raise and clarify social issues and problems, to modify conflicting interests, and to transmit information of mutual concern to parties" (Werner, 1974, p. 95).

The practice of mediation is not confined to Western culture. In fact, mediation has probably been more widely practiced in China and Japan, where religion and philosophy place a strong emphasis on social consensus, moral persuasion, and striking a balance or harmony in human relations (Brown, 1982). Mediation is currently widely practiced in the People's Republic of China through People's Conciliation Committees (Ginsberg, 1978; Li, 1978).

Latin America and other Hispanic cultures also have a history of mediated dispute settlement. Nader (1969) reports on the dispute resolution process in the Mexican village of Ralu'a, where a judge assists the parties in making consensual decisions. Lederach (1984) describes other mediation models in Hispanic culture such as the *Tribunal de las Aguas* (water courts) in Spain.

Mediation is also utilized in Africa, where the *moot court* is a common means for neighbors to resolve disputes (Gulliver, 1971). Mediated settlement is also practiced in some Arab villages in Jordan (Antoun, 1972).

In Melanesia, the Tolai villages in New Britain each have a counselor and committee that meet regularly to hear disputes (Epstein, 1971). The role of the counselor and committee is to "maintain conditions for orderly debate and freedom of argument by the disputants and anyone else who wishes to express opinion" (Gulliver, 1979, p. 27). The process is both a "mode of adjudication" and a "settlement by consensus" of the parties (Epstein, 1971, p. 168).

Mediation also has a long history in the American colonies

and the United States. Auerbach's *Justice Without Law* (1983) is an excellent history that describes the dispute resolution mechanisms of the Puritans, Quakers, and other religious sects; procedures of Chinese and Jewish ethnic groups; and informal alternative dispute resolution efforts.

For the most part, mediation historically and in other cultures has been performed by people with informal training, and the intervenor's role has usually occurred within the context of other functions or duties. Only since the turn of the twentieth century has mediation become formally institutionalized and developed into a recognized profession.

The first arena in which mediation was formally institutionalized in the United States was in labor-management relations (Simkin, 1971). In 1913 the U.S. Department of Labor was established, and a panel, the "commissioners of conciliation," was appointed to handle conflicts between labor and management. This panel subsequently became the United States Conciliation Service, and in 1947 was reconstituted as the Federal Mediation and Conciliation Service. The rationale for initiating mediation procedures in the industrial sector was to promote a "sound and stable industrial peace" and "the settlement of issues between employer and employees through collective bargaining" (Labor-Management Relations Act, 1947). It was expected that mediated settlements would prevent costly strikes or lockouts for workers and employers alike and that the safety, welfare, and wealth of Americans would be improved.

Federal use of mediation in labor disputes has provided a model for many states. Numerous states have passed laws, developed regulations, and trained a cadre of mediators to handle intrastate labor conflicts. The private sector has also initiated labor-management and commercial relations mediation. The American Arbitration Association was founded in 1926 to encourage the use of arbitration and other techniques of voluntary dispute settlement.

Mediation sponsored by government agencies has not been confined to labor-management issues. The U.S. Congress passed the Civil Rights Act of 1964 and created the Community Relations Service (CRS) of the U.S. Department of Justice.

This agency was mandated to help "communities and persons therein in resolving disputes, disagreements, or difficulties relating to discriminatory practices based on race, color, or national origin" (Title X, Civil Rights Act, 1964). The agency assists people in resolving disputes through negotiation and mediation rather than having them utilize the streets or the judicial system. CRS works throughout the country on such issues as school desegregation and public-accommodation cases. In 1978, a team from CRS mediated the dispute that erupted when a neo-Nazi political group announced its intention to demonstrate in Skokie, a predominantly Jewish suburb of Chicago (Salem, 1984).

Diverse state agencies, civil rights commissions, and private agencies also use mediation to handle charges of sex, race, and ethnic discrimination conflicts (Chalmers and Cormick, 1971; Kwartler, 1980; "Municipal Human Relations Commissions . . . ," 1966).

Since the mid 1960s, mediation has grown significantly as a formal and widely practiced approach to dispute resolution. In the community sector, the federal government funds Neighborhood Justice Centers (NJCs) that provide free or low-cost mediation services to the public to resolve disputes efficiently, inexpensively, and informally. Many of these NJCs are institutionalized and have become part of city, court, or district attorney programs for alternative dispute resolution. Some community programs are independent of governmental agencies and offer a grass roots independent dispute resolution service in which community members sit on mediation or conciliation panels and help neighbors resolve their disputes (Shonholtz, 1984).

Mediation is also practiced in schools and institutions of higher education. In this setting, disputes are mediated among students, such as the potentially violent interracial conflict handled by Lincoln (1976); between students and faculty; between faculty members; or between faculty and administration (McCarthy, 1980; McCarthy and others, 1984).

The criminal justice system also utilizes mediation to resolve criminal complaints (Felsteiner and Williams, 1978) and disputes in correctional facilities (Reynolds and Tonry, 1981). Mediation in the latter arena takes the form of both crisis intervention in case of prison riots or hostage negotiations and institutionalized grievance procedures.

Perhaps the fastest-growing arena in which mediation is practiced is in family disputes. Court systems and private practitioners provide mediation to families in child custody and divorce proceedings (Coogler, 1978; Haynes, 1981; Irving, 1980; Saposnek, 1983; Moore, forthcoming); disputes between parents and children (Shaw, 1982; Wixted, 1982), conflicts involving adoption and the termination of parental rights (Mayer, 1985), and spousal disputes in which there is domestic violence (Bethel and Singer, 1982; Orenstein, 1982; Wildau, 1984). In family disputes, mediated and consensual settlements are often more appropriate and satisfying than litigated or imposed outcomes. Models of practice in this area include mandatory court-connected programs in which disputants must try mediation before a judge will hear the case; voluntary court programs; and forms of private practice such as sole practitioners, partnerships, and private nonprofit agencies.

Mediation is also used within and between organizations to handle interpersonal and institutional disputes. The scope of mediation application ranges from mediating one-on-one personnel disputes, managing problems between partners (such as in law or medical practices), interdepartmental conflicts, and altercations between companies (Biddle and others, 1982; Blake and Mouton, 1984; Brett and Goldberg, 1983; Brown, 1983).

Mediation is also applied to a variety of larger disputes over environmental and public policy issues (Talbot, 1983; Bingham, 1984; Carpenter and Kennedy, 1977; Cormick, 1976; Lake, 1980; and Mernitz, 1980). Disputes over power plant siting, dam construction, and land use have all been successfully mediated. Government agencies are experimenting with negotiated rule making in public policy issues (Bingham, 1981; Harter, 1984). The Negotiated Investment Strategy, a mediated procedure initiated by the Kettering Foundation, enables local, state, and federal agencies to coordinate their decisions on program funding (Shanahan and others, 1982).

Mediation is also being applied in landlord-tenant conflicts (Cook, Rochl, and Shepard, 1980), personal injury cases
("AAA Designs . . . ," 1984), police work (Folberg and Taylor,
1984), disputes between elderly residents and nursing home
owners, and consumer disputes (Ray and Smolover, 1983). The
arenas in which mediation is being applied are very broad. If
trends continue, the process will be used to resolve a variety of
disputes in arenas not conceived of today.

Mediation Activities: Moves and Interventions

Negotiation is composed of a series of complex activities
or "moves" people initiate to resolve their differences and
bring the conflict to termination (Goffman, 1969, p. 90). Each
move or action a negotiator conducts involves rational decision
making in which outcomes of alternative actions are assessed according to their relationships to the following factors: the
moves of the other parties, their standards of behavior, their
styles, their perceptiveness and skill, their needs and preferences, their determination, how much information the negotiator has about the conflict, his or her personal attributes, and
resources available.

Mediators, like negotiators, also initiate moves. A *move*
for a mediator is a specific act of intervention or "influence
technique" focused on the people in the dispute that encourages the selection of positive actions and inhibits the selection
of negative actions relative to the issues in conflict (Galtung,
1975b). The mediator, a specialized negotiator, does not *directly* effect changes in the disputants by initiating moves; he or she
is more of a catalyst. Changes are the result of a combination of
the intervenor's moves with the moves of the negotiators (Bonner, 1959).

In negotiations, people in conflict are faced with a variety
of procedural or psychological problems or "critical situations"
(Cohen and Smith, 1972) that they must solve or overcome if
they are to reach a settlement. All problem-solving groups face
these situations, which can be categorized according to size,
type, time, and frequency. The largest categories and most fre-

quent problems are hereafter referred to as *stages* because they constitute major steps that parties must take to reach agreement. There are stages for both negotiation and mediation, which, for the most part, directly correspond to each other.

Mediators make two types of interventions in response to critical situations: *general* or *noncontingent* and *specific* or *contingent* moves (Kochan and Jick, 1978).

Noncontingent moves are general interventions that a mediator initiates in all disputes. These moves are responses to the broadest categories of critical situations and correspond to the stages of mediation. They are linked to the overall pattern of conflict development and resolution. Noncontingent moves enable the mediator to

1. gain entry to the dispute,
2. assist the parties in selecting the appropriate conflict resolution approach and arena,
3. collect data and analyze the conflict,
4. design a mediation plan,
5. practice conciliation,
6. assist the parties in beginning productive negotiations,
7. identify important issues and build an agenda,
8. identify interests,
9. aid the parties in developing settlement options,
10. assist in assessing the options,
11. promote final bargaining, and
12. aid in developing an implementation and monitoring plan.

I will examine these moves and stages in more detail later in this chapter.

Smaller noncontingent moves are initiated by mediators within each stage. Examples of this level of moves include activities to build credibility for the process, promote rapport between the parties and the mediator, and frame issues into a more manageable form, as well as develop procedures to conduct cost-benefit evaluations on settlement options.

Contingent moves are responses to special or idiosyncratic problems that occur in some negotiations. Interventions

to manage intense anger, bluffing, bargaining in bad faith, mistrust, or miscommunication are all in this category of specific
interventions. While some contingent moves, such as the caucus—
private meetings between the parties and the mediators—are
quite common, they are still in the contingent category because
they do not happen in all negotiations.

Hypothesis Building and Mediation Interventions

For a mediator to be effective, he or she needs to be able
to analyze and assess critical situations and design effective interventions to counteract the causes of the conflict. Conflicts,
however, do not come in neat packages with their causes and
component parts labeled so that the parties, or the intervenor,
know how to creatively respond to them. The causes are often
obscured and clouded by the dynamics of the interaction.

To work effectively on conflicts, the intervenor needs a
conceptual road map or "conflict map" of the dispute (Wehr,
1979) that should detail why a conflict is occurring, should
identify barriers to settlement, and should indicate procedures
to manage or resolve the dispute.

Most conflicts have multiple causes; usually it is a combination of problems in the relations of the disputants that leads
to a dispute. The principal tasks of the mediator and the parties
are to identify central causes of the conflict and take action to
alleviate them. The mediator and participants in a dispute accomplish this by trial-and-error experimentation in which they
generate and test hypotheses about the conflict.

First, the parties and the mediator observe the aspects of
the dispute. They examine attitudinal or behavioral problems in
the interactions of the disputants, disagreements over "facts,"
compatible and competing interests, interaction dynamics,
power relations, and value similarities and differences. From the
observations, the mediator tries to identify the central critical
situations or causes of the dispute. He or she often uses a framework of explanatory causes and suggested interventions such as
those identified in Figure 2. Once the mediator believes that a
central cause has been identified, he or she builds a hypothesis.

Figure 2. Sphere of Conflict—Causes and Interventions.

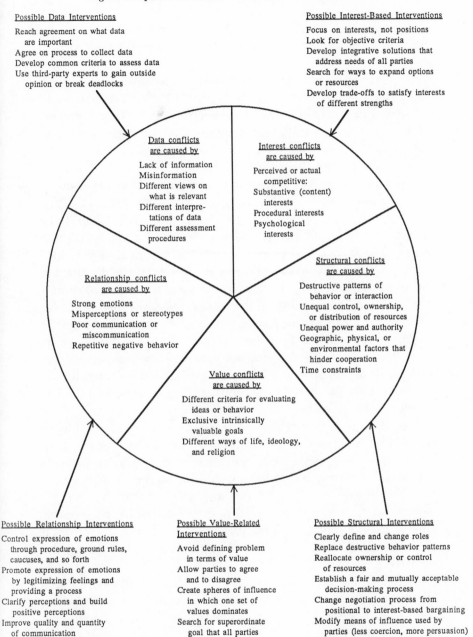

Possible Data Interventions

Reach agreement on what data
  are important
Agree on process to collect data
Develop common criteria to assess data
Use third-party experts to gain outside
  opinion or break deadlocks

Possible Interest-Based Interventions

Focus on interests, not positions
Look for objective criteria
Develop integrative solutions that
  address needs of all parties
Search for ways to expand options
  or resources
Develop trade-offs to satisfy interests
  of different strengths

Data conflicts
are caused by

Lack of information
Misinformation
Different views on
  what is relevant
Different interpre-
  tations of data
Different assessment
  procedures

Interest conflicts
are caused by

Perceived or actual
  competitive:
Substantive (content)
  interests
Procedural interests
Psychological
  interests

Structural conflicts
are caused by

Destructive patterns of
  behavior or interaction
Unequal control, ownership,
  or distribution of resources
Unequal power and authority
Geographic, physical, or
  environmental factors that
  hinder cooperation
Time constraints

Relationship conflicts
are caused by

Strong emotions
Misperceptions or stereotypes
Poor communication or
  miscommunication
Repetitive negative behavior

Value conflicts
are caused by

Different criteria for evaluating
  ideas or behavior
Exclusive intrinsically
  valuable goals
Different ways of life, ideology,
  and religion

Possible Relationship Interventions

Control expression of emotions
  through procedure, ground rules,
  caucuses, and so forth
Promote expression of emotions
  by legitimizing feelings and
  providing a process
Clarify perceptions and build
  positive perceptions
Improve quality and quantity
  of communication
Block negative repetitive
  behavior by changing structure
Encourage positive problem-
  solving attitudes

Possible Value-Related
Interventions

Avoid defining problem
  in terms of value
Allow parties to agree
  and to disagree
Create spheres of influence
  in which one set of
  values dominates
Search for superordinate
  goal that all parties
  share

Possible Structural Interventions

Clearly define and change roles
Replace destructive behavior patterns
Reallocate ownership or control
  of resources
Establish a fair and mutually acceptable
  decision-making process
Change negotiation process from
  positional to interest-based bargaining
Modify means of influence used by
  parties (less coercion, more persuasion)
Change physical and environmental
  relationships of parties (closeness
  and distance)
Modify external pressures on parties
Change time constraints (more or
  less time)

"This conflict is caused by *a,* and if *b* is changed, the parties will be able to move toward agreement." The hypothesis must then be tested.

Testing hypotheses about conflicts involves designing interventions that challenge or modify the attitudes, behaviors, or structural relationship of the disputants. These interventions are often grounded in a theory that identifies a particular cause for the conflict and suggests prescriptive actions. For example, one theory about the cause of conflict has communication as its base. Most communication theories propose that conflict is the result of poor communication in either quality, quantity, or form. The theory postulates that if the *quality* of the information exchanged can be improved, the right *quantity* of communication can be attained, and if these data are put into the *correct form,* the causes of the dispute will be addressed and the participants will move toward resolution.

A mediator following the communications theory of conflict might begin by observing disputants communicating very poorly: One can hardly speak without the other interrupting, they have difficulty focusing on present issues and constantly digress to arguments over past wrongs that tend to escalate the conflict, and the dispute develops into a shouting match. The mediator observes the interaction, hypothesizes that one cause of the dispute is the inability of the disputants to talk with each other in a constructive and restrained manner, and proceeds to experiment with modifications of their communication patterns (quality, quantity, and form) to see if he or she can change the conflict dynamics. The mediator may suggest that they discuss one topic at a time, may obtain their permission to monitor them, may establish ground rules about insults, or may even separate them so that they can communicate only through the mediator.

Each intervention is a test of the theory and a hypothesis that part of the dispute is caused by communication problems, and that if these difficulties can be lessened or eliminated, the parties will have a better chance of reaching settlement. If the desired effect is not achieved, the intervenor may reject the specific move as ineffective and try another. If several interventions based on one theory do not work, the intervenor may shift to another theory and begin trial-and-error testing again. The cycle of hypothesis building and testing is the basic process of intervention and conflict resolution (see Figure 3).

Figure 3. Mediator Process of Building and Testing a Hypothesis.

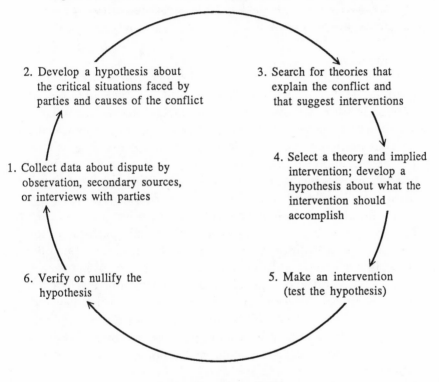

2. Develop a hypothesis about the critical situations faced by parties and causes of the conflict

3. Search for theories that explain the conflict and that suggest interventions

1. Collect data about dispute by observation, secondary sources, or interviews with parties

4. Select a theory and implied intervention; develop a hypothesis about what the intervention should accomplish

6. Verify or nullify the hypothesis

5. Make an intervention (test the hypothesis)

The Stages of Mediation

One of the broadest spheres of mediator hypothesis building occurs in the process of conceptualizing the stages of mediation and designing appropriate interventions based on the stage of development that a particular dispute has reached.

The stages of mediation are often difficult to identify. Mediator and negotiator moves seem to blend together into an undifferentiated continuum of interaction. Only through careful observation of negotiations and mediated interventions can distinct stages composed of general moves be identified and hypotheses generated about the critical situations that the disputants will experience.

The stages of mediator intervention fall into roughly two broad categories: work that the mediator performs before joining the parties in joint session, and moves made once the mediator has entered into formal negotiations. Five stages occur in the prenegotiation work of the mediator, and seven stages occur after the mediator begins to work jointly with the disputants (see Figure 4).

In each of the twelve stages the mediator will design hypotheses and appropriate strategies and will execute specific moves. These moves are both sequential and developmental and are designed to assist disputing parties in accomplishing specific tasks at particular times in the negotiation process. If a task has not been completed either by the negotiators alone or with the assistance of a mediator, the parties generally encounter great difficulties in moving on to the next stage of negotiation.

Regardless of when a mediator enters negotiations—at the beginning, middle, or end—he or she will usually perform all the general or noncontingent moves. Naturally, the amount of time spent in each stage and the emphasis on each set of moves will vary considerably according to variables that will be discussed in the remaining section of this chapter—level of conflict development, timing of entry, productive conflict resolution capabilities of the disputants, power and influence relations of the parties, negotiation procedures being used, complexity of the issues, and definition of the mediator's task.

Variables That Influence Mediation Strategies and Moves

Although mediators make a variety of interventions to help parties move through the negotiation and mediation stages, their moves are not perfectly identical from case to case. While there are general patterns of moves, each mediator will have to modify his or her activities according to variables present in the case. The most critical variables that influence interventions are

1. The level of conflict development and the timing of a mediator's entry.
2. The capability of negotiators to resolve their own dispute.
3. The power equality of the disputants and the mediator's role as a power balancer and agent of empowerment.
4. The negotiation procedures used by the parties.
5. The complexity of the issues negotiated.
6. The role and tasks of the mediator as mutually defined by the parties and the intervenor.

I will examine each of these variables and how they affect the role of the mediator and his or her application of general and specific strategies.

Conflict Development and Timing of Entry. The stage of conflict development and the degree of emotional intensity of the parties influence the tasks that negotiators have to perform. If a mediator enters a dispute in its early stages before extreme issue polarization or the development of intense emotions, he or she will use a different strategy and set of moves to assist the parties than if he or she arrives at a later stage when the parties have been negotiating and have reached a substantive impasse. In viewing mediation as a general process, however, the change in strategy and moves is primarily one of emphasis rather than a specific change in the type of move. Conciliation, for example, generally must occur more at the beginning of negotiations rather than later. If, however, a mediator enters in the later phases of a negotiation, after impasse, for example, he or she will probably still have to conciliate. The mediator will generally have to complete this phase prior to pursuing developmental moves more appropriate to the stage in which the parties have reached impasse.

Capability of Disputants to Resolve Their Own Disputes. Whether the disputants are capable of resolving their own dispute also strongly affects the mediator's intervention strategies. Parties who are able to negotiate rationally, who are aware of problem-solving procedures, and who appear to be progressing toward a settlement will require little assistance from a mediator. In this situation, the mediator may lend support to the

Figure 4. Twelve Stages of Mediator Moves and Critical Situations
to Be Handled.

Stage 1: Initial Contacts with the Disputing Parties
- Making initial contacts with the parties
- Building credibility
- Promoting rapport
- Educating the parties about the process
- Increasing commitment to the procedure

Stage 2: Selecting a Strategy to Guide Mediation
- Assisting the parties to assess various approaches
  to conflict management and resolution
- Assisting the parties to select an approach
- Coordinating the approaches of the parties

Stage 3: Collecting and Analyzing Background Information
- Collecting and analyzing relevant data about the people,
  dynamics, and substance of a conflict
- Verifying accuracy of data
- Minimizing the impact of inaccurate or unavailable data

Stage 4: Designing a Detailed Plan for Mediation
- Identifying strategies and consequent noncontingent moves that
  will enable the parties to move toward agreement
- Identifying contingent moves to respond to situations peculiar
  to the specific conflict

Stage 5: Building Trust and Cooperation
- Preparing disputants psychologically to participate in
  negotiations on substantive issues
- Handling strong emotions
- Checking perceptions and minimizing effects of stereotypes
- Building recognition of the legitimacy of the parties and issues
- Building trust
- Clarifying communications

Stage 6: Beginning the Mediation Session
- Opening negotiation between the parties
- Establishing an open and positive tone
- Establishing ground rules and behavioral guidelines
- Assisting the parties in venting emotions
- Delimiting topic areas and issues for discussion
- Assisting the parties in exploring commitments, salience,
  and influence

Stage 7: Defining Issues and Setting an Agenda
- Identifying broad topic areas of concern to the parties
- Obtaining agreement on the issues to be discussed
- Determining the sequence for handling the issues

Stage 8: Uncovering Hidden Interests of the Disputing Parties
- Identifying the substantive, procedural, and psychological interests of the parties
- Educating the parties about each other's interests

Stage 9: Generating Options for Settlement
- Developing an awareness among the parties of the need for options
- Lowering commitment to positions or sole alternatives
- Generating options using either positional or interest-based bargaining

Stage 10: Assessing Options for Settlement
- Reviewing the interests of the parties
- Assessing how interests can be met by available options
- Assessing the costs and benefits of selecting options

Stage 11: Final Bargaining
- Reaching agreement through either incremental convergence of positions, final leaps to package settlements, development of a consensual formula, or establishment of a procedural means to reach a substantive agreement

Stage 12: Achieving Formal Settlement
- Identifying procedural steps to operationalize the agreement
- Establishing an evaluation and monitoring procedure
- Formalizing the settlement and creating an enforcement and commitment mechanism

work of the parties merely by his or her presence or by minimal support of the principal negotiators (Perez, 1959; Kolb, 1983). On the other hand, if parties are in the grip of intense emotions, do not have skills or expertise in negotiations or problem-solving procedures, or have reached an impasse on substantive issues, the mediator will probably be more active and more visible in the negotiations. He or she may assist the parties in productively venting strong emotions, narrowing the bargaining range, creating agendas, generating and assessing options, and initiating a variety of other procedures or moves that assist the parties in reaching a settlement.

Power Equality Between Disputants. In order to derive mutually satisfactory and acceptable decisions from negotiations, all parties must have some means of influence, either positive or negative, on other disputants at the table. This is a prerequisite for a settlement that recognizes mutual needs (Lovell, 1952). If the power or influence potentials of the parties are well developed, fairly equal in strength, and recognized by all disputants, the mediator's job will be to assist parties in using their influence effectively while producing mutually satisfactory results. If, however, influence on each other is not equal and one party has the ability to impose an unsatisfactory settlement on another, an agreement that will not hold over time, or a resolution that will result in renewed conflict later, the mediator will have to decide whether and how to assist the weaker party.

Assistance or possible empowerment of the weaker party by the mediator requires very specific intervention moves—activities that shift the mediator's function dangerously close to advocacy. This problem in mediation has been debated among mediators (Bernard, Folger, Weingarten, and Zumeta, 1984). One argument states that a mediator has an obligation to create just settlements and must therefore help empower the underdog to reach equitable and fair agreements (Laue and Cormick, 1978; Suskind, 1981; Haynes, 1981). Another school argues that mediators should not do anything to influence the power relations of disputing parties because it taints the intervenor's impartiality (Bellman, 1982; Stulberg, 1981b).

In examining this question and how it affects the mediator's choice of intervention moves, it is important to distinguish between a mediator assisting in recognizing, organizing, and marshaling existing power of a disputant and a mediator becoming an advocate and assisting in generating new power and influence. The latter strategy clearly shifts the mediator out of his or her impartial position, while the former keeps the mediator within the power boundaries established by the parties. There is no easy answer to this strategic and ethical problem, but it does have an important impact on the types of moves a mediator initiates.

Negotiation Procedures. Negotiation is a form of joint problem solving. The topical problems that negotiators focus on are often called *issues.* An issue exists because the parties do not agree on a particular topic and because they have perceived or actual exclusive needs or interests.

In the Singson-Whittamore case described in Chapter One, the issues about which the two people will negotiate include: (1) Can Whittamore continue to practice medicine in a town in which he wishes to live? (2) Will there be a penalty for breaking the contract? (3) If there is a penalty, how much will it be? (4) How will the penalty be calculated, and what factors should be considered? (5) Is there a way that Whittamore can stay at the clinic and still maintain some distance from his estranged wife? (This, after all, is the crux of the problem.) Note that the framing, or description, of the issues above is in neutral terms that favor neither party, and that the wording describes a problem to be solved rather than a particular alternative to be forced by one bargainer on another.

Parties to a conflict select one of two major negotiation procedures to handle issues in dispute: *positional bargaining* or *interest-based bargaining* (Fisher and Ury, 1981). Positional bargaining usually occurs when a negotiator perceives that contested resources are limited and a distributive solution, one that allocates shares of gains and losses to each party, is the only possible outcome (Walton and McKersie, 1965). Interest-based bargaining, on the other hand, occurs when negotiators seek integrative solutions that meet as many of the needs of both parties as possible (Walton and McKersie, 1965). Generally, interest-based bargaining occurs when parties do not see resources as limited and solutions can be found in which all parties can have at least some of their needs met.

Positional bargaining derives its name from the practice of selecting a series of positions—particular settlement options that meet a party's interests—and presenting these to an opponent as the solution to the issue in question. A party's position may or may not be responsive to the needs or interests of other negotiators. Positions are generally ordered sequentially so that the first position is a large demand and represents a negotiator's maximum expectation of gain should his or her opponent acquiesce. Each subsequent position demands less of an opponent and results in fewer benefits for the initiating party. Characteristically, positional bargaining often commits parties early in negotiations to very specific solutions to issues in dispute and often reduces flexibility to generate other equally acceptable options.

In the Singson-Whittamore case, Whittamore's possible positions might include: "I refuse to pay any penalty for breaking the contract because the no-competition clause is not constitutional." Singson might respond with counter-positions: "Pay the penalty fee immediately or move out of town," or "You must pay the penalty, but we can negotiate when it is due."

Disputants often adopt positional bargaining when

- The stakes for winning are high.
- The resources (time, money, psychological benefits, and so forth) are perceived to be limited.
- A win for one side will mean a loss for another.
- Interests of the parties are not interdependent or are contradictory.
- Future relationships have a lower priority than immediate substantive gain.
- All major parties have enough power to damage the others if an impasse in the negotiations occurs (Moore, 1982b).

Interest-based bargaining, in contrast to positional bargaining, is based on different assumptions about the substantive issues to be negotiated, the contents of an acceptable solution, and the process by which an agreement is to be reached.

In interest-based bargaining, the negotiators do not necessarily assume that the substantive resource in question—money, time, behavior, and so forth—is necessarily limited. They do not assume that the resource must be divided into shares in which one bargainer is a winner and the other a loser. The attitude of the interest-based bargainer is that of a problem solver. The goal of negotiation is to find a solution that is mutually satisfactory and results in a win-win outcome.

Interest-based bargainers believe that settlements in negotiations are reached because a party has succeeded in having his or her interests satisfied. *Interests* are specific conditions (or gains) that a party must obtain for an acceptable settlement to occur. Interests are of three broad types: substantive, procedural, and psychological. *Substantive interests* refer to the needs that an individual has for particular tangible objects such as money and time. Substantive interests are usually the central needs on which negotiations focus.

Procedural interests refer to the preferences that a negotiator has for the *way* that the parties discuss their differences and the *manner* in which the bargaining outcome is implemented. Possible procedural interests may be that each person have the opportunity to speak his or her mind, that negotiations occur in an orderly and timely manner, that the parties avoid derogatory verbal attacks, that the plan for implementing the agreement be worked out in detail prior to final settlement, and that a written document or contract should result from bargaining.

Psychological interests refer to the emotional and relationship needs that a negotiator has both during and as a result of negotiations. Negotiators want to have high self-esteem, want to be respected by their opponent, and do not want to be degraded in negotiations. If the relationship is to be ongoing, the negotiators may want to have ongoing positive regard from the other party for their openness to future communication.

In the Singson-Whittamore case, Whittamore's interests include: (1) a desire to remain in town so that he can see and parent his children, (2) a desire to continue practicing his profession, (3) a desire to avoid contact with his estranged wife, (4) a preference for maintaining amicable relations with the clinic and its staff, and (5) a need to minimize the amount of initial penalty payments to the clinic so that he has enough money to start his own practice.

Some of Singson's interests include: (1) avoidance of monetary loss and patient attrition when a doctor leaves the staff, (2) maintenance of clinic management's prerogative to set the terms of an employment contract, (3) avoidance of a precedent in which a doctor leaves the clinic before the expiration of a contract and begins a practice in town, and (4) avoidance of a law suit.

Interest-based bargaining begins with an understanding of each of the interests of the two parties, not statements of positions. Often the parties identify their interests and those of other disputants in private and then hold a joint meeting to share their results. Parties discuss and modify their interests based on these early discussions. Once the interests have been revealed, explored, and accepted at least in principle, the parties can begin a mutual search for solutions that will meet their needs. Reaching an agreement requires negotiators to develop settlement options that meet at least some of the combination of substantive, procedural, and psychological needs of all parties.

Interest-based bargaining focuses on the satisfaction of particular interests rather than advocacy of a particular position that may or may not meet the needs of the individuals, as is the case in positional bargaining. The procedure in interest-based bargaining is one of mutual problem solving, similar to the process involved in putting together a puzzle. The parties sit side by side and attempt to develop a mutually acceptable settlement.

Mediators can help parties conduct either positional or interest-based bargaining more efficiently and effectively. Since the goal of mediation is to help parties reach a mutually acceptable settlement, mediators generally have a bias toward interest-based and integrative solutions. Often parties are engaged in a positional process that is destructive to their relationships, is not generating creative options, and is not resulting in wise decisions. One of the mediator's major contributions to the dispute resolution process is assisting the negotiators in making the transition from positional to interest-based bargaining.

Complexity of the Case and Issues Negotiated. Disputes come in a variety of levels of complexity. The simple-issue landlord-tenant case in which two parties argue over a security deposit is very different from the complexity of a child custody and divorce dispute that involves multiple issues and very complex psychodynamics between the disputants. The latter case may in its own right be very uncomplicated when compared to a multiparty case that involves American Telephone and Telegraph, a local Bell company, multiple independent phone companies, the Public Utilities Commission, and numerous consumer or public interest groups and that centers around multiple and complex technical issues.

Mediators entering disputes must design intervention strategies that respond to the complexity of a specific dispute. In one case, detailed data collection procedures may be required to understand the causes and dynamics of the conflict, while in another case a simple intake interview at the first joint session with the parties is sufficient. In some cases the mediator must break a particularly difficult impasse, and, when successful, may withdraw and return the parties to negotiations on their own. In other cases, the mediator may play an active role throughout negotiations and provide the major procedural framework for negotiations. In exploring the stages of mediation in later chapters, it is important to consider the complexity of the dispute to determine the amount of detail required in the intervention.

Definition of the Mediator's Role and Types of Interventions. The final variable that affects the noncontingent and contingent moves of a mediator is the definition of the tasks and role that the mediator is to perform in the negotiations. Mediators differ significantly when deciding their role and involvement in promoting successful negotiations. The division usually occurs when determining how much the mediator should focus on process and substance.

One school argues that mediators should focus primarily on the process of negotiations and leave decisions about the substantive content as the exclusive domain of the parties (Stulberg, 1981b). Procedurally oriented mediators define their role this way for a variety of reasons. First, mediators often believe that the parties are better informed about the substantive issues in dispute than any third party could ever be. These intervenors believe that the best quality decision is that determined by the parties. Second, mediators from this school believe that what the parties need is procedural help, not a substantive suggestion or decision. Third, these intervenors believe that the parties' commitment to implement and adhere to a settlement will be enhanced if they make the substantive decisions themselves, as opposed to having the deal decided or forged by the intervenor. Finally, the mediators of this school believe that a focus on the process and an impartial stance toward substance builds trust between the intervenor and disputants, decreases the risk to the parties of involving another party in the dispute, and makes them more open to procedural assistance.

Many labor-management mediators, especially intervenors from the Federal Mediation and Conciliation Service, subscribe to this role for the mediator (Kolb, 1983). They see themselves as "orchestrators" of a process that enables the parties to make their own substantive decisions.

Some environmental mediators also follow this procedurally oriented definition of the mediator's role. Bellman (1982) generally does not try to influence the substantive outcome of a dispute even if he ethically disagrees with the outcome, considers the settlement environmentally unsound, or believes that it is based on inaccurate or inadequate information. He sees himself purely as a process consultant.

Some family mediators also adhere to the procedurally oriented approach to intervention. They argue that in a divorce, for example, the parents generally know what is best for both the children and the family system as a whole (Phear, 1984; Saposnek, 1985). The parents do not need a substantive expert to tell them what to do. What they need is procedural help to assist them in problem solving.

The other school of thought argues that although the mediator is impartial and neutral, this does not mean that he or she should not work with the parties directly on substantive matters to develop a fair and just decision according to the intervenor's values. Suskind (1981, pp. 46–47), an environmental mediator, argues that intervenors should be involved in substantive decisions when (1) "the impacts of negotiated agreement [will affect] under represented or unrepresented groups," (2) there is "the possibility that joint net gains have not been maximized," (3) the parties are not aware of the "long term spill-over effects of the settlements," and (4) the precedents that they set "may be detrimental to the parties or the broader public." Suskind further notes that "although such intervention may make it difficult to retain the appearance of neutrality and the trust of the active parties, environmental mediators cannot fulfill their responsibilities to the community-at-large if they remain passive" (p. 47). Some labor-management mediators also belong to this school. These "deal-makers" intervene substantively when the parties are uninformed, ill-prepared to negotiate, or unaware of mutually acceptable substantive settlements (Kolb, 1983).

Child custody and divorce mediators also have advocates in the second school. Saposnek (1983) argues that the mediator should advocate the unrepresented interests of the children in negotiations between the parents and believes that the mediator should intervene and influence the substantive outcome if those interests are violated and not taken into consideration. Coogler (1978) also urges the mediator to engage in substantive negotiations and advocates that the intervenor write a letter of nonconcurrence that is sent to the court if the mediator seriously disagrees with the settlement.

Haynes (1981), another family mediator, believes that the intervenor should be active in power balancing help to define the terms of the substantive decision. Haynes, Coogler, and Saposnek directly disregard the concept of substantive impartiality as a critical component of the mediator's role.

There is a spectrum along which mediators place themselves in defining their degree of involvement in the procedure and substance of negotiations. On one side are those who advocate mostly procedural interventions; on the other side are advocates of substantive involvement by the mediator that may include actually forging the decision. Between them are mediators who pursue a role with mixed involvement in process and substance.

I lean strongly toward the process end of the spectrum because I believe that the parties should have the primary responsibility for self-determination. On rare occasions, however, the mediator has an ethical responsibility to raise critical questions about substantive options under consideration by the parties. These situations include cases where the agreement appears to be extremely inequitable to one or more of the parties, does not look as if it will hold over time, seems likely to result in renewed conflict at a later date, or where the terms of settlement are so loose (or confining) that implementation is not feasible. I believe the mediator should also intervene in cases involving the potential for violence or actual violence to one or more parties, either primary or secondary.

Depending on the role that the mediator or the mediator and the parties assign the intervenor, he or she will have to decide which types of interventions he or she will perform. In defining interventions, the mediator must decide on (1) the level of intervention, (2) the target of intervention, (3) the focus of intervention, and (4) the intensity of intervention.

The *level of intervention* refers to how much the mediator concentrates on helping negotiators move through the general critical situation, for example, the stages of bargaining, versus a focus on particular idiosyncratic problems that are pushing the parties toward impasse. In some disputes the parties may need assistance to break a particular deadlock, while others will need mediator assistance throughout the bargaining process.

The *target of intervention* refers to the person or people to whom the mediator directs his or her moves. Should moves be directed to all parties, to a relationship within the group such as a subgroup or team, or to a particular person? In a postmarital dispute, for example, should the mediator focus on changing the ex-wife's move, the ex-husband's, or both, or should he or she focus on the entire family system, including children, ex-spouses, stepparents, and grandparents? In a community dispute, should the mediator focus on the spokespeople, specific team members, the team as a whole, or the constituents of the parties?

The *focus of intervention* refers to the particular critical situations at which the mediator directs his or her moves. The mediator may focus his or her energies on changing the *psychological relationship* of parties to each other. This is often referred to as a conciliation. He or she may aim at creating the psychological conditions that are necessary for productive negotiations. The mediator may also focus on changing the *negotiation process* or the procedure that is being used by one or more people to solve the dispute. The focus may be on the process for moving through the stages of solving a specific problem, such as how to help a party make a proposal that will be acceptable to the other side.

The focus may also be on changing the *substance* or *content* of the dispute. The mediator may look for ways to explore data, to expand the number of acceptable options on the negotiation table, to narrow the choices when the parties are overwhelmed with possibilities, or to integrate proposals made by the disputants.

Finally, the intervenor may focus on changing the relationship *structure* among the parties. This may mean influencing their personal or interactive relationship in regard to such factors as power, communication patterns, face-to-face versus private negotiations, team structure, or a party's relationship to its constituents.

I will now turn to a detailed examination of the stages of mediation and the general moves mediators initiate to assist in reaching agreement.

THREE

Initial Contacts
with the
Disputing Parties

Mediators enter disputes as a result of (1) direct initiation by the parties, (2) referrals by secondary parties, (3) direct initiation by the mediator, or (4) appointment by a recognized authority such as a government official or agency. Each of these means of entry poses specific strategic choices regarding mediator activities and may affect the quality, type, and probability of a settlement.

Direct initiation by a party or parties is probably the most common means used by disputants to obtain a mediator's services. The request for mediation may come from a single party, a subgroup or coalition of parties, or all the disputants. The request may be initiated before or after the start of negotiations. The source of the request and the timing of the proposal for mediation may have a significant effect on the dynamics of negotiations. I will first explore requests for entry of a mediator made by single parties and subgroups of disputants and then examine requests made by all involved parties.

A request for mediation by a single party, whether an individual or a team, can have a variety of effects on the dynamics of negotiation and on subsequent strategies of the negotiators. One party commonly either proposes mediation to an opponent or makes a unilateral initiative to obtain a mediator. For exam-

44

ple, a husband may call a mediator and request help in negotiating custody arrangements with his estranged wife, or a government agency may request assistance in negotiating with a public interest group. If the parties have not started to negotiate, the request for mediation may mean that discussions are preferable to avoidance, stalemate, or competitive approaches to dispute resolution. A request for mediation may also signal a desire to cooperate for mutual benefit, a willingness to make concessions, or a belief that total victory is not possible.

People in conflict are often reluctant to ask for a third party's assistance. Parties are afraid that their request for intervention will weaken their negotiating position and damage the possibility of a satisfactory outcome. Reluctance to call a mediator is especially strong once parties are in the midst of negotiations and have reached an impasse. Theodore Kheel, a labor mediator, describes the problem faced by a party who is initiating the entry of a mediator: "If you've reached an impasse, it can be assumed that both sides have put forth what they claim will be their final offers. In that situation a proposal by one side or the other to bring in a mediator is obviously a signal that that side is willing to go still further" and grant more concessions, for instance (Shapiro, 1970, pp. 41-42). Reluctance to appear weak or to make additional offers often discourages a request for a mediator. If the party does ask for third-party assistance, he or she is probably following the traditional negotiator rule: "Always save something for the mediator" (Downing, 1960, p. 62).

Similar problems to those described above hold true for subgroups or coalitions of parties who request mediation. Risks, however, may be blunted when more than one party make such requests. The initiative can be framed in terms of the needs of all disputants rather than those of a single party, thus lowering the expectation of new concession making.

A proposal for mediation, especially in interpersonal or community disputes, raises the possibility of procedural rejection by another party. Several studies have examined the rate of refusal to initiate mediation in community and interpersonal disputes. Cook, Rochl, and Shepard (1980) found that people refused mediation services in 1,898 of 3,911 cases—a refusal rate of 48 percent.

Pearson (1982) found a rejection rate of 50 percent among divorcing couples in Denver, Colorado, who were offered free mediation services. Davis, Tichane, and Grayson (1980) found that in felony offenses among acquaintances, 32 percent of those referred to mediation failed to report and 12 percent refused outright to participate in the process.

Researchers have attributed the rejection of mediation services to (1) unfamiliarity with the process, (2) rigid adherence to a win-lose approach to dispute resolution, (3) intense emotions that block communication, and (4) habitual attachment to judicial means of dispute settlement (Cook, Rochl, and Shepard, 1980). Single-party requests for mediation services generally seem to result in fewer instances of mediation.

Given the above data on rejection rates, what should the mediator do if approached by only one party? After talking with the initiator, the intervenor must contact the responding party. Often the mediator or agency will mail a letter to the responding party, explaining the process of mediation and its advantages, liabilities, and cost, and notifying the party that the mediator will call within a short time to answer any questions and to discuss whether the party is interested in using the process. This letter helps the mediator avoid calling spontaneously and without introductions, forewarns the responding party of the intervenor's imminent call, and gives the disputant an opportunity to consider the viability of mediation before talking to the mediator.

When the mediator calls the respondent, the intervenor should not assume that the party wants to mediate. Since many people are not familiar with the process, the mediator may need to educate the respondents before obtaining a commitment to mediate. He or she should allow adequate time to explain the process and answer any questions. Care should be taken not to "hard sell" mediation. The respondent should select the option and not feel pressured to use the mediator's services. The party's personal commitment is crucial to successful settlement.

One mediator has used a paradoxical approach to explain

the viability of mediation: He asks the respondent to explain why he or she should use mediation, instead of promoting the process himself. This intervenor places the respondent, not the mediator, in the position of mediation advocate.

In cases in which the mediator is approached by both parties, a significant psychological step toward a cooperative resolution to the dispute has been made. "Implicit in such an invited third-party role are two assumptions: first, the disputants are sufficiently motivated to address their conflict that one or both of them are willing to enlist the services of a third party; and second, the third party is regarded as sufficiently attractive by one or both disputants that this party is invited to intervene rather than some other individual. From the third party's vantage point, an invited role is desirable both because it suggests that the disputants are ready to work and because the third party is placed in a unique position to exercise influence" (Rubin, 1981, p. 11).

To date, no data exist that correlate joint initiation of mediation to successful intervention. Mediators, however, generally find that a cooperative initiation of mediation by all parties usually minimizes escalatory dynamics between the disputants at the beginning of the intervention and indicates willingness to solve the dispute to the satisfaction of all.

Referrals by interested secondary parties, people who are not principal actors in disputes, are another way that people obtain mediation services. Secondary parties include two categories of persons or groups: first, parties who have no direct stake in the settlement of a dispute but are concerned about the general ramifications of continued conflict; and second, parties who, although they are not principal actors, do have tangible investment in the settlement of a dispute.

Examples of the first type of referral include close friends or neighbors who refer parties to a mediator or the intervenor to the parties, or a foundation that is concerned about general community turmoil that could result from escalating conflict (Lansford, 1983). These parties do not have a direct stake in the outcome but do want the dispute settled.

Secondary parties who have a more direct interest in the

settlement also initiate activities that facilitate mediator entry. The following workplace dispute illustrates such action: Two managers were in conflict over how a job was to be performed. A third manager—a peer—was uncomfortable with tension in the office. He talked to a fourth person in the office, a woman with no authority over the disputing managers, and asked her to intervene.

Lincoln (1976) described a school desegregation conflict in which a mediator was invited by the mayor and the school superintendent to mediate between two hostile groups of students—one group black, and the other white—that were threatening to vandalize school property and physically harm each other. Although the secondary parties were not directly involved in the negotiations, they clearly had high stakes in the outcome.

Secondary parties occasionally have authority over the people in conflict and will intervene to encourage disputants to mediate. Mediation organizations often establish referral relationships with judges, lawyers, court clerks, police officers, and personnel in planning departments, social service agencies, and educational and public interest organizations to route disputes to mediation.

Secondary parties not only refer cases to mediation but may also influence the probability of settlement. Bench referrals by judges, prosecutors, public attorneys, and police officers have a higher rate of settlement than referrals from community social service agencies, legal aid organizations, or governmental agencies (Cook, Rochl, and Shepard, 1980). The prospect of a litigious alternative is probably a significant factor in the influence of a referral source on the probability of settlement. Parties realize that if they do not reach an agreement in mediation, the case will probably go to court, an undesirable alternative in many instances.

Interventions initiated by the mediator are common in complex community disputes that are public in nature, involve multiple parties, and do not have a set of defined primary actors who can request mediation. In this form of entry, the mediator usually learns of the dispute from published written material or an interested secondary party. After careful examination of the dispute, the mediator takes the initiative to contact one or more disputants and offer his or her services. Entry of this type is complicated by the fact that the mediator may have difficulty building credibility with disputants, may lack their psychological commitment, may be subject to ethical issues involving association of his or her intervention with "ambulance chasing," and will need to consider the possible effect of the intervention on the coalescence of power among the parties involved.

Gerald Cormick and Jane McCarthy, mediators of an environmental dispute involving flood control and land use along the Snoqualmie River in Washington State, used this approach. They entered the conflict on their own initiative and assisted the primary parties in identifying and including additional disputants. "In determining whether mediation would be acceptable to the disputants, Cormick and McCarthy discovered who the key participants were by asking everyone involved: 'Can you name 10 or 12 persons who if they could agree on something, would have stature and influence enough so that you, who are in disagreement, could reasonably support them and any agreement they might reach?' Those named most often became part of the group that would meet with Cormick and McCarthy to work out a compromise" (Dembart and Kwartler, 1980, p. 47).

This uninvited form of entry is often the only one available to mediators who perceive that they may be helpful to disputants who may not be aware of mediation as a means of dispute resolution. More will be said about targeting parties and entry in Chapter Five.

Appointing a mediator is another means of entry. In institutionalized labor disputes, mediation is often legally required before the parties can proceed to other means of dispute resolution, and mediators are appointed by state or federal agencies. There are some interpersonal and community disputes in which government agencies may mandate the process, appoint mediators, or do both.

In the marital conciliation court system of California, for

example, parties in child custody cases are required to try mediation before court action (Comeau, 1982). There are also instances in which elected officials have appointed a mediator to respond to a community dispute (Dembart and Kwartler, 1980; Lansford, 1983; Clark-McGlennon Associates, 1982), but in most cases of this type, appointment appears to be merely official recognition of what has previously been arranged and accepted by the disputants themselves.

Tasks of the Mediator in the Entry Stage

Regardless of how a mediator enters a dispute, he or she must accomplish certain specific intervention tasks. These include (1) building personal, institutional, and procedural credibility; (2) establishing rapport with the disputants; (3) educating participants about the negotiation process, the role of the mediator, and the function of mediation; and (4) gaining a commitment to begin mediating.

Building Credibility. Mediators must build credibility with those in conflict by developing their expectations that the mediator and the mediation process will help them resolve the dispute. There are three types of credibility: personal, institutional, and procedural.

Personal credibility refers to the mediator's possession of particular personal characteristics that mediators and disputants have long attributed to the success of the intervention process. Landsberger (1956) found that disputing parties in labor negotiations, when evaluating successful mediator attributes, included originality of ideas, an appropriate sense of humor, the ability to act unobtrusively in a conflict, the ability to create the feeling of being "at one" with the disputants and concerned with their well-being, a willingness to be a vigorous salesperson when necessary, control over his or her feelings, persistent and patient effort, the ability to understand quickly the dynamics and complexities of a dispute, and some specific knowledge of the field in which he or she is mediating. Activities by mediators that allow them to personally exhibit these qualities will generally reinforce beliefs held by disputing parties that the mediator has personal attributes that will assist them in resolving the dispute.

Institutional credibility refers to the reputation of the organization that employs the mediator. Institutional credibility is based on an organization's history of successful performance in the field of dispute resolution for which a mediator is needed, a history of unblemished impartiality among personnel, and often a background of neutral or at least not overtly biased sources of funding. Institutional credibility may be a crucial factor in the acceptance or rejection of mediators or mediation organizations. Mediators wishing to build institutional credibility (1) may produce brochures describing their expertise and services, (2) may present a list of former clients to prospective users (subject, of course, to client approval and the limits of confidentiality), (3) may explain past cases that illustrate the types of disputes the intervenor has mediated, (4) may present credentials of membership in recognized dispute resolution associations, or (6) may disclose organizational funding sources to demonstrate institutional impartiality.

Two case examples illustrate the importance of building institutional credibility. A company executive who was a party to a dispute considered using a mediation service to assist him in settling a community dispute. The mediation firm was asked to make a presentation describing its services to some of the involved parties. During the meeting, the executive looked at the firm's brochure and began to put pluses and minuses next to the names of the firm's board members based on his perception of whether they would be positively or negatively disposed toward his interests in the dispute. When he checked the marks, he noticed that they came out even, and he accepted the firm's claim to impartiality.

In another case, an environmental group wanted the names and telephone numbers of other public interest groups that had used a certain mediation organization to settle conflicts over mining. The organization provided the data to build institutional credibility.

Procedural credibility refers to beliefs held by the disputants that the process the mediator has proposed to resolve the conflict has a strong likelihood of success. Some mediators are reluctant to describe the procedures by which they propose to resolve a dispute. By claiming that they respond differently to each conflict or by arguing that mediation is an art form rather than a series of scientific interventions, some mediators shroud their practice in secrecy and leave the disputants ignorant of the mediation process. Procedural credibility in this instance might be enhanced by demystifying the mediation process.

Clouding the mediation process has been sharply criticized by other mediators, and I advocate a candid education of the parties about general mediation procedures that might be used in their dispute. Clear procedural descriptions enable the parties to make informed judgments about the viability of the process and will demonstrate how the procedure might work for them. In building procedural credibility, the mediator should stress that successful resolution rests primarily on the disputants themselves and that the best possible process will not guarantee that recalcitrant parties will come to terms.

An example of procedural credibility building occurred in 1985 when mediators from the Center for Dispute Resolution were asked to intervene by the Public Utilities Commission of Colorado in a dispute over the creation of a new rule on telephone access charges. As the process of negotiated and mediated rule making had a very limited history in Colorado and none of the major parties had ever engaged in such a process, the mediators initiated an educational session for the disputants in which case histories and procedures used for regulatory rule making in other settings were presented. Successful case studies built procedural credibility and enabled the parties to visualize how the process might work for them.

Establishing Rapport with the Disputants. Personal, institutional, and procedural credibility is merely the starting point for a mediator's entry into a dispute. The greatest factor in the acceptability of an intervenor is probably the rapport established between the mediator and the disputants. *Rapport* refers to the ability to communicate freely, the level of comfort of the parties, the degree of precision in the communication, and the quality of human contact. Rapport is clearly influenced by the mediator's personal style, manner of speech, dress, and social background; common interests, friends, or associates; and the degree of communication between the mediator and the disputants. Mediators often talk about the need to develop some form of bond with the parties. This may be accomplished by identifying common personal experiences early in the mediation such as recreation, travel, children, associates, and so forth that the mediator and disputants share; talking about common values; genuinely affirming a disputant's attribute or activity; or demonstrating the sincerity of the mediator through behavior.

Kakwirakeron, a Mohawk leader in a dispute involving Native American land claims at Moss Lake in upstate New York, described the manner of Rowley, a mediator with the American Arbitration Association, as follows: "When I first met Rowley I remember the white hair which he has, and the type of face he has is to me an honest face. And he always had the ready smile, which is a genuine smile, not just for the show of it. He had a manner, a very easy manner which is easy for us to identify. He really doesn't have a mask on. He is not trying to put on a show or an air of importance. He is just honest and straightforward and our first impression of him held up all the way through" (Kwartler, 1980, pp. 15-16).

Educating Participants About the Mediation Process. To build initial procedural credibility, the mediator should explain enough about his or her role and mediation procedures that disputants are willing to try the process. In the later phases of a mediator's efforts to enter a dispute, he or she will spend additional time educating the parties about the particular negotiation and mediation process. This educational effort should be undertaken to (1) minimize surprises that might result from misunderstandings about the negotiation and mediation processes, (2) clarify the sequence of steps so that disputants know what to expect and know what roles they will be playing, and (3) gain both conscious and unconscious feedback from the participants about their feelings and reservations about the intervention procedure. Although mediation is not primarily an edu-

cational exercise, disputants must have at least a minimal understanding of the process for the intervenor to be successful. Some
of the procedures that the parties should understand include:

- The impartial role of the mediator
- How data will be collected
- The procedure that will be used to "work" on each issue
- The limits of confidentiality in the mediation process
- The potential use of caucuses or private meetings
- The possible forms that a settlement, if reached, might take

Parties should assess all the procedures available to them
to resolve the dispute and decide on mediation before beginning
the process. Careful explanation and evaluation of the alternative approaches enhance the probability that mediation, if it is
selected as the preferred dispute resolution process, will be successful.

Gaining a Commitment to Mediate. The mediator must
believe that there is a common commitment by the parties both
to the process of negotiation and mediation as means of resolving their dispute and to the mediator as an assistant in this effort. The commitment to the process and to an intervenor has
been referred to in organizational development literature as a
"psychological contract" (Schein, 1969, pp. 81–88). A psychological contract consists of the terms and expectations of the
relationship between the mediator and disputant such as openness, honesty, and commitment to settlement.

Mediators at this point usually have to make a strategic
decision about how explicit or formal the commitment process
should be and what contractual form it should take. Formal
contracts often specify fees, expected time expenditure, and
specific services to be or not to be performed. Mediators vary
considerably on the degree of formality in mediation contracts.
Some mediators want an explicit signed statement that the parties are committed to achieving a jointly satisfactory solution
with the mediator's assistance (Coogler, 1978; Folberg and Taylor, 1984; Ricci, 1980). Other mediators rely exclusively on
more informal, verbal psychological contracts.

In some disputes an attempt to gain overt commitment to mediation, either oral or written, may lead to a failure to begin negotiations at all. Mediators occasionally defer explicit initial formal commitment to the process in favor of tentative or preliminary negotiations. They delay asking the parties to commit to mediation until a series of successful procedural and substantive decisions have been made. Commitment will be formalized later. In this approach to achieving commitment, mediators gain an initial agreement to talk with one or more parties alone or in informal joint meetings. In conversations, the mediator and disputants may discover common interests that can be built on to develop rapport between the parties and later, perhaps, to form substantive agreements. Common interests are later used to initiate formal discussions.

Between these two extremes of explicit written or verbal informal commitment is a strategic third option. Through questioning of and discussion with the disputants, a mediator may discover specific conditions under which conflicting parties will be willing to negotiate. These might include guidelines for how the parties will interact in negotiation, times and locations of sessions, or specific symbolic gestures required to initiate discussions. The mediator may work with the parties to meet these behavioral preconditions for negotiation. By setting the stage and building a commitment contract, the mediator can encourage involvement without seeking a formal statement to that end. This approach has the advantage that parties do not have to overtly commit to the process to begin dialogue but has the drawbacks that a precedent may be established that requires the mediator to constantly overcome limits or hurdles thrown up by participants who may not be committed to the process, or that the parties may not be willing to formalize their commitment to any agreements.

Implementing Entry

So far I have explained the four general means of entry and the tasks to be accomplished by the mediator during this stage of intervention. I now turn to specific ways that mediators initiate contact with disputants. These include letters, phone calls, personal visits, and third-party introductions. Depending on the mediator, institution, type of dispute, and characteristics of the disputants, various combinations of the above may be effective. Some mediation organizations make their first contact with clients by phone, while others rely more heavily on personal interviews. Frequently a combination of letter, brochure, and phone call is used to build credibility, describe the process, and gain commitment to mediate. (See Resource B for a sample contact letter.)

In complex disputes—such as volatile community conflicts or cases involving highly bureaucratic and hierarchical organizations—in which access to the main actors is tightly controlled or limited by some barrier such as race, channels of authority, or even physical inaccessibility, a secondary party may be used to introduce the mediator to one or more disputants. These introductions may be invaluable to the intervenor seeking entry into a closed dispute.

Timing of Entry

Two levels of intervention activity are usually weighed when considering the point at which a mediator should enter a dispute: (1) the timing of data collection regarding the case and (2) the initiation of problem-solving mediation activities. While both types of intervention require entry by the mediator, their impacts on the dispute are quite different.

Data Collection. Entry to gather preliminary data about a conflict can be initiated at almost any time in the development of a dispute, although information may be more difficult to collect during certain phases of conflict development, such as the early escalation stage before the actual decisions of the parties to negotiate, or the stage in which negotiations have commenced but parties do not believe the mediator is necessary. The mediator's entry to collect data about the conflict usually does not change the power relations between the parties.

The major strategic decisions about intervention for data collection focus primarily on whom to talk to, the sequence of interviews, and the content of interviews. More will be said about entry strategies for data collection in Chapter Five.

Initiation of Mediation and Problem Solving. The timing of mediator intervention to solve problems, as opposed to collecting data, is one of the most intensely debated topics in the dispute resolution field (Simkin, 1971; Kerr, 1954; Carpenter and Kennedy, 1979; and Pearson, 1984). Some mediators argue that early intervention limits hostility and emotional damage. Early entry by the mediator may also alleviate the tendency for parties to polarize on substantive issues. Early entry may enable the mediator to prevent a party's hard-line commitment to alternatives that are unacceptable to other disputants.

Another argument for early intervention concerns procedural advantages. Polarization often results when disputants fail to understand productive means or procedures to resolve their controversies. Early intervention can discourage unproductive negotiation behavior, can route the parties toward behavior or procedures that will result in settlement, and can discourage energy-draining responses that may escalate a dispute and create barriers to settlement due to poor process rather than substantive differences.

Arguments for later mediator entry into a dispute center on the needs for parties to mobilize their power, to equalize the means they have to influence each other, and to occasionally demonstrate their coercive power before negotiations. Later entry may also allow for polarization to develop that often clarifies issues, provides time for the parties to vent emotions, and allows the parties themselves to request the assistance of an impartial mediator after they have exhausted their own procedural and substantive options.

Proponents of later intervention argue that parties need time to mobilize their forces and gather their means of influence in order to affect the other parties involved (Cormick, 1982; Crowfoot, 1980). They claim that early entry hinders this process; that the weaker party, who is not as well prepared for the conflict and therefore has less influence, may be overwhelmed; and that an unfair settlement may be either reached or imposed. Therefore, they believe that disputants should have adequate time to mobilize their power before starting negotiations or engaging a mediator's services. Examples of mobilization of resources might include visiting a lawyer and obtaining advice on the strength of a legal case, conducting research necessary for informed negotiations, mobilizing a community group to protest a particular policy, filing a case in court, or planning a strike.

Early-entry adherents generally do not disagree with those advocating late entry about the needs of parties to mobilize and, whenever possible, equalize power. Failure to gather the necessary data before negotiations is tantamount to playing a game of poker without looking at the cards. Failure to assess legal power or, when appropriate, extralegal action before negotiations can cause one party to be taken advantage of by another.

Advocates of early entry diverge from their colleagues who advocate late entry on the question of demonstrating coercive power. They argue that mobilization and exercise of coercion should be separated. Advocates of early entry point to experimental research (Rubin and Brown, 1975) demonstrating that the exercise of coercive power, although it may promote negotiations, does not necessarily promote cooperative behavior. This finding seems to be corroborated by research on outcomes of actual negotiations. Pearson (1984), for example, found that couples in divorce settlement mediation who had used coercive court mechanisms to obtain temporary orders had a lower rate of settlement than those who had not used legal coercion before settlement negotiations.

Late-entry advocates counter with valid case examples in which the exercise of force—legal suits, strikes, or demonstrations—has been necessary to demonstrate a party's power and, in some cases, to force an opponent to negotiate. Last-minute pressure has clearly inclined parties toward agreement and has motivated them to request a mediator's assistance.

Mediators who look for easy answers regarding questions of power and timing of the impartial party's entry will probably find none. The best answer is that these factors depend on the case. If parties can mobilize power so that they are informed and so that the other side knows that they are dealing with a prepared adversary, the power may never need to be exercised, and the mediator may be able to intervene before there is a crisis. Early entry in this case may prevent unnecessary damage to either of the disputing parties.

On the other hand, if the parties have unequal power, need a confrontation to mobilize resources, or must test each other's strength before bargaining in good faith can begin, mediators are advised to delay entry. This may enable the parties to test and balance their power and may place them in a position to bargain from a position of strength.

The argument for a period to vent emotions is also not contested by early-entry proponents. They do, however, maintain that unstructured and prolonged venting, which may occur if the mediator delays entry, may result in hostile or unproductive behavior that causes unnecessary psychological barriers. The final argument, which relates to the "ripeness" of a dispute for settlement, is an extremely important strategic issue concerned directly with the timing of intervention. Numerous mediators and negotiators have observed that disputes go through specific cycles and that resolution of issues in disputes often cannot occur until disputants have performed ritual acts (Douglas, 1962). Mediator entry too early in a dispute, it is claimed, damages this developmental cycle.

Late-entry proponents argue that parties are not psychologically or strategically prepared to use an intervenor's services until they have reached an impasse and recognize that they cannot reach a settlement without third-party assistance (Perez, 1959, p. 717).

> The safest rule postulates that a mediator should not enter a negotiation until there is a bona fide deadlock. The reason is self-evident. A premature intervention by the mediator relieves the parties of the pressure under which they are working. The reciprocal pressure is the basic force that keeps the parties moving through proposals and counter-

proposals. Entering the situation before a genuine deadlock is reached creates an atmosphere of relaxation in the parties, and consequently, the mediator has no basic element to keep the parties moving. Requesting the services of a mediator before the bona fide deadlock is usually a trick used by one or both parties to extend the negotiations. An intervention at this time will discourage the parties from reaching an agreement. One or both parties will relax their efforts while the mediator gets his fingers burned.

Proponents of early entry, on the other hand, argue that psychological readiness and motivation for settlement can often be accelerated by an efficient mediation process introduced early into a dispute. Early introduction of mediation can decrease levels of frustration, can diminish polarization, and can promote positive results. Success, rather than mutual frustration, can then become the driving force for negotiations.

The timing of entry is clearly an important strategic decision for mediators. At the current stage of research, not enough is known to specify in an unqualified manner the conditions under which early entry is superior to later intervention. Mediators should assess whether they believe early entry will be more detrimental to the disputants than delay. If their answer is no, an early intervention is probably the safer route.

FOUR

Selecting a Strategy to Guide Mediation

In Chapter One I presented several approaches to conflict management and resolution. These spanned a continuum with conflict avoidance at one extreme and physical violence at the other. As one moved from left to right in the diagram (see Figure 1), the approaches became progressively more assertive and coercive. My concern in this chapter is with the process people use in conflict to select a particular approach or combination of approaches along this continuum. Of particular concern is how and under what circumstances people select mediated negotiations as the principal way to manage or resolve conflict.

Selection of an arena is related to selection of a dispute management approach. Arenas or locales vary according to the degrees of several dimensions: publicness and privacy, informality and formality, institutionalization and noninstitutionalization, and voluntariness and coercion. Any given approach can be acted out in a variety of arenas. For example, mediation can occur in a private setting that is informal, voluntary, and un-institutionalized—as in child custody and divorce settlements. Mediation can also be conducted in a highly public setting with standardized behaviors and rituals. An example of large-scale public negotiations is the Negotiated Investment Strategy sessions sponsored by the Kettering Foundation that enabled federal, state, and city agencies to develop coordinated policies on issues ranging from site-specific land use matters to citywide social service policies (Shanahan and others, 1982).

61

Parties need to select both the approach and arena that they think will best meet their needs and satisfy their interests. Approach and arena selection is a relational procedure in that it occurs as a result of interaction between the people in conflict. Parties may use the same approach and arena, may partially coordinate their approaches or arenas, or may use entirely different approaches and arenas. To achieve a termination of the conflict, the parties must usually coordinate their dispute resolution activities.

A mediator can assist parties in selecting and coordinating approaches and arenas. He or she is often more aware of approaches and arenas than are the disputing parties and can educate them about alternatives in this early stage of prenegotiation and assist them in selecting an appropriate means of dispute settlement that will best meet their needs and capabilities.

Mediator-Disputant Relationship for Making Decisions

The mediator's role in assisting disputants in making decisions about conflict approaches and arenas is similar to role decisions faced by lawyers. Hamilton (1972, p. 41) outlines three philosophical stances that a lawyer may take in advising and counseling clients:

A. Collect the facts, explain how the law applies, analyze, recommend a best course, or courses, of action and argue for its adoption.
B. Collect the facts, explain how the law applies, analyze, explain the course of action open to the client and leave the decision entirely to him.
C. "B" above, except with discussion of the ramifications of the course of action and the situation until the client is able to make his decision.

Mediators must choose among the same three stances, with the exception that they do not interpret the law.

The majority of mediators probably see their role as defined by option C, in which the task of the mediator is to assist disputants in making their own informed decision based on data and knowledge of procedural opportunities available through various approaches and arenas outlined by the mediator. Most mediators view the mediator-disputant relationship as collaborative, in which information is shared to develop the wisest and most considered decisions possible.

Approach and Arena Decision:
General Move Categories

Mediators should not automatically assume at this stage of intervention that mediated negotiation is the best approach for conflict management. It is only through a careful assessment process that the disputants and the mediator may jointly arrive at this conclusion.

There is no one procedure that is appropriate in all disputes to decide if mediation is the best approach for dispute resolution. Mediators can, however, assist people in conflict in accomplishing some of the following tasks:

1. Identify the interests or goals that must be satisfied in a potential settlement.
2. Consider the range of possible and acceptable dispute outcomes.
3. Identify the conflict approaches that may assist disputants in reaching individual, subgroup, or collective goals.
4. Identify and assess criteria for selecting an approach.
5. Select and make a commitment to an acceptable approach.
6. Coordinate approaches between disputants, if necessary.

In the following sections I will explain each point in more detail.

Identification of Interests

The mediator at this point will usually talk with the parties separately and will encourage them to carefully examine their own interests and those of other parties to arrive at answers to the following questions:

1. What interests (substantive, procedural, and psychological) must be met by a conflict management approach and settlement?
2. What interests are mutually incompatible or overlap with the interests of other parties?
3. What interest is there in an ongoing relationship?
4. What forms of actual or potential power do the parties have that would allow them to impose their interests on other disputants?
5. How important or salient are the various interests to each actor in the dispute?

The analysis of interests enables the parties and the intervenor to determine whether any common interests exist and to assess the purity of the dispute (Kriesberg, 1973). *Purity* refers to the exclusivity or commonality of interests. A pure conflict is one in which all interests are incompatible—for example, no settlement options are available that can satisfy one party's interests without sacrificing those of another. A mixed conflict allows for some satisfaction of all interests. If a conflict is pure, parties have little to negotiate. If it is mixed, negotiation and mediation are appropriate approaches to dispute resolution.

For example, if a couple both demand legal custody of their child and there are no provisions in their state for joint custody, the conflict could be pure: Neither party can win legal custody without the other losing. On the other hand, if both parents want to share their relationship with the child and are interested in allocating nonconflicting time fairly between themselves, then the conflict is mixed and suitable for negotiation.

Dispute Outcomes

After identifying the interests involved in the conflict, mediators usually work with each party separately to assess potential and, in some cases, probable conflict outcomes. Thomas (1976) identifies five possible outcomes to any given issue in dispute. Clark and Cummings (1981) elaborate on Thomas's themes. Their combined results are represented in Figure 5. For the sake of clarity this figure represents a dispute with only two sides and illustrates a conflict from the viewpoint of Party A.

Figure 5. Possible Outcomes of a Dispute as Viewed by Party A.

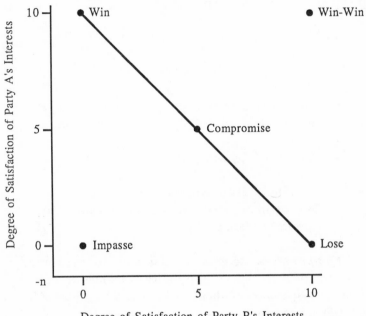

Degree of Satisfaction of Party B's Interests

Win-lose outcomes occur in the upper left and lower right corners of the chart. The difference is in which party wins. Here, Party A wins, its interests are satisfied, and Party B loses. Win-lose outcomes are most common when

- One party has overwhelming power.
- Future relationships are not of great concern.
- The stakes for winning are high.
- One party is extremely assertive and the other is passive or not as aggressive as the "winner."
- Satisfaction of the interests of the disputants is not dependent on their mutual cooperation.

- One or more parties are uncooperative [Moore, 1982b, p. V-3].

Impasse outcomes are present in the lower left corner. These outcomes result when parties are not able to come to an agreement. They occur when

- Both parties choose to avoid the conflict for whatever reason.
- Neither party has enough power to force the issue.
- There is lack of trust, poor communication, excessive emotion, or an inadequate resolution process.
- The stakes for winning are low or neither party cares about the dispute.
- The interests of the parties are not related.
- One or more of the parties are uncooperative [Moore, 1982b, p. V-3].

Compromise outcomes are illustrated by the central portion of the diagonal line. Compromise outcomes occur when all parties give up some of their goals to obtain others. They are likely to happen when

- Neither party has the power necessary to win totally.
- The future positive relationship of the disputants is important but they do not trust each other enough to work together.
- The stakes for winning are moderately high.
- Both parties are assertive.
- The interests of both parties are mutually interdependent.
- The parties have some leeway for cooperation, bargaining and tradeoffs [Moore, 1982b, p. V-3].

Win-win outcomes occur when all parties feel that their interests have been satisfied. Conditions for win-win outcomes are present when

- Both parties are not engaged in a power struggle.
- A future positive relationship is important.
- The stakes are high for producing a mutually satisfactory solution.
- Both parties are assertive problem solvers.
- The interests of all parties are mutually interdependent.
- Parties are free to cooperate and to engage in joint problem solving [Moore, 1982b, p. V–3].

Mediators discuss with parties various possible outcomes and how they meet the interests of the parties. The outcomes and interests should match.

Conflict Strategies and Approaches

Once a party has assessed its interests and those of other parties and reviewed potential dispute outcomes, it must select a particular approach to reach the desired end. Approach selection depends on a variety of criteria. One of the most important criteria is the strategy that a party plans to pursue. Mediators review either explicitly or implicitly general strategy options open to the parties and how these strategies may be applied within the context of a given approach. Strategy assessment is usually conducted by the mediator privately with each party.

There are five general strategy options: (1) competition, (2) avoidance, (3) accommodation, (4) negotiated compromise, and (5) interest-based negotiation. Figure 6 describes strategy options as viewed by Party A.

Competition: The Way to Win-Lose Settlements. In some situations, a party's interests are so narrow that they can be met by only a few solutions, none of which are acceptable to other parties. A party may choose a competitive approach and strive

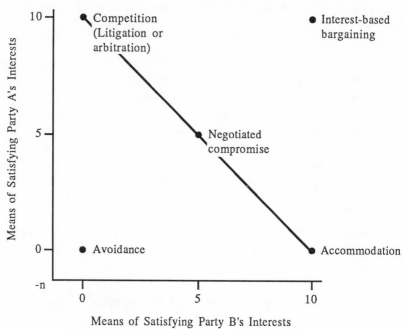

Figure 6. Conflict Strategies as Viewed by Party A.

for a win-lose outcome, especially when it has more power than its opponent. Competitive approaches include litigation, arbitration, and extralegal activities such as nonviolent direct action and violence.

In deciding to use a competitive approach, a party should weigh the costs as well as the benefits of its conflict behavior:

- Will the party get what it wants over the long term as well as short run?
- Will competitive behavior destroy relationships that will be important in the future?
- Does the party have enough power to guarantee a win? What happens if it loses?
- Will competition provoke competition in other areas?
- Will a competitive strategy lead to the most desirable solution? [Moore, 1982b, p. V-4].

Avoidance or Stalemate. Conflict avoidance can be either productive or unproductive to dispute settlement. People avoid conflict for a variety of reasons: fear, lack of knowledge of management processes, absence of interdependent interests, indifference to the issues in the dispute, or belief that agreement is not possible and conflict is not desirable.

Blake, Shepard, and Mouton (1964) noted that avoidance approaches have different levels. The first may be to claim a position of *neutrality.* Stating "We have no position on this issue at this time" is a way to avoid being drawn into a dispute.

In the second level of avoidance, *isolation,* disputants pursue their interests independently of another group with limited interaction. Groups are allowed to have their "spheres of interests" if they do not impinge on another's domain. This strategy is used frequently when a conflict of interest exists, but overt conflict is not desirable. For example, some parents agree to spheres of interest in custody arrangements. When the child is at one parent's house he or she is expected to behave a certain way, and at the other's the rules may change. The parties agree to disagree on parenting styles while respecting the other's style and contract not to fight each other on this issue.

People or groups that have been defeated repeatedly use *withdrawal* to ensure their continued existence and to avoid any conflict that might lead to another defeat. Withdrawal means total dissociation of disputants. This strategy is not helpful to mediated negotiations.

Accommodation: Providing for the Other's Interests. Accommodation occurs when one party agrees to meet the interests of another at the expense of its own needs. Accommodative strategy is pursued when

- Sacrifice of some interests is required to maintain a positive relationship.
- It is desirable to demonstrate or foster cooperation.
- Interests are extremely interdependent [Moore, 1982b, p. V-5].

A positive accommodative approach may be pursued when there is hope that a more collaborative process or traded benefits may occur later on other issues. For example, when a developer voluntarily agrees to spend additional funds to add an amenity demanded by a dissatisfied homeowners' group, he is accommodating himself to their needs. He did not have to spend the money but decided that a positive ongoing relationship was worth the expenditure.

Accommodation may also be pursued for negative reasons:

- Parties lack the power necessary to pursue an alternative strategy.
- Parties are passive or unassertive.
- Parties have a low investment in the outcome [Moore, 1982b, p. V-5].

Negotiated Compromise: A Strategy of Education and Sharing Profits and Losses. Bargaining or compromise is selected because

- The parties do not perceive the possibility of a win/win situation that will meet their needs and have decided to divide up what they see as a limited resource.
- Interests are not seen as interdependent or compatible.
- The parties do not trust each other enough to enter into joint problem solving.
- Parties are sufficiently equal in power so that neither can force the issue in its favor [Moore, 1982b, p. V-5].

Many out-of-court settlements are negotiated compromises. A judicial decision is risky for both sides because it is not clear who will win. Lawyers split the difference to ensure that their clients each get some of what they want, and each party shares some of the loss.

Interest-Based Negotiation: Meeting the Needs of All Parties. In contrast to competition and compromise, in which the outcome is seen as division of fixed resources, interest-based negotiation seeks to enlarge the range of alternatives so that the needs of all parties are met.

Interest-based negotiation works best when

- Parties have at least a minimal level of trust in each other.
- Parties have some mutually interdependent interests.
- Equal, but not necessarily similar, means of influence exist or the party with the superior power is willing to curtail the exercise of power and work toward cooperative solutions.
- Parties have a high investment in mutually satisfactory outcome because of mutual fear of potential costs that might result from impasse, or desire for a positive future relationship [Moore, 1982b, p. V-5].

Each of the strategies listed above can be pursued in the context of several approaches and arenas.

Parties must match the strategy with their interests and link it with an approach that will best assist the parties in satisfying them. Mediators should individually help parties to decide if they want to compete, avoid, accommodate, compromise, or seek a cooperative settlement. Once the party has selected a general strategy, it also chooses an approach that best implements the strategy. General strategies of compromise, accommodation, and interest-based negotiation are most compatible with negotiation as an approach.

Selection of a general strategy to guide a negotiation approach does not mean that other strategies will not be used to respond to particular aspects of a dispute. For example, a party may choose to compete on central or core issues and may decide to avoid or accommodate others. Selection of a general strategy is merely a guide for subsequent negotiations. Strategy will often change once the parties have started discussions and have become more informed about issues, interests, and means of influence of other parties. Parties commonly select a competitive strategy, decide to negotiate, and then shift to a strategy of compromise or interest-based negotiations.

Mediators aid parties in matching interests, strategies, and approaches by helping them identify and assess an approach's potential for reaching a satisfactory outcome. Generally, a mediator should suggest and help a party assess more than one strategy and approach so that it does not appear that the intervenor is advocating a particular method of resolution. The mediator may also discuss possible arenas that may be combined with an approach. For example, a party might consider litigation as a means of forcing a party to negotiate. The locale becomes the legal system and the courthouse, and the combined approaches become litigation and negotiation.

Criteria for Selecting an Approach and Arena

After identifying possible approaches and arenas available to the party, mediators usually assist the parties in identifying relevant criteria that should be considered in selecting an approach and arena. Criteria may be different for interpersonal, organizational, or community disputes. There are, however, many similarities. Some of the criteria or variables for selecting an approach or arena are cost, time, the relationship between the disputants, the internal dynamics of the dispute, and power.

Cost

- What will be the financial cost of pursuing each approach or arena alternative (direct costs, salary costs, delay costs, lawyer fees, and so forth)?

Time

- How long will it take to settle the dispute using each approach or arena?
- Is a rapid or a delayed settlement desirable?

- Are there any critical deadlines or time restraints on the parties? Do these deadlines pose an opportunity or a crisis for one of the parties?
- What is the most advantageous time to settle?
- Do the parties need more time to mobilize resources or build credibility and commitment among a constituency for a particular course of action?

Relationship Between Disputants

- Is the conflict a single-encounter dispute or is the conflict occurring in the context of an ongoing relationship?
- What type of relationship is desired at the end of the dispute?
- How will the use of various approaches and arenas affect the ongoing relationship?
- Do any of the proposed approaches and arenas seem unfair or in conflict with relationship or community norms?
- What effect will selection of the various approaches or arenas have on the public image of the party or parties? Do they enhance or detract from public credibility?
- Will the selection of a particular approach or arena affect future conflicts of this type?

Internal Dynamics (Crowfoot, 1980)

- Is the individual or organization stable and effective enough to pursue various approaches?
- Will the approaches involve the membership of the organizations? How and at what costs or benefits?
- Will a particular approach or arena build or unify membership and the organization?
- Does a particular approach build self-acceptance, confirmation, essentiality, and a psychological feeling of success or failure (Argyris, 1970)?
- Do the individuals or organizations have the necessary leadership and skills to pursue a particular course of action?
- Do the individuals or organizations have the time, energy, and financial and emotional resources to pursue a particular course of action?

Power (Simokaitis, n.d.)

- What power or means of influence do disputants have to make the other side give them what they want?
- How powerful does the party believe the other side perceives it to be?
- What possible allies and other sources of power might the party be able to tap?
- What might happen to limit the party's power?
- What are the limits on the power of the other disputants?

Once decision criteria or variables are identified, the mediator should assist a disputant in assessing how important each criterion is and how it affects or will be affected by the selection of a particular approach and arena. Mediators may assist parties in making this analysis by providing a structure to do a cost-benefit analysis (Moore, 1982b), by developing a decision tree (Behn and Vaupel, 1982) that identifies strategic choices and possible outcomes, or by helping participants assess probabilities of outcomes through an analysis of similar cases or trends (Bellows and Moulton, 1981).

There are cases in which parties originally state that they want to mediate, but a careful assessment of interests and criteria for selecting an approach and arena reveals that they are not willing to make the substantive, procedural, or psychological concessions that would make a negotiated settlement possible. In these situations the mediator should advise the parties that other approaches to resolving the conflict may be more appropriate.

Selecting and Making a Commitment
to an Approach and Arena

Once all approaches and arenas have been compared, according to the criteria and desired outcome, the mediator should assist the parties in making a final decision to pursue a particular approach or arena. Careful assessment of valid information about potential outcomes from each procedure usually helps people build internal commitment to a choice of action. "Internal commitment means the course of action or choice that has been internalized by each member so that he experiences a high degree of ownership and has a feeling of responsibility about the choice and its implications. Internal commitment means that the individual has reached a point where he is acting on the choice because it fulfills his own needs and sense of responsibility, as well as those of the system" (Argyris, 1970, p. 20).

Internal commitment to negotiation with the assistance of a mediator will help the people in dispute to struggle together to reach an agreement. If the mediator has done his or her job well, assisting the parties in selecting mediated negotiations will have inclined them closer to settlement.

Coordination of Approaches and Arenas

Approach and arena selection by one disputant does not mean that the same approach or arena will be selected by other disputants. The approach and arena assessment process must be conducted with all of the primary parties in a dispute.

Mediators may assist parties who are operating with different approaches or in different arenas in coordinating their conflict resolution efforts so that they can cooperatively reach a solution rather than spend unnecessary time, money, physical energy, or emotional effort on unproductive conflict activity. For example, Party A wants to negotiate a settlement on one issue but not while litigation is being conducted on another. The mediator may help Party A defer litigation until after the negotiable issues have been discussed.

In disputes involving collective bargaining in which negotiation is the accepted and preferred means of settling conflicts, the parties do not have the same degree of coordination problems that is present in interpersonal, organizational, or community disputes. In the latter types of conflict, disputants often lack either a common approach or arena. They may in fact have no prior history of interaction and therefore have no traditional or accepted way of resolving conflicts. In these types of disputes, the mediator can play a critical function in assisting the parties in coordinating their conflict resolution efforts.

There are, however, situations early in the negotiation

process in which perfectly coordinated procedures are not attainable. These situations arise when

- Parties are not psychologically prepared to commit themselves to a particular approach.
- Parties are not dissatisfied with a current approach.
- Parties want to try noncoordinated activity to push for a
  win-lose outcome in their favor before cooperating.
- Parties feel that a coordinated approach offers them no advantage.
- Parties feel that they do not have equal influence or power
  that can be effectively used if a coordinated conflict resolution approach is pursued.
- Parties do not have the resources to engage in a coordinated
  effort.

When faced with parties who are not prepared to coordinate their conflict resolution approaches, the mediator has several strategy options:

1. If coordinating efforts has no advantage to a disputant, the
   mediator can encourage the parties to pursue their chosen
   approaches and inform them that if it is advantageous to
   negotiate or mediate at a later time, the option remains
   open. This approach should be conducted so that the mediator refers to the various costs and benefits identified by
   the disputant of pursuing this uncoordinated course.
2. The mediator can negotiate a procedural approach to the
   dispute in which the parties agree to begin negotiations
   while retaining their right to pursue other approaches or
   arenas of dispute resolution, or without ceasing hostilities.
3. The mediator may begin negotiations with fewer parties in
   the hope that others may be persuaded to join later or be
   impelled to join because of the fear that a settlement will
   be reached without them.
4. The mediator may obtain a tentative commitment to explore negotiation or mediation through a prenegotiation
   conference. This conference may have as its goal concilia-

tion or negotiation of a mutual and cooperative conflict management procedure.

5. The mediator may continue with efforts to persuade the parties to begin negotiations.

6. The mediator may seek additional parties who may be able to influence the principal disputants to try negotiation.

FIVE

Collecting and Analyzing Background Information

Data collection and conflict analysis enable a mediator and disputants to understand the identities of the parties in conflict, what issues and interests are important to them, and what relationships and dynamics—historical and current—exist between them. The process of identifying the components and dynamics of a conflict is *data collection*; the integration and interpretation of that information are *analysis*.

Through data collection and analysis the mediator will

- Develop a mediation plan or conflict strategy that meets the requirements of the specific situation and the needs of all parties.
- Avoid entering a dispute with a conflict resolution or management procedure that is inappropriate for the stage of development or level of intensity that the dispute has reached.
- Operate from an accurate information base that will prevent unnecessary conflicts due to miscommunication, misperception, or misleading data.
- Clarify which issues are most important.

Note: The conceptual outline for this chapter was originally published in 1982 by ACCORD Associates as part of their training manual, *Natural Resources Conflict Management,* by Christopher W. Moore, in collaboration with other ACCORD staff. The author gratefully acknowledges the permission to use some of the original outline and concepts first presented in *Natural Resources Conflict Management.*

78

- Identify the key people involved and the dynamics of their relationships.

The first part of this chapter will examine methods of data collection. The second part will explore how this information is integrated and analyzed. This chapter focuses primarily on data collection and analysis of disputes between more than two people or parties. However, the process is basically the same for conflicts between only two individuals.

The amount of time spent on data collection depends on the complexity of the dispute. An interpersonal conflict clearly requires less time expended in data collection, perhaps a half-hour with each party, than a complex social policy dispute in which months may be needed to gather appropriate information.

Data collection can be conducted before negotiation or once negotiation has begun. Because I prefer to perform preliminary data collection before joint sessions, I will assume in this chapter that the mediator is meeting with the parties separately before starting formal mediation.

Useful and accurate data collection depends on several factors:

- A framework for analysis and adequate background information
- An appropriate method of data collection
- An appropriate person to collect the data
- A strategy for data collection and the means that will be used to build rapport and credibility with involved parties
- Appropriate interviewing approaches that encourage valid responses
- Appropriate questions and listening process during interviews

Framework for Analysis

All conflicts involve specific people, relatively predictable dynamics of development, competing interests, and tangible and intangible issues. These common components of disputes allow a general framework to be created that is useful in generating questions and explanatory hypotheses about a given dispute.

Mediators may use categories in Figure 2 as a basic framework for analyzing a conflict. Relationship problems, data disagreements, competing interests, structural barriers, and value differences should be considered potential causes of conflicts. In addition, factors that promote positive relationships, points of data on which the parties agree, compatible or nonexclusive interests, structural variables that enhance constructive interaction, and common or superordinate values should be identified as factors that may be encouraged or enhanced to promote agreement.

Selecting an Appropriate Data Collection Method

Mediators use several procedures to collect data: direct observation, secondary sources, and interviewing. These procedures are used either individually or in combination to provide more accurate or complete information about a given conflict.

Direct Observation. A mediator may watch a couple fighting at the beginning of a mediation session, may attend and observe a public meeting, may visit a proposed development site, or may attend a company briefing to gather firsthand information on how the parties react and interact in a conflict.

Observation goals vary from dispute to dispute. The focus can be on three levels: individual behavior, interaction within subgroups, or interaction between groups. From observation, the mediator can determine social class, status, power, and influence relationships; communications patterns; and group routines that will influence the conduct of a conflict.

Secondary Sources. Secondary sources are materials that provide information about a dispute without direct observation or interviews. Helpful secondary sources may include financial records, minutes of meetings, maps, organizational or government reports, newspaper or magazine articles, tape recorded or videotaped presentations at meetings, and research conducted on the issues or people involved in a dispute.

Interviewing. The most common way for mediators to gain information is to interview. There are two broad types of interviews that may be used in mediation: data collection interviews and persuasive interviews (Stewart and Cash, 1974). The first type is used to collect relevant information, the second to persuade disputants that a particular procedure or outcome is desirable. The focus of this discussion will be on data collection interviews.

These interviews may be conducted at two different times: (1) before or (2) during joint meetings. Some mediators prefer to hold a preliminary data collection interview with each individual or party before a joint meeting. This provides the interviewer with information necessary to understand some of the people, issues, and dynamics of the conflict before interacting in a joint session. Preliminary interviews also provide the mediator with more information about the dispute than is known by one party. This knowledge enables the mediator to plan how the people will educate each other in joint sessions, and identifies the information that when exchanged will clarify misperceptions, fill in data gaps, and help the parties reach agreement.

Data collection interviews also introduce the participants to the mediator. The personal and organizational rapport and credibility that are built between the mediator and the disputants during the interview strongly influence the amount and quality of information gathered and the receptivity of the disputant to the mediator's later intervention. Rapport is often more easily developed in one-on-one interviews than in joint sessions.

Finally, data collection interviews allow an exchange of information about the mediation process. A mediator can use the data collection interview to describe his or her proposed process in more detail, or he or she may solicit procedural suggestions from interviewees. A dialogue on processes for conflict management may be the first step toward collaborative problem solving.

Data collection interviews may also be conducted at the start of joint meetings. Data collection is now conducted in the presence of all involved parties. These interviews allow the parties to educate each other, provide an opportunity for the mediator to watch how the disputants interact, and enable the intervenor to verify that information presented in the joint meeting is consistent with that provided in the earlier private interviews.

Selecting the Appropriate Data Collector

Many mediators do not conduct the initial interview, but may assign an "intake" worker whose primary responsibility is to perform the initial round of data collection. A written case file is then given to the mediator. While this format may save time for mediators, it may also hinder the development of rapport and credibility between the mediator and the disputants during later phases. Usually the mediator will also have to conduct a brief data collection interview to build rapport with the disputants.

In some conflicts, mediators or their agencies may prefer to collect and mediate in teams. Male-female or lawyer-therapist teams are often utilized in child custody and divorce cases. In complex public policy or environmental disputes, interviewer-mediator teams may be involved. Co-mediators should take care in data collection to work together as much as possible, to frequently exchange any information that they obtain individually, and to minimize the possibility of working at cross purposes.

In some disputes, assignment of mediators to a particular type of conflict or interviewee may be an important move in obtaining additional information from a respondent. Gender, age, race, social class, status, and previous relationship with the interviewer may influence how much information can be gained from a respondent. For example, a woman disputant may feel more comfortable relating an incident of domestic violence if one of the mediators is a woman. In some interracial disputes, a minority mediator's presence has made a difference in the willingness of parties to cooperate.

Usually, the more the respondent identifies with the interviewer or mediator, the better he or she will respond. Mediators determine their own dress, speech, and manners, and can use these attributes to enhance the possibility of interviewer-respondent identification.

Data Collection Strategy Selection

In many interpersonal or organizational disputes, parties are easy to identify, and the mediator can easily determine whom to interview. In divorce cases, for example, usually the husband, wife, and perhaps children or extended family members will be targeted for interviews.

In conflicts in which there are multiple disputants and the parties are not well organized or highly visible, the mediator may have to identify main actors before data collection. In community disputes, mediators use procedures similar to those researchers use in community power-structure research (Aiken and Mott, 1970). The methods listed below are used alone or in combination to assist mediators in identifying critical individuals, groups, and organizations in a dispute.

The *positional approach* (Jennings, 1964; D'Antonio, Loomis, Form, and Erickson, 1961) identifies the main formal institutions or organizations involved and targets the people who fill their key roles. The chief executive officer of a company, members of a county commission, and the director of a department all occupy positions of authority. The assumption of this approach is that those in key formal positions of authority in the institutions or organizations in a dispute are those who will make decisions about the conflict. In many cases this may be true, although potential power may never actually be exercised on a specific issue. Leaders from social, economic, and political institutions may not be as important as an individual who can mobilize a group of supporters, make a technical decision, or initiate a lawsuit.

The assumption of the second identification method, the *reputational approach* (Walton, 1966; Hunter, 1953), is that people with a reputation for having power are indeed powerful. Mediators ask a group of reliable informants, "Who are the central people who should be interviewed about this conflict?" These informants are usually secondary resource people who know about the dispute but are not directly involved. Names gathered in this process are cross-referenced, and the people receiving the most "votes" are considered central to the dispute.

One of this method's strengths is that it identifies those whom informed observers perceive as possessing power. The weakness, as in the positional approach, is that perceived power does not necessarily mean actual power. Only through interviews can the two aspects of power be correlated.

The third identification method is the *decision-making approach* (Polsby, 1960; Dahl, 1961). In this method, the mediator investigates to determine who within an organization or group has been involved in—and at what level he or she has been involved in—a decision made on previous issues similar to that in question. The assumption is that the same people are likely to be involved this time. This method depends on the mediator's ability to review representative previous decisions and to identify the people who took part in them. It focuses on those participating in a conflict, the processes they have used in the past to influence decisions, and the development of conflict relationships over time.

All these approaches for identifying key people in conflict have merits and weaknesses, both in their theoretical assumptions and in their applications. Mediators will usually find that a combination of these approaches produces the most accurate collection of potential interviewees.

Appropriate Sequence of Interviews. After the interviewees have been targeted, mediators should consider the sequence of interviews. In interpersonal disputes and occasionally in other conflicts, the party that initiates mediation is interviewed first. This gives the mediator background information that will be useful in interviewing the other party or parties. Since data collection in conflict situations requires mediators to obtain information from individuals under actual or potential emotional stress, great care should be taken to determine a sequence of interviews that will not antagonize anyone.

In multiparty disputes, the mediator may have to develop a more detailed process for sequencing interviews. Often he or she may have to contact secondary parties before talking to the principals. This helps the mediator gain a more accurate picture of the conflict, identify disputants, practice questioning techniques, and obtain valuable information on the approach to interviewing before interviewing main actors. Secondary parties are invaluable resources in disputes, since they often have a more objective view and may also be able to introduce the interviewer to other parties to the conflict.

The mediator should frequently ask a secondary party, "Who is it important for me to talk with?" and "Who should be talked to first?" Including interviewees in interview sequencing decisions often gives the mediator valuable information about those most central to the dispute. In some instances, an interviewee may offer to call a friend and provide an introduction.

When secondary sources have provided sufficient data for the mediator, he or she should develop a strategy and a sequence for interviewing central people. Questions that frequently guide the sequencing include:

- Who are the most powerful or influential people in the dispute?
- Who will be offended if he or she is not interviewed or is not interviewed first?
- Who should be interviewed earlier so that his or her cooperation can be used to induce others to participate in interviews?
- Who is the person most likely to talk about the problem?

Before interviewing the central people, the mediator may conduct some specific research on what roles they play in the conflict, what positions they have held on similar issues, their likes and dislikes, and their personal traits. These data may enable the mediator to obtain more data in the interview than if he or she were unfamiliar with them.

Timing of Data Collection Interviews. Data collection can be conducted before or at the time of joint sessions. Questions that mediators can ask themselves to determine if a premediation data collection interview is necessary include:

1. Are the parties extremely hostile toward each other? Is there a potential for violence?
2. Do the parties have widely divergent viewpoints on the issues in conflict?
3. Do their styles of communication in joint session inhibit a clear exchange of views on the issues in dispute?

4. Are multiple issues involved?
5. Are issues extremely complex?
6. Is there a likelihood that additional data or factual information may be needed before a joint session?
7. Does one of the parties appear to be weaker than another?
8. Does one party express fears of being dominated by another party?
9. Is one party unclear about the mediation process or the role of the mediator?

If a mediator answers yes to any of the above questions, a premediation interview for data collection may be appropriate.

If a mediator decides to use a premediation conference, he or she should carefully explain to all parties the purpose of the interview, its duration, the scope of issues to be covered, and limits of confidentiality of data revealed in the sessions. Most mediators maintain that information exchanged in the premediation data collection meeting and in later separate caucuses is confidential and will only be revealed publicly or in joint session with the consent of the disputants. Some mediators, however, make exceptions to this rule, most notably on criminal conduct, child abuse, or risk of physical harm.

Some mediators opt to conduct all their initial interviews in joint session with all disputants present. This option may be based on strategy, convenience, time constraints, complexity, limits on confidentiality, or a desire to avoid suspicions of partiality. The mediation may also be constrained by the wishes of the disputants themselves, who cannot meet separately because of emotional or political reasons. More will be said about conducting data collection interviews at the start of a joint session in Chapter Eight.

Building Rapport and Credibility. The first five minutes of any data collection interview may be the most critical in the process of building rapport and establishing personal credibility. This has been called the "social" stage of the interview (Survey Research Center, 1969). In this brief period of informal conversation the mediator should try to present himself or herself as an open, warm, intelligent, and interested person. A mediator should make informal conversation positive and genuine in tone and content. It should not include subjects that might create distance between the mediator and the disputant.

Once the initial phase of developing rapport has been completed, mediators begin the process of credibility building mentioned in Chapter Three. Mediators build credibility from the moment they make their first phone call or send a confirmation letter, but the interview provides an additional opportunity to intensify the process through a face-to-face encounter. Mediators usually decide how much to explain about themselves, the mediation organization, and the process before direct questioning. The disputant may need to know more before he or she can trust the mediator.

The mediator must also motivate the participant to respond. This can be easy or difficult depending on the participant's disposition toward the issue, the procedure, or the mediator. Some of the motivation strategies that mediators can use to elicit information include

- Explaining the importance and worth of the data to the mediation process so that the disputant feels that he or she can make a genuine contribution toward a positive change.
- Appealing for the need to hear all views, especially that of the interviewee.
- Explaining the benefits of participation.
- Answering questions that may decrease resistance to participation.
- Demonstrating a positive personal interest in the disputant's concerns, problems, or viewpoints.

Most mediators use a combination of these motivation strategies.

The Appropriate Interviewing Approach

In some data collection interviews, the mediator determines specific areas about which he or she wants to obtain information through secondary source analysis. In other cases, mediators are more interested in conducting general exploratory interviews that may become more focused after the disputant has shared his or her perception of the conflict.

Advantages to specific interviews include

- The ability to focus on issues that are important to the mediator.
- The ease of filtering extraneous or irrelevant information that results because the disputant does not understand the major focus of the interview.
- The ability to gain the most helpful information in the shortest amount of time.

The major drawbacks are that

- The mediator may bias the information received by encouraging the disputant to give answers he or she thinks the interviewer wants.
- The mediator may miss valuable information the participant would have supplied if the questioning had been more comprehensive.
- The mediator's conception of the conflict may become the framework for viewing the conflict instead of the dispute participant's conception.
- The mediator may not have time or may have constraints that prevent extensive interviewing on specific topics.

A mediator should carefully decide what he or she needs to know and then design an interview format that will achieve those goals.

Structure of the Interview. Mediators usually use two types of interview formats to collect data from disputants or other parties with relevant information: (1) structured interviews and (2) nonstructured interviews.

Structured interviews are designed to collect the same or similar information from each of the disputants so that their answers are quantifiable and comparable. This requires a list of standardized questions or categories of information.

Nonstructured interviews are used for exploratory data

collection in which the same information is not required from each disputant, when there may be resistance to structure by the interviewee, or when the mediator has not accumulated enough information to narrow the focus to specific categories or questions. Nonstructured interviews resemble ordinary conversations except that they have more focus and less equal exchange. In this form of interview both the mediator and the disputant have greater freedom to influence the information exchange's direction.

In selecting the most appropriate interview format, mediators consider which type of interview will produce the desired information, induce the respondent to share knowledge, and create the rapport necessary for later information gathering or intervention.

The Interview Format. Mediators should plan a format for both individual and joint data collection interviews. While formats may differ somewhat for these two interventions, many of the strategic questions are the same. The following considerations should be addressed:

- In joint meetings, who should speak first to either make an opening statement or present his or her story?
- What information exchange format should be used?
- What time constraints should be placed on speakers?
- How will the mediator gain a procedural agreement on the data collection process?
- How acceptable is emotional expression?
- How will disagreements or discrepancies in data be managed?
- In joint sessions, how will the mediator prevent psychological burnout or boredom in the party who is not speaking?
- How will interruptions be managed?

While there is not enough space to answer all these questions, several of the most critical ones are addressed here.

Who speaks first? This question applies only to joint data collection meetings. Mediators use several criteria for determining who presents his or her view first: Who initiated the dispute or conflict? Who wishes to change the status quo? Who is not emotionally capable of waiting to explain his or her case? Who is the weaker party? General practice usually allows the initiator or claimant to go first, as this party has brought the dispute to mediation (Stulberg, 1981a). Often the first party to speak is the one who wishes to change the status quo. An exception may be made when one of the parties is so emotionally engaged in the conflict that the party cannot wait for another party to present its viewpoint first, when one party is weaker and may gain some internal psychological strength from going first, or by mutual agreement of the disputants.

What format should be used for information exchange and data collection? There does not seem to be one format that mediators use consistently. One common procedure is to allow each party a certain delineated period of time in joint session to present its case to the mediator and the other party. The only interruptions allowed are requests for clarification from the mediator. In joint meetings the other party or parties may also be allowed to obtain clarification at the end of each interview.

Another procedure used in group disputes is for a disputant whom most of the parties trust to tell the history and outline of the dispute while other parties identify data on which they disagree. These points of disagreement may later become agenda items for discussion.

How are anger, interruptions, and disagreements over data to be managed in joint session? Since data collection usually occurs either before joint sessions, at the start of negotiations, or after the mediator has entered a dispute as the result of an impasse, the parties usually experience tension. In individual interviews, mediators may accept emotional expression more than in joint sessions. More will be said about this in Chapter Seven.

Interviewing: Appropriate Questions
and the Listening Process

Effective interviews require both good questions and good listening on the part of the mediator. The balance between these communications skills, of course, depends on the purpose and structure of the interview. In both structured and nonstructured interviews, there is a great degree of variety in how questions are asked and the degree of mediator directiveness (see Table 1). Questions generally are of two types: closed and open-ended (Stewart and Cash, 1974).

Table 1. Types of Questions.

Type of Response	Definition	Example
Elaboration Question	A request for more information related to something respondent has already said.	A. We are interested in co-parenting but don't know what it entails. Q. Can you say more about what concerns you?
Active Listening	An exact statement or paraphrase of what the respondent has said. The response is often to the emotional content of a message and is more of a response than question.	A. I'm very upset about the condition of the road and what they did to it. A. You are outraged that they damaged your property.
Direct Clarification Question	A direct request for information to clarify vague or ambiguous information.	A. We do not want multiple-family homes in our neighborhood. It spoils our single-family home life-style. Q. Is it the idea of multiple family homes that bothers you or the number of people or units in each one that is important?
Inferred Clarification Question	Clarification of information that was implicit in previous response.	A. The meeting was held over at the Federal Building. Q. At Frank Williams's office?
Summary Question	A question that summarizes previously stated information and requests that the respondent verify the data.	A. We purchased the property as a cooperative venture, wrote an agreement that required an equal input of money, and they

(continued on next page)

Table 1. Types of Questions, Cont'd.

Type of Response	Definition	Example
		subsequently violated it by not making agreed payments.
		Q. You purchased property, made a financing agreement, and then the partners failed to follow through?
Confrontation	A question that points out a discrepancy in data presented by the respondent. (This should be used with care because it can create resistance from the interviewee.)	A. I want to have Smith pay for the cost of replacing my windshield and all the trouble he has caused me. That amounts to $250.
		Q. You say you want to have him pay $250 in damages, yet you stated earlier that your brother handled the installation and that the glass cost only $100. What exactly were your time and energy expenditures on this problem?
Repetition Question	An exact restatement of a previous question.	Q. How much will impact mitigation cost to restore the land to its previous state?
		A. Oh, I'm not sure with the price of water, seed . . .
		Q. How much will impact mitigation cost to restore the land to its previous state?

Closed Questions. Closed questions allow the mediator to narrow the focus in order to obtain smaller pieces of information from the respondent by asking for more specific information regarding when, why, or how something happened. The most closed format is a leading question such as, "Didn't you see the people move the truck onto the site the afternoon of August 27th?" Mediators usually avoid leading questions because they may create hostility between the mediator and the respondent (Richardson, Dohrenwend, and Klein, 1965).

Closed questions are usually asked later in interviews when a mediator wants to gain more detailed information about a disputant's views. Premature use of closed questions can limit the amount and quality of information that a party reveals to the mediator.

Open-Ended Questions. The mediator wants to gather as much information about the conflict as possible and to identify the disputant's perceptions. That information is frequently difficult to obtain because of distrust or guardedness of people in conflict, or because the respondents have not defined the situation in the same terms as the mediator. Mediators use open-ended questions to help overcome these limitations. This type of question allows the interviewee to share as much of the information as he or she wishes without feeling pressured. In addition, open-ended questions allow interviewees to share their perception of reality with the mediator without the imposition of an alien framework of analysis; there are no probing questions with an implied or prescribed answer to disturb them.

When conducting an open-ended question interview, mediators should not create a highly structured discussion. The goal is for the interviewee to do most of the talking. Mediators ask an open-ended question and then listen. Active listening (see Table 1) with content or emotional feedback may be useful as a clarifying technique (Gordon, 1978).

Sample open-ended questions include

- What is the background to this situation? (*Situation* is preferable because of the negative connotation that *conflict* may produce.)
- What are the problems or issues that concern you?
- What kind of decision is to be made?
- Who are the people, agencies, or groups involved in the situation? What do they think about the problem?

- What common interests or concerns do the people in this situation have?
- What do you think should be done to avoid or resolve this situation? Are you willing to work with the other people on this?

It should be noted that most of these questions begin with *what* and *how* rather than *why*. Asking *why* questions requires a person to justify his or her belief and may put him or her on the defensive (Richardson and Margulis, 1984).

When Respondents Fail to Answer Questions. Occasionally an interviewee will fail to answer a mediator's question. Reasons for failure to respond are numerous:

- Not understanding the question.
- Complex wording of the question.
- Too many questions at once (multiple questions asked in one sentence).
- Scope or complexity of the problem is too large for a single response.
- Disputant does not want to reveal private or privileged information.
- Thinking is blocked by intense emotion.
- Lack of trust between disputant and mediator.

By carefully recording questions, observing nonverbal behavior, or questioning directly, the mediator should be able to determine why a respondent does not answer.

Recording Information in Interviews. A mediator often receives more information in an interview than can possibly be remembered. To prevent losing important data, mediators usually decide before the session what data recording methods they plan to use. The two primary recording techniques are written notes and tape recordings. Each method has its benefits and costs.

Written notes require rapid notation so that content and emotions can be easily retrieved during analysis. The writing method must be accurate enough that points of information are not lost but unobtrusive enough that the writing does not distract from the interview. Some guidelines for mediators using written recording include:

- Ask permission of the disputants to take notes about what they have to say.
- Clarify with the disputants how notes will be used and whether the data are confidential or will be open to the public.
- If an interview has a planned sequence of informational categories, have a prelabeled page for each category.
- Take notes in an abbreviated or shorthand form.
- Maintain eye contact (if this is culturally appropriate) with the respondent as much as possible during the interview and do not concentrate on taking notes.
- Take notes consistently throughout the interview. Do not write in a noticeably different manner when an especially important or complex point is explained by the respondent. This prevents biasing the disputant through special attention to a particular area of questioning.
- Read the notes back to verify accuracy.
- If appropriate, use a team consisting of one interviewer and one recorder. The roles can be reversed during the interview.

Tape recording interviews is another way to obtain complete interview records. Tape recording is by far the most accurate data collection and storage system, but it is often time consuming to listen to the entire playback and costly to transcribe it. In addition, respondents may be reluctant to have their statements recorded when they cannot control use of the tape.

If sessions are to be recorded, mediators should obtain permission from disputants and explain how the tape will be used and who will have access to it. Mediators may gain more cooperation if they offer to turn off the recorder if a disputant is uncomfortable discussing a particular subject.

Conflict Analysis

Conflict analysis is the synthesis and interpretation of data collected by the mediator from interviews, direct observation, or an examination of secondary sources. The mediator's central task during this stage is to integrate and understand the elements of the dispute: people, dynamics, issues, and interests.

The moves of conflict analysis are often difficult to identify as a separate component of mediation because many mediators do not perform any visible or external activities to indicate that they are analyzing a dispute. From all appearances, they often move from data collection to proposing an acceptable mediation procedure. Nevertheless, conflict analysis and designing an intervention plan are important cognitive steps that prepare mediators and disputants for later activities.

Data Reporting

Data reporting refers to the exchange of interview information between interviewers or mediators if more than one person is collecting data. Several techniques are used to facilitate reporting. The simplest approach is probably a periodic team meeting in which mediators make brief oral reports on people they have interviewed and information they have obtained. Time should be allowed to clarify questions from other interviewers or to suggest modifications of the interview procedure and format to improve the process. Formal meetings, however, may take up too much time if there are many interviewers or interviews and the dispute demands rapid intervention.

Alternative methods of disseminating information include circulation of written transcripts or recordings of interviews or the interviewer's impressions of the sessions. Mediators often find that recording their reflections while traveling from an interview is an effective procedure for interpreting data and sharing them with others. This technique promotes synthesis and summarization of salient points into a manageable form.

Integrating the Information

In complex disputes, a tremendous quantity of information is often generated by interviews. Structured recording and cross-referencing systems may have to be used. There are a variety of tools that mediators use to integrate the data.

Integrating Information About People. One way to organize data about the people in a dispute is to make a *participant list* that identifies names of potential and past interviewees and organizations with which they are associated. This list helps mediators determine those who have been interviewed, when they were interviewed, and who remains to be questioned. It also allows mediators to determine when individuals representing a particular category of disputant—such as another family member, a company representative, a local city council member, a lawyer, or a federal regulator—should be interviewed to balance an issue and to ensure that all viewpoints have been presented. Additional factors that mediators may consider particularly helpful in listing participants are the name of the interest group to which the person belongs and the degree to which he or she can influence the course or outcome of the dispute (Table 2).

Integrating Information About Relationships and Dynamics. The second category of information to be integrated is the relationships of the conflicting parties. In order to understand a dispute, the mediator must have a grasp of historical events and trends that have led to the present conflict. Two tools are often used to describe the development of conflict relationships: timelines and case study scenarios (Coover, Deacon, Esser, and Moore, 1977).

The timeline is a chart on which a mediator has recorded significant events that have influenced a conflict's development (see Figure 7). Timeline entries include specific communications, failures to communicate, interviews, press releases, public meetings, elections, direct actions, or the initiation of litigation. Timelines may also include larger events such as changes in public awareness on an issue, economic trends, a major government

Table 2. Interest Group or Individual Participant List.

	Industry Group		Government Group		Public Interest Group	
	Person	*Interview Date*	*Person*	*Interview Date*	*Person*	*Interview Date*
Main Groups or Individuals with High Influence						
1	_____	__/__/__	_____	__/__/__	_____	__/__/__
2	_____	__/__/__	_____	__/__/__	_____	__/__/__
3	_____	__/__/__	_____	__/__/__	_____	__/__/__
4	_____	__/__/__	_____	__/__/__	_____	__/__/__
Secondary Groups or Individuals with Moderate Influence						
1	_____	__/__/__	_____		_____	__/__/__
2	_____	__/__/__	_____		_____	__/__/__
3	_____	__/__/__	_____		_____	__/__/__
4	_____	__/__/__	_____		_____	__/__/__
Interested Parties with No or Low Influence						
1	_____	__/__/__	_____		_____	
2	_____	__/__/__	_____		_____	
3	_____	__/__/__	_____		_____	
4	_____	__/__/__	_____		_____	

Figure 7. One-Month Timeline.

Parties	Time and Events			
	Week 1	Week 2	Week 3	Week 4
1. Company	Files plans with planning department	Visits to affected homeowners		Attend public hearings
2. Planning Department	Reception of plans			Hold public hearings
3. Public Interest Group	Meeting to discuss company plans	Develops counter-position and press release	Meets with homeowners	Attends public hearings
4. County Commissioners		Notified by planning department of citizen opposition to project	Talk with citizens	
5. Local Landowners	House meetings to discuss company plans	Meet with company	Meetings with public interest group	Attend public hearings

policy change, or international events that influence the dynamics of the dispute. Timelines may also project into the future
and identify critical data or action that will affect the conflict
dynamics.

Some mediators also write brief dispute case histories to
help them identify and order historical events. The mediator
may use these case studies or scenarios later to explain to the
parties perceptions of how the conflict developed and to create
a common view of the background of the dispute.

Integrating Information About Substantive Issues. The final category of data that must be organized and integrated per-

tains to the substance of a dispute: issues, positions, interests, and potential settlement options.

One tool that mediators use to order and analyze conflicting interests is an issue, position, interest, alternative chart. This chart is used to plot a disputant's stated issues and positions in a linear format and then identify the underlying interests that have promoted the position. This chart also identifies potential settlement alternatives. By identifying the interests the mediator can assist the parties in generating alternative solutions that may be mutually acceptable.

Verifying Data

Data collection, especially when conducted in separate meetings, may result in contradictory information. Data may have been incorrectly heard or recorded by the mediator, or the respondent may have intentionally or unintentionally given misinformation. Disputants may also have different perceptions or definitions of the problem. The mediator must try to understand and correct the information if a successful intervention is to be launched.

The first step in verifying discrepant data is to determine if the incongruity is due to a problem in the questioning process by reviewing original notes, cross-referencing interviewee responses, referring to secondary sources, or conducting follow-up interviews or questions.

Occasionally, mediators may confront a disputant to clarify a point. This is usually done in a low-key manner, without placing judgment or blame on the disputant. For example, "I don't understand; there seem to be two explanations of this point. Can you clarify this for me?" would be appropriate to challenge a discrepancy in the information. The respondent always needs a way to maintain dignity in the process of clarifying conflicting data.

Interpreting Data

So far, most of the conflict analysis procedures discussed pertain to data organization. I will now discuss the most difficult aspect of conflict analysis: the interpretation of information. In order to proceed, the mediator must create a conceptual map of the conflict and develop a set of hypotheses such as those discussed in Chapter Two. There is no one procedure used by mediators to interpret information about a dispute. Listed below are several thought processes that may be useful depending on the type of dispute. These procedures are linked to the categories presented in Figure 2.

Some mediators begin to dissect and analyze a conflict by dividing the unnecessary or unrealistic causes from those that are genuine or realistic (Coser, 1956). *Unrealistic causes of conflict* include strong emotions that are not based in objective reality, misperceptions about motivations of negotiators, stereotypes, miscommunication, unproductive repetitive behavior that negatively affects another party, attempts to force an agreement on values when concurrence is not required for settlement, confusion over data, or competitive behavior induced by a misperception that interests are mutually exclusive.

Genuine causes of conflict include real differences over what data are important; how they are collected or assessed; actual competing substantive, procedural, or psychological interests; structural constraints on the parties such as competing roles, unequal power, or authority; destructive behavior patterns caused by external forces such as environment or time constraints; and different value systems that are difficult to reconcile but must be addressed to reach settlement. By dividing the causes of conflict into unnecessary and genuine categories, the mediator can first address the problems that are tangential—the unrealistic ones, for instance—and then focus on the realistic causes of the dispute.

A second analysis process requires the mediator to carefully analyze the causation categories described in each sector of Figure 2 and then target the cause that is integral to initiating successful dispute resolution. For example, in a complex issue involving closure of a local school because of declining enrollment, the structure for parents to express grievances may include only a hearing process before the school board. Public hearings frequently promote conflict because of their one-way communication structure and the tendency of participants to voice extreme positions. A new forum or structure is needed for the community and education officials to discuss the impacts of the closure on the neighborhood and the system. By providing a new structure, productive dispute resolution may be induced.

This same procedure can be used if a dispute over data was deemed to be the primary cause. For example, in a complex water dispute in Colorado, the parties disagreed over critical basic data—how much water was available, how much was needed, and where resources were located. Negotiations could not proceed until these issues were resolved. One party had much of the information in a computer model, but would not disclose it because it was proprietary and would affect the party's economic capacity to obtain additional resources. The mediator worked with the parties to help develop a parallel computer model that would answer the necessary questions about water resources, but would not require disclosure of privileged information. Both models were submitted to an independent and mutually acceptable water resource consultant for comparison. The consultant verified that each model was based on valid premises and came up with similar conclusions regarding the amount of water available and the location of sources. The group was able to use assumptions developed through the computer modeling process to agree on basic data without violating proprietary constraints.

Conflict analysis is complex and will be different for each case. This step, however, is critical to designing an intervention plan.

SIX

Designing a Detailed Plan for Mediation

Once a mediator has gained a commitment from the parties to mediate and data have been collected and analyzed, the task that remains before any directive intervention is designing a mediation plan. A *mediation plan* is a sequence of procedural steps initiated by the intervenor that will assist conflicting negotiators in reaching an agreement. The plan's detail depends on the type and complexity of the conflict, how much the mediator knows about the dispute, available planning time, and how much control over the negotiation process the disputants have delegated to the intervenor.

Mediation planning occurs throughout a dispute, but in the beginning of the intervention the mediator may be especially active. If the mediator has scheduled separate data collection interviews with disputants before joining them in negotiations, the mediator may have time to reflect and develop a plan before working with the parties together. If, however, the first data collection is performed when all the parties are together and they expect to progress in the same session, the mediation plan may have to be spontaneously designed. Many mediators prefer a more deliberative planning process that allows them time to consider all the alternatives and formulate a comprehensive strategy. Other intervenors prefer to design the plan as the issues and dynamics unfold. Clearly there is not one right way to design a mediation plan. Mediators must assess the process with which they are most comfortable, or that the particular situation allows, and then proceed.

The mediator may develop mediation plans alone or in cooperation with the disputants. Two conditions exist under which the mediator may design a mediation plan without consulting or involving the disputants (Argyris, 1970). First, if the issue or problem under discussion is not very important and "does not involve the clients' feelings of self-acceptance and competence and where the problem is clearly out of range of competence of the clients" (p. 27), the mediator may want to intervene unilaterally. Second, if the dispute is extremely intense and the disputants feel hopeless or paralyzed in their efforts to change their interactions, the mediator may take control of the process.

The mediator's design of the process may mean that the commitment of the parties to the procedure will be external to them. Commitment is stronger when the parties have designed the procedures themselves in cooperation with the third party. Whenever possible, the parties should be involved in the design of the mediation plan. An example of joint procedural planning by the mediator and the parties occurred in the telephone access charge negotiations mentioned earlier. The mediators asked each party to designate a representative to sit on a process design task group. The function of this group was to design, with the mediator, the procedures by which issues in dispute were to be discussed. Once developed, procedural proposals were submitted to the group as a whole for approval and implementation. Direct involvement in designing the negotiation procedures and mediation plan tremendously enhanced the parties' commitment to the process and created strong advocates for the interventions that were suggested by the mediators.

In the process of designing a mediation plan, mediators should consider certain critical questions:

1. Who should be involved in the mediation effort?
2. What is the best setting for mediation?
3. What procedures will be used?
4. What issues, interests, and settlement options are important to the parties?

5. What are the psychological conditions of the parties?
6. What is the general plan for the first joint negotiations in the mediator's presence?
7. How will specific agenda items be identified and ordered?
8. How will rules or behavioral guidelines be established?
9. How will parties be educated about the process and agree to proceed with negotiations?
10. What possible deadlocks could occur and how will they be overcome?

This chapter will examine the points above and discuss planning of activities assuming that they will be accomplished before the first joint session conducted in the mediator's presence. This approach will allow us to examine the design of mediation plans in more detail. Chapter Ten will focus on the implementation of the activities designed in this stage.

Participants in Negotiations

In many disputes, the parties who should participate in negotiations are readily apparent. In divorces, husband and wife should be present; in labor-management disputes, union and management representatives should attend. In other disputes, however, the identities of the central parties are not as clear. For example, in a child custody case concerning visitation rights revision, the second wife of the divorced husband may want to participate in negotiations. In large-scale community land use disputes, multiple parties may be interested in the issues and may want to participate.

While the mediator usually should not choose who the disputants are or who will participate in negotiations, he or she may help the parties decide who should be present. Occasionally, a mediator may assist a party in selecting a spokesperson or identifying a person who will be both effective and acceptable to the other side. When a group or organization is disorganized, the mediator may also assist in designing a decision-making process to select a negotiating team or spokesperson.

Participants in the negotiation should include those who

- Have the power or authority to make a decision.
- Have the capacity, if they are not involved, to reverse or damage a negotiated settlement.
- Know and understand the issues in dispute.
- Have negotiating skills.
- Have control of their emotions.
- Are acceptable to other parties.
- Have demonstrated or can demonstrate bargaining in good faith.

An example of a mediator's assistance in selecting representatives of disputing parties may illustrate this point. A mediator in a city-sponsored housing mediation project was asked to intervene in a dispute between a landlord and numerous tenants in a large apartment complex. The mediator entered the apartment building's common room, where the residents had gathered. They were vocal, angry, and prepared to harass the landlord. The mediator asked the tenants who their spokespersons were. They had not thought to choose anyone. She asked for a list of issues they wanted to discuss, and they shouted out a few items. The mediator told the group that their meeting and show of force had demonstrated their seriousness to the landlord, but they now had to organize themselves to be effective in negotiation. She suggested that they select four or five people who could speak for the group and would have authority to negotiate. She mentioned some of the criteria listed above, and after some resistance and milling around, the tenants selected a team. Compromises had to be made on membership to ensure that all views were represented and that no one would work against the group's interests. Once the team was selected, the mediator asked the representatives to identify the issues deemed important and to prepare to negotiate on them.

As part of a bargaining strategy, one party occasionally may refuse to send a representative who has the authority to make a final decision. This action may be an attempt to insult the other party, an indication that one party does not consider the issue as important as the other party does, or a means of insulating a decision maker from the dynamics and direct pressure of negotiation (Schelling, 1960). Negotiation etiquette usually requires people of equal rank or status to be present. When faced by a discrepancy in decision-making authority between negotiators, mediators may (1) push for a redecision concerning the presence of a decision maker with equal authority or (2) make explicit differences in authority between two or more sides and develop an understanding of the decision-making and ratification structure to be used by the party without a decision maker present. Clarification of the decision-making process for parties with absent decision makers before negotiations can minimize unnecessary conflicts and later claims of bargaining in bad faith.

Friends, Witnesses, Constituents, and Secondary Parties. Parties often want to have friends, witnesses, constituents, or secondary parties present at negotiations. There is no one rule or practice mediators follow to respond to these requests. Some mediators request that friends, witnesses, and constituents remain outside negotiations unless they have a particular function or role to perform (Stulberg, 1981a). Other mediators allow observers who are informed of the limits of their participation. The mediator occasionally may not have a preference or procedural rule regarding the presence of additional parties at negotiations, and may refer the question to the disputants.

Mediators usually request the presence of (1) parties with direct involvement in a dispute as defined by their central interests in the outcome, (2) parties with decision-making authority, (3) parties that contribute positively to decision making, and (4) parties that will respect negotiating etiquette.

Lawyers, Therapists, and Other Resource Persons. Disputants often want resource persons with specialized skills present in negotiations. These secondary parties may assist the disputants in exchanging accurate information, may provide emotional support, or may participate as surrogate negotiators.

Lawyers are a special category of resource persons. They provide numerous types of services to disputants (Bronstein, 1982; Riskin, 1982). They may be legal advisers providing information about possible settlement ranges or patterns should a dispute be brought to court for settlement, strategists, advisers, or surrogate negotiators for disputants who are disinclined or unable to represent themselves.

Lawyers who advise or coach may or may not be present in negotiations. The mediator should encourage parties who are negotiating issues that involve legal questions without legal counsel present to consult with a lawyer before, during, and after negotiations to ensure that the disputants are conscious of their legal rights and possible settlement parameters. The mediator may request that lawyers who are not directly negotiating on behalf of a client remain silent in joint session and confine consultations with their clients to caucuses or private meetings, or they may be allowed to participate fully. Their degree of involvement depends on the case, the parties, and the intervenor's style.

Lawyers who participate in negotiations as representatives of clients and who negotiate on their behalf may create special problems for mediators. While many lawyers have a cooperative style and are experienced in interest-based bargaining, others are familiar only with hard-line positional bargaining (Williams, 1983). Lawyers are generally trained to develop a case for a particular solution or position and may couch settlement options in terms of right and wrong solutions or options that can be answered in a yes or no fashion. Negotiation depends on cooperative and integrative decisions rather than either/or options for success. The different demands of litigation and negotiation often strain the lawyer's role in mediation.

Mediators may decrease adversarial tendencies in mediation by encouraging parties to retain lawyers for legal advice but not as surrogate negotiators. Currently, the preference of mediators for—and their strategy to respond to—the presence of lawyers vary widely (Folberg, 1982). Insufficient research has been conducted to determine how lawyers affect the settlement of disputes either by their presence or by direct participation.

Disputants may also request the presence of therapists in negotiations. This is not unusual in family or interpersonal disputes. Although mediation is not a therapeutic process, it may benefit from the presence of resource persons who can pro-

Can you make it therapeutic?

vide emotional support or psychodynamic insight. Mediators should be open to the involvement of therapists in negotiations if it is acceptable to all parties and if it can be demonstrated that the therapist can help disputants with emotional and psychological problems (Haynes, 1981). However, some restrictions applied above to lawyers may be appropriate for therapists.

Disputants may also request that accountants, technical experts, and researchers be allowed to participate in negotiations. Resource persons may provide disputants with a new perspective from a professional from another discipline (Fisher, 1978), may provide information that will prevent unnecessary conflict over inaccurate or conflicting data, or may provide a way to mediate data disputes (Straus, 1979). Mediators often suggest that specialized resource persons such as property assessors, accountants, or scientific experts be introduced into mediation to provide new information to disputants.

Media. Mediation in the U.S. is generally considered to be a private means of dispute resolution. In fact, research evidence indicates that negotiation is effective because of the private nature of the controlled communication (Folberg and Taylor, 1984; Freedman, Haile, and Bookstaff, 1985). Private negotiations may allow for greater candor and may decrease the need for posturing so often found in public adversarial relationships.

Before mediating a dispute of public interest, the mediator and the parties should decide how they will manage inquiries from the news media about media presence in and reporting of negotiations and how reporters can obtain information about the negotiations. The media are often excluded from negotiation because of the potential negative effect they may have on the behavior of disputants or the public. The presence of reporters often encourages posturing for a constituency rather than serious negotiation. Premature or inaccurate revelation to the public of the substance of negotiation can create conditions that make joint problem solving impossible. Privacy may be a critical factor in obtaining agreement.

In disputes such as those involving public policy or in which large interested and involved constituencies are present, maintaining privacy may be difficult or impossible. Public de-

cision makers may be precluded from participating in closed
negotiations by "sunshine laws" that require all discussions to
be public. While mediators and many negotiators generally assume that closed negotiations are crucial, significant negotiations have been successfully executed in the public view. The
Negotiated Investment Strategy, sponsored by the Kettering
Foundation to settle disputes over allocation and use of public
resources by various government levels, has conducted all its
negotiation meetings under public scrutiny. Negotiations in
Columbus, Ohio; St. Paul, Minnesota; Gary, Indiana; and Connecticut between representatives of local, state, and federal
decision makers for allocation of funds to various government-
sponsored programs indicate that open meetings can result in
successful settlements.

There has also been some experimentation with open
negotiations on the interpersonal level. The Community Boards
in California (Shonholtz, 1984) and several Canadian mediators
(McWhinney and Metcalf, 1984) have conducted open mediation with significant success. However, open meetings are the
exception rather than rule for most mediations (Vorenberg,
1982).

Mediators should assist the parties in determining if negotiations are to be closed or open to the public and to design,
when appropriate, public education about the substance and the
procedure disputants use to resolve their differences. If meetings are to be closed, the mediators may propose specific procedures to release information (Lansford, 1983). Parties often
agree to a common press release issued by the group as a whole
and announced by the mediator. Other publicity about mediation progress may include periodic meetings with the press and
public presentations by the parties outside the negotiation sessions.

Location of Negotiations

The location chosen for negotiations may significantly affect the interaction of the negotiators. In considering where to
meet, a mediator should select, or persuade the parties to select,
a neutral location where neither party nas strong emotional

identification or physical control of the space. The benefits and costs to the parties and the mediator of neutral locations are listed below.

Benefits

- Interruptions can be controlled.
- Neither side can manipulate the use of space.
- Distance from the site of the conflict and other distractions can be maintained.
- Distance from the usual environment may encourage the psychological distance needed for an open-minded exploration of issues.
- Use of time can be dictated by negotiators rather than the location.
- Possibility of bugging or eavesdropping is limited.
- All parties have the same psychological handicap of being in a new location.

Costs

- Separation from information that might be needed.
- Separation from an emotional support system.
- Parties may have to bear the cost of renting facilities.

Disputants occasionally refuse to negotiate at a neutral site and want to mediate in their own territory, or want to continue negotiations at a site established before the mediator's entry. Parties who demand to negotiate in their own territory usually assess the opportunities and costs of this option with the following criteria:

Benefits

- They feel relaxed and comfortable.
- They can control the environment and use it to their advantage.
- They have easy access to information.
- They have control of the physical arrangement of negotiation facilities.
- They can arrange or control strategic interruptions.

Costs

- It is difficult to remove an opponent from the negotiation site.
- It is difficult to turn down requests for information that is readily available.

Mediators have two major strategic options when confronted with a negotiator who insists on meeting in his or her own territory. They can (1) discuss and make explicit the costs and benefits of such a decision, stressing the possible negative impacts on settlement; or (2) persuade other parties to accept the recalcitrant party's request while identifying costs or benefits to the party who is not on its own territory.

Benefits

- The guest party can demonstrate its good faith and willingness to compromise.
- Asking the host party for information may be easier, and it may be more difficult for him or her to refuse.
- The guest party can occupy the host party's time and space if the host party does not cooperate.

Costs

- Unfamiliar surroundings may disorient the guest party.
- Lack of access to information from its sources may weaken its case.
- The host party can be interrupted and called away at any time.
- The host party can receive strategic phone calls.

The mediator may also refuse to mediate the case, but this response is extremely rare.

Physical Arrangement of the Setting

Physical arrangement of the negotiation setting may also affect the dynamics and outcome of negotiations. The disputes that erupted over seating arrangements and the shape of the table at the Vietnam peace negotiations held in Paris in the early seventies indicate the impact that physical arrangement can have on negotiations.

Physical arrangement refers to seating patterns, shape of the table, amount of physical space allocated to and between disputants, physical objects that indicate authority or differences in power, and space for public or private interaction. Social science research presents important findings on seating arrangements and conflict behavior. Filley (1975) observes that adversaries tend to seat themselves opposite each other and that this physical arrangement seems to produce more polarized and competitive behavior than side-by-side seating. Sommer (1965, 1969) postulates that undifferentiated seating locations for disputants, so that they neither are arranged opposite each other nor possess seats that indicate greater or lesser power, produce more evenly distributed leadership and less one-sided exercise of power.

Tables, or the lack of tables, and the use of other barriers between disputants is another variable. The following case illustrates the psychological effect of tables: The intervenor conducted several sessions in an informal setting without a table. One day mediation was scheduled in a conference room with a large wooden table. One disputant remarked, "Well, we now have a negotiating table. We can get down to business." They did, and settled that day.

The table's shape may be used to indicate the status of a party as a discrete entity with its own "side." A physical place at the table may grant recognition and legitimacy to a party and its views. Such was the case in the Paris peace talks to end the Vietnam War.

In volatile disputes, maintaining a safe distance and using a table as a physical barrier may be crucial in preventing dispute escalation and physical violence. The effect of tables and space on the escalation of a dispute is illustrated in this example: Several years ago the U.S. Air Force Academy negotiated with a union that provided services to the facility. The negotiations were protracted and became heated. Finally one negotiator reached across the narrow negotiating table, seized the position paper of his opposite, and tore it into small pieces. A negotiator from the other party reciprocated. The table prevented physical violence but was not large enough to prevent this negative interchange.

In addition, the shape of the table and seating arrangements may be used to blur differences between disputants. Round tables are often used by mediators because there is no physical indication of a boundary between representatives of the disputing parties.

In some disputes, mediators may eliminate tables or barriers between disputants to increase physical proximity or to promote informality (Stulberg, 1981a). In interpersonal disputes, a living room setting without tables may be more appropriate than a formal conference room.

Additional important physical arrangements are waiting rooms and facilities for caucuses (Stulberg, 1981a). Mediators need waiting rooms so that the intervenor does not have to associate publicly with one of the parties before joint meetings. Disputants may perceive this fraternization as partial behavior. In volatile situations, mediators may also use separate waiting rooms for antagonistic or hostile parties.

Caucus rooms are facilities where mediation participants can meet privately during negotiations. Caucus rooms should be near the site of joint negotiations but far enough removed so that they provide visual and auditory privacy. Caucus rooms are crucial in managing conflicts in which intense emotions are displayed or in which a potential for violence exists (Schreiber, 1971). Mediators often use entirely separate rooms for each party in disputes that involve actual or potential violence. The mediator can carry messages and work out a settlement between disputants, and, if necessary, the parties might never actually meet.

Mediators should consider the type of dispute and the psychological and emotional conditions of the disputants, and should select a physical arrangement that will be conducive to resolution. When physical arrangements are a given factor due to previous negotiations in a particular setting before a mediator's entry, the mediator may try to make minor modifications to induce psychological shifts in the disputants, or may move them to an entirely new setting.

Negotiation Procedures

Before developing a mediation plan for joint negotiations, mediators should evaluate what the conflicting parties know about negotiation procedures and ascertain approaches—positional or interest-based bargaining—that have been used or that they are likely to use. If the mediator conducts private meetings to collect data before the joint sessions, this information is usually easy to obtain. If it is not possible to collect data on the preferred negotiation procedure of the parties, the mediator should design a series of contingency plans that will enable him or her to respond to any combination of negotiation procedures.

There are four possible combinations in a two-party dispute: (1) both parties use positional bargaining, (2) both parties use interest-based bargaining, (3) one party uses predominantly positional bargaining and the other uses predominantly interest-based bargaining, and (4) both parties use a mixed procedure depending on the issue and their interests. If the dispute involves more than two parties, the number and combinations increase.

Mediators usually have a procedural bias toward interest-based negotiation procedures because the interests of all parties are more likely to be satisfied with this process. When mediators encounter parties who have previously engaged or are planning to engage in positional bargaining, they should, when possible, develop a mediation plan that will incline the parties toward interest-based bargaining as rapidly as possible. I will discuss mediator moves designed to accomplish this task in later chapters.

Issues, Interests, and Settlement Options

Designing a mediation plan requires a mediator to identify issues and interests with which disputants are concerned, the salience or importance of these issues and interests, and potential settlement options. Anticipating these components of the dispute enables the mediator to design an effective procedural plan but not a specific mediation settlement. Mediators differ considerably on how specifically they link the interests of the parties to a plan that produces a particular settlement that the mediators create. Some intervenors, often called "deal-makers," design a plan that will lead toward specific solutions that they have identified. Other mediators, often referred to as "orchestrators," design a plan in which the parties identify their interests and develop their own negotiation procedure (Kolb, 1983). I usually prefer the latter procedure.

Psychological Conditions of the Parties

An assessment of the psychological readiness of the disputants to negotiate should accompany a mediator's consideration of substantive concerns and procedural preferences of the parties. The mediator should review some of the relationship variables—level of emotions, accuracy of perception, amount of miscommunication, and repetitive negative behaviors—that will influence or have influenced the dynamics of the negotiations, and design appropriate procedures to reduce potential negative impacts and enhance positive ones. More will be said on these topics in Chapter Seven.

The mediation plan includes developing a tentative sequence of activities for the first joint negotiations. The structure is tentative because the parties must accept the proposed activities before it can be implemented. I will now explain possible activities that a mediator can plan to set the tone, define an agenda, establish rules or behavioral guidelines, and obtain commitment to negotiate.

It is important to establish a positive and harmonious tone at the start of negotiations. Positive working relationships between the parties depend on their attitudes toward themselves and each other. The presence of a neutral third party helps facilitate the development of a positive, open, direct, and businesslike approach.

Tone setting usually begins with introductions. Setting the stage for the first joint session should include scheduling time for the mediator and the parties to introduce themselves. In cases in which parties in dispute are groups or organizations, the mediator may also provide time for descriptions of group affiliation and concerns.

After introductions the mediator will usually structure time for his or her opening statement, a description of what is to come. Stulberg (1981a, pp. 42–43) lists the advantages of conducting an effective opening statement:

A. It establishes the ground rules and your role in the hearing.
B. It establishes your control over the hearing.
C. It serves to put people at ease.
D. It conveys to the parties a sense that the mediator is confident and skilled, thereby inviting them to trust both the mediator and the process.
E. It serves to reconcile any conflicting expectations regarding what the party believes he could obtain through mediation and the reality of it.

Mediators often begin their opening remarks with a congratulatory statement that applauds the willingness of the disputants to negotiate and to try to cooperatively solve their problems. A reference to their interdependence is often mentioned at this time. Stulberg maintains that "The very first sentence or question in mediation needs to address what the individuals have in common or what they like and respect about each other. Emphasizing mutual dependence on one another heightens the need for overcoming the obstacles that brought them in. It also helps participants to look for the good in each other rather than letting their anger blind them. Conflict is much easier to handle if it rests on a positive foundation" (1981a, p. 22).

After planning tone-setting activities, the mediator may allow time to review how he or she was asked to assist the parties in the dispute. If the mediator represents a mediation agency, he or she may explain the procedures and goals of the agency and the services that it provides. The mediator may also describe his or her background and qualifications, but mediators usually try to convey their qualifications by their manner rather than reviewing their professional work, educational background, or affiliations.

In this phase of intervention planning, mediators should demonstrate personal credibility, trust, and a businesslike manner by explaining, for instance, what mediation is and the mediator's role. The manner and process of explanation will convey the mediator's command of negotiation procedures.

Mediators commonly cover the following items in their description of mediation and the mediator's role (Moore, 1981):

- Mediation is a process whereby a third party or an independent person helps people in conflict to identify issues about which they disagree, uncover needs which must be met by a settlement, generate possible solutions, and reach decisions.
- Mediation is voluntary. The people are there by choice, and the mediator has no power to force a decision on the parties involved.
- The people in the conflict will decide how the conflict will be terminated.
- A mediator is impartial. He or she has no investment in a particular substantive settlement. The mediator is a facilitator of the process, not a judge on the issues.
- A mediator is neutral in that he or she has no relationship with any of the parties which might bias his or her impartiality.

Mediators should also inform parties of their procedural legal rights. Providing this type of legal information should not, however, be construed as legal advice or the practice of law. Disputants do not lose their right to cease negotiations and pursue a legal route to redress their grievances until they sign an agreement that may become a legal contract. Participation in negotiation or mediation does not deny a party the right to consult legal counsel. Disputants can confer with a lawyer at any time, and many mediators request that all decisions be reviewed and perhaps be drafted by counsel before the parties sign the document (Folberg and Taylor, 1984).

In addition, mediators should explain the limits of confidentiality of the proceedings. Information exchanged between negotiators or the negotiators and the mediator in joint sessions or in caucuses is usually confidential. Mediators often have parties sign release forms in which the parties state that they will not subpoena a mediator or records of the negotiations for a later court case.

Establishing Ground Rules or Behavioral Guidelines

In some negotiations, a carefully designed procedure may be enough to incline disputants toward a productive resolution. In other disputes, the negotiators may need to establish behavioral guidelines that detail how they will act toward each other and how the parties will handle particular problems that arise in the course of negotiations.

Behavioral guidelines that should be considered by mediators and parties include:

- Decisions about how the background of the problem will be examined.
- Speaking order of the disputants.
- How disagreements over data will be managed.
- Time frame for the negotiation session or sessions.
- Agreements on observers and witnesses.
- Rules preventing attribution of motives or slanderous statements.
- Rules regarding interruptions.
- Procedures for intermissions.
- Procedures for initiating caucuses or private meetings.

Behavioral guidelines may be proposed either by the mediator or by disputants. If they are initiated by the mediator, the parties must agree to their implementation. If the mediator suggests guidelines, he or she should be careful not to create a dynamic in which he or she is the authority and the parties are obedient subjects. Guidelines must be agreed on by consensus to work effectively.

Behavioral guideline agreement may be structured as the first step in mediation. Parties may be willing to discuss behavioral guidelines and agenda formation procedures for a variety of reasons. Focusing on behavioral guidelines and procedures at the beginning of negotiations

- Enables the parties to establish rules for interaction that may make the parties feel safer.
- Allows parties to practice making agreements on problems that are neither substantively important nor as emotionally charged as the issues in dispute.
- Demonstrates that agreement is possible [Moore, 1982b, p. VI-33].

I will explore the process of negotiating behavioral guidelines in more detail in Chapter Eight.

The amount and detail of guidelines vary tremendously among mediators. Coogler (1978), a leader in divorce mediation, has incorporated the explanation of procedures and guidelines as an elaborate component of the mediation process. He has catalogued and defined his procedural description and mediation guidelines in a list of sixty rules that disputants with whom he mediates must agree to before starting negotiations. While Coogler occupies an extreme position, establishing behavioral guidelines is common practice, and most mediators may suggest a few to provide safety and direction for the parties.

Establishing a Tentative Agenda

Once the mediator has planned the first joint session's general format, he or she should define the process for identification of specific agenda items. The mediator usually has enough information from data collection and conflict analysis that he or she can formulate a proposed negotiating agenda.

In most cases, mediators should plan a procedure that provides the parties with an opportunity to make their own opening statements—presentations at the start of negotiations in which the parties present the problem or conflict history, identify the needs they must have met for a satisfactory settlement, and, occasionally, express strong emotions. Opening statements may be the first opportunity for the mediator to watch the disputants interact face to face. Mediators learn much about disputants, issues, interests, positions, alternatives, and conflict styles by observation at this stage. Foreknowledge of the issues and interests that parties will focus on in the opening statement assists the mediator in planning the order in which issues will be managed and what the subsequent problem-solving process will be for each item. One agenda-planning procedure many mediators use follows (adapted from Moore, 1982b, pp. VII-18-19):

1. The mediator should gather all potential agenda items from disputants prior to the negotiation session. This may be done orally or in written form.

2. The mediator should clarify in his or her own mind the goals or outcomes desired by the parties for each item. He then should determine which items are information-sharing items, discussion items, or issues which require a decision.

3. The mediator should make a tentative judgment about which are high-priority items, medium-priority, low-priority, and which could be held over for a later session. In defining priority, the mediator should take into consideration time value of the item (does this decision have to be made tomorrow so that work can proceed next week?), importance of the issue (substantive importance and emotional importance), and to whom it is important (all parties, a subgroup, an individual, or a superior). High-priority issues should usually be scheduled to be discussed at least in principle at the first session and are not deferred.

4. The mediator should make an estimate of how long it will take to achieve the defined goal for each agenda item and establish possible time blocks for the topics.

5. Agenda items should be ranked according to how difficult they will be for the parties to achieve the defined goal: hard, medium, and easy.

6. The first item on the agenda should usually be one of high or medium priority to most of the disputants, either in substantive, emotional, or time value, and one the mediator expects will not require a long time to reach an agreement or to achieve the stated goal. This item should be easy for the parties to work on. The mediator should place the item with these qualities first because he or she wants the dis-

putants to have a chance to achieve success in a short time early in negotiations. An early success will make the disputants feel more positive toward the process and toward their ability to work together, and it will indicate the possibility of future success in negotiations.

7. The second item often concerns a more difficult topic and may take longer to reach the goal. Successful completion of the first item will prepare people for work on more complex issues.

8. Short and long and hard and easy items may be alternated so that the participants feel that the negotiations are progressing toward a productive end.

9. Time for identification of issues to be discussed at a later time and future logistics should be allowed for at some point in the agenda.

Educating the Parties and
Gaining a Commitment to Begin

After completing a mediation plan, the mediator should decide how he or she will educate the parties about the process and gain their commitment to try it. If the mediator has worked with disputants to design the plan, gaining final approval is not a problem, but if disputants are not familiar with negotiation procedures, or are too embroiled in the substantive issues in the dispute to focus on procedure, the mediator may have to educate the parties about the process he or she has designed.

Mediators occasionally take an active educational role before joint sessions to prepare disputants for what they can expect to occur. These mediators try to gain the commitment of the parties to the procedure before the joint session. Other mediators make their procedural proposals or suggestions during the first session and assume that they will be accepted or that alternative procedures will be negotiated with disputants. Neither method seems to be more effective than the other. The procedure for agreement on process usually depends on the particular parties involved, the issues in dispute, and the conflict dynamics of the case.

Identifying Special Problems

The final aspect of designing an intervention plan is the mediator's identification of potential problem areas that may cause an impasse. Fisher (1978) identifies several problem areas that often deadlock negotiations: (1) substantive problems, such as too few or too many favorable options, that make it difficult to select one; (2) procedural problems, such as no process or the wrong process; and (3) problems with people, such as strong emotions, stereotypical labeling, or miscommunication. Early identification of potential problems and contingency plans to avoid or overcome them are central to mediation planning. Mediators can prepare for unexpected or special problems by imagining problems that might occur in the joint session and then developing several contingent plans for solving each of them. I will discuss a variety of problems listed by Fisher and moves mediators use to counter them in future chapters.

SEVEN

Building Trust
and Cooperation

Negotiation has long been recognized as a psychological process. Rubin and Brown (1975) identify over five hundred recent studies on negotiation that examine individual psychological variables and group dynamics. In this chapter I will discuss mediator activities that minimize unnecessary conflict and build a positive psychological relationship between disputing parties. This process is called conciliation.

"Conciliation is essentially an applied psychological tactic aimed at correcting perceptions, reducing unreasonable fears, and improving communication to an extent that permits reasonable discussion to take place and, in fact, makes rational bargaining possible" (Curle, 1971, p. 177). *Conciliation* is the psychological component of mediation in which the third party attempts to create an atmosphere of trust and cooperation that is conducive to negotiation.

Although I will discuss conciliation here as a separate stage of negotiation and mediation, conciliation in practice is an ongoing process that occurs throughout negotiation. My discussion will focus on conciliatory moves often practiced by negotiators as well as mediators.

Five types of problems commonly create negative psychological dynamics in negotiations: (1) strong emotions, (2) misperceptions or stereotypes held by one or more parties of each other or of issues in dispute, (3) legitimacy problems,

124

(4) lack of trust, and (5) poor communication. I will discuss each of these problems in turn and explore the most common intervenor moves employed to respond to and change them.

Strong Emotions

Several authors have noted the different emotional stages that disputants move through in the process of conflict development, de-escalation, and settlement (Douglas, 1962; Kessler, 1978; Ricci, 1980). People at the start of negotiations often feel angry, hurt, frustrated, distrustful, alienated, hopeless, resentful, betrayed, fearful, or resigned to unsatisfactory conditions. For rational discussions on substantive issues to occur, the impact of negative emotions must be managed and minimized by either the disputants themselves or by an intervenor. If emotions are not managed early in negotiation, feelings either openly manifested or felt and not spoken will probably later block a substantive settlement.

For a mediator to assist parties in reaching an agreeable solution, he or she must at least minimize or neutralize the effects of negative emotions and, if possible, create positive feelings between disputants. Before examining conciliation procedures used to influence emotions of disputants, I will diverge briefly to examine two sources of emotions in conflict.

Unrealistic and Realistic Conflict and Emotions. Coser (1956) distinguishes between unrealistic and realistic conflict. Unrealistic conflict exists when parties act as if they are in dispute when no actual objective conditions for conflict exist. Realistic conflict is the result of genuine conflicts of interest. Coser's concepts of unrealistic and realistic conflict can also be applied to human emotions. Frequently, parties in conflict have unusually strong feelings that may not be merited by the actual situation. A conflict without a realistic base for negative emotions is in direct contrast to a dispute in which the cause produces logically predictable emotional response.

Many people have had the experience of meeting someone for the first time and immediately forming an intense dislike for the person. There is no previous relationship between the people and yet there is an intense negative emotional reaction. This dynamic has been variously referred to as restimulation (Jackins, 1978) or negative transference (Freud, [1920] 1943).

Restimulation refers to the surfacing of feelings similar to those generated by a relationship or events in the past. Old feelings are triggered by the new encounter that may or may not be similar to the earlier relationship or event. The new situation may not provide an objective base for restimulated feelings, but it may be the trigger mechanism that is necessary to resurrect past emotions in the disputant.

An example may illustrate restimulation more clearly. An environmental group spokesperson became angry when she learned that a public utility with which the group had struggled over construction of a hydroelectric dam was planning to build another, and that the group would have to expend time and energy on the same issue that it had struggled for and won in the previous conflict. Many feelings surfaced about the people on the other side with whom she would have to negotiate. Ironically, the other side was not composed of the same actors that the spokesperson had negotiated with before. She experienced restimulation of past negative feelings that were not necessarily connected with the current conflict.

Transference, and in particular negative transference, is the carryover or generalization of learned responses from one particular relationship to another. In the Freudian sense, transference occurs when the power dynamic of a previous relationship is transferred by one person to another relationship. The new relationship may or may not be similar to the earlier one. For example, in a couple's dispute the wife may transfer emotions about a controlling father onto her husband even though the interpersonal dynamics between the spouses are not the same as the previous parent-child relationship.

Restimulation and transference may result in an escalation of feelings that may or may not be merited by the objective conditions of the disputants. Mediators need to know how to respond to this source of strong emotions. More will be said on this point later in this chapter.

Realistic feelings, in contrast to restimulated feelings, are the direct result of clear and present conditions that would normally be expected to cause a conflict or intensify emotions. For example, if two parties in negotiation begin to yell at each other and make derogatory remarks about each other's integrity, the direct insult will usually result in strong emotions. This activity does not produce restimulation but emotions that are a direct result of the insult. (Obviously a person could also be restimulated if he or she has been directly insulted in the past, but the current events do merit the strong emotions that the disputant feels.)

Ideally parties will manage realistic and restimulated feelings caused by current negative events. However, when people feel strong emotions, a third party may be needed to mitigate the damages caused by emotional expression. Although the mediator is not a therapist, he or she must be familiar with psychological techniques to assist the parties in managing their emotions.

Responding to Intense Emotions. For the most part, conflicts involve negative rather than positive feelings. In considering conciliation strategies, I will focus attention on mediator interventions that neutralize negative emotions or enhance positive ones between disputants.

Emotions are highly complex physiological and psychological responses to external stimuli. Emotions may manifest themselves in neuromuscular, cardiovascular, respiratory, hormonal, or other bodily changes. The mediator must often respond to both the physiological and the psychological basis of emotions, and he or she should consider that feelings cannot be "resolved" in that emotions cannot necessarily be dispelled by objective solutions. Mediator responses to emotions consist of three separate steps: recognizing that a party has a strong emotion, diagnosing the emotion, and selecting an appropriate intervention strategy to assist the party in managing the emotion. Mediators should watch for signs of strong emotions that may hinder productive bargaining. Tone of voice, pacing of words, facial expressions, changes in posture, or body movements are all clues to the presence of underlying emotions.

Mediators frequently have little difficulty recognizing that a party is experiencing an emotion, but may not be able to identify it or determine how intensely the party feels about the subject under discussion. Active listening often facilitates identification and diagnosis of emotions. Rogers (1945) first identified this form of communication and interaction as a means of conducting social research, and Gordon (1978) and Creighton (1972) later elaborated on it as a method of responding to the emotions of people in conflict. *Active listening* is a communication technique in which a listener decodes a verbal message, identifies the precise emotion being expressed, and then restates the emotional content of the message to the speaker using the same or similar words used by the speaker. For example, the mediator might respond, "You were really frustrated and hurt when the city did not respond rapidly to your permit request." The disputant then has an opportunity to verify the accuracy of the mediator's perceptions of his or her feelings: "Yes, I felt frustrated! I had complied with all the requirements but they still wanted more data." It is important that the listener accept the speaker's emotions without necessarily agreeing with the speaker or holding the same beliefs about the issues in question.

Active listening performs several functions in responding to people's feelings:

1. It ensures that the speaker has indeed been heard.
2. It allows the speaker and listener to verify that the precise meaning of the message has been heard.
3. It demonstrates the acceptability of expressing emotions.
4. It allows the speaker to explore his or her emotions about a subject and to clarify what he or she really feels and why.
5. It may also perform the physiological function of encouraging the release of tension through expressing emotions.

Mediators can use active listening in caucuses and joint sessions to assess whether the expression of emotions is a negotiation tactic to bluff or influence another party to make concessions, whether it is posturing for other disputants or constituents, or whether it is a genuine expression of feelings. The more the mediator and disputant interact, the more difficult it is for disputants to maintain insincere emotional postures.

Once the mediator has accurately diagnosed the content and intensity of a disputant's emotions, the intervenor should decide the response to be used to assist the party in managing his or her feelings productively. Although conciliatory moves are close to the practice of therapy, the mediator is in fact not attempting to change or rehabilitate a disputant through a clinical, custodial, or casework approach. The mediator should merely assist a party in managing his or her emotions so that the party can negotiate on the specific issues in dispute.

There are three general categories of strategies to respond to intense emotions: (1) approaches that provide creative opportunities for parties to express their emotions, (2) strategies for suppressing emotions, and (3) strategies for removing the objective cause of the emotions by meeting substantive needs or interests. I will discuss the first two strategies in this chapter. Strategies for removing the objective cause of emotions will be discussed in Chapters Nine through Fourteen.

Strategies for Venting Emotions. Strategies for venting strong emotions are usually pursued because the mediator believes that (1) the party needs a physiological release for repressed emotions and is unable to focus on substantive issues in dispute until this physiological release has occurred (Jackins, 1978; Bach and Goldberg, 1974), or (2) the party needs to express his or her emotions to another party as an educational move to demonstrate how strongly he or she feels about an issue. If a mediator decides that parties need to vent emotions for either of these two reasons, he or she usually decides when, where, and how the emotions might best be expressed.

Emotions that may be highly destructive to a delicate negotiation process, strong emotions that are the result of restimulation, or manipulative expression of emotions are often best expressed in a caucus between the mediator and the party. Emotions are also channeled into a caucus when the recipient of the emotions may not be capable of responding to a direct expression. In this format, the emotions are vented safely in the presence of the mediator, but not in the presence of other parties. Physiological release can be attained, an assessment can be conducted of what is real or genuine emotion versus what are restimulated emotions, and the expression of manipulative comments can be curbed without risking the damage that could result from a direct negative interchange. Mediators often initiate a caucus to vent emotions once parties have begun negative venting in joint session. Mediators also initiate caucuses specifically for the purpose of provoking parties to release emotions.

Venting in joint session may also be a functional process important for achieving productive negotiations. Douglas (1962) observed that ritualized venting in the early stages of labor-management disputes appeared to be almost a prerequisite for the parties to move toward negotiation of substantive issues. If the mediator decides to encourage the parties to vent their emotions or if venting occurs spontaneously in joint session, his or her central concerns should be how to prevent venting from escalating and how to prevent negative dynamics in the relationship of the parties.

Several intervention strategies for response to this problem are common. Mediators may encourage parties to establish ground rules regarding acceptable behavior. These rules may exclude character assassination, attribution, or direct personal attacks. Mediators may also encourage parties to vent about the *interests* in dispute and not about the *people* who advocate interests (Fisher and Ury, 1981). A third approach is for the mediator to verbally identify unproductive venting and to encourage or suggest ways that disputants can express the same concerns in a less volatile manner. This strategy often means preparing a party in caucus for a verbal interchange in joint session. Humor is a fourth way that mediators can assist parties in venting and yet limit the negative effects of anger (Landsberger, 1956). By making encouraging remarks or telling jokes that are not at the expense of any party, the mediator may be able to release tensions of the disputants through laughter. The mediator may also call for a break to allow parties to gain psychological distance from each other.

Venting in joint session is only productive if it provides a productive physiological release for one or more parties and does not damage the delicate relationship between disputants, or if it serves to educate a party about the value or intensity of emotion about a particular issue. When venting is conducted to punish another party, it will probably result in a deterioration of the relationship of the parties. When this occurs, the mediator should encourage the parties to hold a caucus both as a defensive measure and as a measure that will channel the destructive feelings into a private forum.

So far I have related the value of venting emotions almost synonymously with a change of attitude. While this may be a valuable strategy in some cases, there is no concrete evidence that emotional release necessarily has a direct correlation to a perceptual or attitudinal shift. The one incontrovertible effect of venting is, however, an inclination toward increased relaxation after an emotional outburst. This physiological effect alone may be worth the efforts of a mediator to provide an opportunity for parties to vent.

Strategies for Suppressing Emotions. I have discussed mediator strategies that encourage emotional expression as a means of furthering better communications and removing sources of unnecessary conflicts. In some situations, however, encouragement either in joint session or in caucus may be counterproductive and may produce unnecessary escalation (Berkowitz, 1973; Hokanson, 1970; Steinmetz and Straus, 1974). Straus (1977, p. 233) argues that "in general, aggression against another (either verbally or physically) tends to (a) produce counter aggression, (b) impedes getting to the real problem, and (c) if it does succeed in squelching the other person, reinforces the use of aggression as a mode of interaction." When there is a history of violence, when one or more parties have a low degree of impulse control, or when the mediator does not believe that he or she can control an escalation of emotions, it may be preferable to structure the negotiation sessions to limit emotional expression. Structures that limit emotional exchange include strict guidelines about how parties will communicate, rules that limit communication between disputants and allow them to talk only to the mediator, and physically separating the parties so that they have few or no face-to-face meetings. The mediator in this last model performs a type of shuttle diplomacy and conveys messages between the parties.

Misperceptions or Stereotypes

Conflicts are often escalated or de-escalated based on a party's perception of another party. The mediator's role in the conciliation phase is to decrease perceptual barriers to negotiation. This is usually accomplished in four stages:

- Identifying perceptions held by a party.
- Assessing whether the perceptions appear to be accurate or inaccurate.
- Assessing whether the perceptions are hindering or furthering a productive substantive, procedural, or emotional settlement.
- Assisting parties in revising their perception of other disputants when they have characterized the disputants with stereotypes or other image distortions, and in minimizing the negative impacts of such misperceptions.

The Mask-Mirage Analogy. Curle (1971, p. 209) observes that "many of man's feelings about others derive from his feelings about himself. Since these feelings are often intricate, contradictory, and not fully grasped at the conscious level, his attitudes toward others are correspondingly obscure and irrational." Curle explains that individuals conceal from themselves and others true representations of themselves and produce a mask in place of these that represents how they would like to perceive themselves or how they would like to have others perceive them.

Curle argues that when a person uses a mask, the image he or she holds of other disputants is often that of another mask or a mirage. A mirage is a false image based on the psychic needs of the observer rather than real or objective characteristics of the observed.

How does the mediator recognize this mask-mirage dynamic? First, through interaction with disputants, the mediator will often be able to penetrate the fronts the disputing parties initiate and to identify the discrepancies between who the disputants are, what they want, and how they are being perceived by other combatants. Because the mediator does not have an investment in a particular outcome and because he or she cannot dictate a settlement of a dispute, disputants are often honest with him or her because they either have a genuine desire for an agreement or have little to lose from exposing their real selves to the mediator (Goffman, 1959). (This does not mean that parties always let down their masks for mediators. Mediators too can misperceive by viewing disputants in terms of false images they project. Mediators should take great care not to be drawn into believing that an image is the real person when in reality it is a mask.) Because mediators have this access, they may have an unusual opportunity to view disputants speaking and acting sincerely. These observations allow them to identify the presence of misperceptions between disputants and assess the accuracy of their views.

Several types of activities are available to parties and mediators to modify the perception of other parties. The disputants or mediator can (1) demonstrate that a party shares similar attitudes toward an object, event, idea, or third person; (2) encourage common association between parties to provide an opportunity to reveal undisclosed commonalities; and (3) encourage a party to associate or disassociate with objects, ideas, or people that his or her opposite does or does not like.

Demonstrating Similar Attitudes. "Similar attitudes toward an object (event, idea, third person) set up forces toward attraction between persons" (Walton and McKersie, 1965, p. 225). Similar attitudes can be created by identifying personal points in common, using similar language, defining a common problem, focusing on the benefits to both parties that will result from mutual success, emphasizing a common view of outsiders, and de-emphasizing differences between the parties.

Personal points in common may include common geographical or educational background or similar intellectual, recreational, or religious concerns. For example, several disputants in an energy development project modified their perceptions toward each other when they discovered that they had all been involved as participants or coaches of high school wrestling teams. The common view toward a mutually engaging sport blurred the adversarial relationship between them. Parties themselves can often identify personal points in common, but if they do not, the mediator may initiate moves that make the parties aware of their commonalities. Mediator moves may be either indirect, such as the casual mention of a common factor, or more direct, structured means to induce information sharing. Some family mediators, for example, ask divorcing couples to describe how they first met and what they liked about each other to create a sense of positive history for a current negative relationship.

Parties often hold misperceptions of each other because they use different language. They may be using different words to convey the same meanings or may actually be speaking from an entirely different world view. Coordination of the languages of the parties may also align their perceptions.

The mediator can encourage parties to use the same language or translate the meanings of the various parties to encourage mutual understanding. The mediator may often assist a party in reframing or restating a message in another way to facilitate accurate communication and positive reception. This process will be explored in more detail in Chapter Nine.

Identifying a dispute as a common problem that can only be resolved for any party through mutual cooperation can also induce a positive attitudinal shift. For example, identifying common problems of landlords and tenants as "stability of living situation and rent" may enable them to reach agreement on the terms of a lease. Mediators often must point out these common problems to a party who is trapped in an adversarial mirage and who sees little in common with an opponent.

Identifying mutual benefits of success is closely related to identifying common problems. Divorcing parents may modify their perception of each other if they believe that their children may benefit from an amicable rather than hostile divorce. Disputing spouses may see having happy and well-adjusted children as a mutual benefit. Mediators often must directly identify mutual benefits to be gained by common action because the parties may not recognize them.

The way that an event, idea, or third person is described can promote either discord or common attraction of parties in dispute. By de-emphasizing differences, a party can minimize the amount of negative perception an opponent has toward him or her. Mediators often perform the valuable function of minimizing differences by easing disagreements between parties.

Encouraging Common Association. Parties can be induced to change their perception of each other by inducing common positive associations. Mediators should determine if parties have undisclosed commonalities that will be revealed or enhanced by increasing their interaction. If this is the case, parties may be encouraged to work together. The opposite, however, may also be true. If the parties have few similarities, association may increase polarization. Mediators may separate and maintain the distance of parties who have little in common or traits or beliefs that may escalate the conflict.

Association and Disassociation with Objects, Ideas, or People. Parties can either associate or disassociate themselves from objects, ideas, or people that another disputant likes or dislikes. Mediators may encourage either association or disassociation, depending on their assessment of various perceptions of the parties. In some instances, association may be more important and positive than disassociation, while in other disputes, the opposite may be true.

Reinforcing Perceptual Change. Another approach to perceptual change focuses on rewarding or punishing a party's behavior to induce perceptual change. This approach has three central premises: (1) the more frequently one person's activity rewards the behavior of another, the more often the latter will demonstrate the behavior, (2) the more valuable the reward activity is to a person, the more often the person will demonstrate the rewarded behavior, and (3) if one person's activity punishes the behavior of another, the punished behavior will probably be suppressed (Walton and McKersie, 1965).

This approach assumes that by rewarding positive behavior and punishing negative behavior, a person can influence the

behavior if not the perception of another. Procedures for rewarding an opponent's behavior include extending compli-
ments, expressing appreciation, returning favors, and increasing
or stressing positive benefits (Walton and McKersie, 1965).
Punishment behaviors include reminding an opponent of his or
her role obligations, threatening the opponent's self-concept,
and issuing direct threats and sanctions (Walton and McKersie,
1965).

Positive reinforcement or rewards are moves usually preferred by mediators and ideally by negotiators because they do
not trigger as many negative reactions (Stevens, 1963). Mediators should stress the benefits of agreeing with the other party
before stressing the costs of not doing so. Emphasis on the positive can incline parties toward agreement while emphasis on the
costs of not settling may set up resistance because of negative
pressure or sanctions.

Occasionally, however, mediators must stress possible
negative measures of reinforcement. The utility of a mediator's reference to a party's use of negative means of reinforcement or possible negative consequences of a continued behavior
depends on several variables.

Punishment or threat of punishment seems to work only
in specific situations. If, for example, a party has anticipated
the costs or punishment that he or she might receive as a result
of a particular action, has factored them into the overall calcu-
lation of what the activity will cost, and has found the punishment to be manageable, the threat is likely to have little effect.

Fisher (1964, p. 32) observes that "other considerations
... suggest that inflicting pain on an adversary may be worse
than useless. There is a common tendency to treat sunken costs
as invested capital. The greater the costs we impose upon our
adversary, the greater the amount they will regard themselves as
having committed to this course of action." Parties therefore resist settlement because of the energy and resources they have invested in a conflict. Mediators may assist parties in rationalizing
a change in resource expenditure so that settlement can be
reached. Mediators should take great care when emphasizing the
negative consequences of a failure to settle. Stressing the nega-

tive, even when the one party has the capacity and will to carry out a coercive threat and the other is incapable of defending himself or herself, may create resistance on the part of the latter and escalate the dispute. Mediators often use soft or negative reinforcement by implying, not directly stating, a threat made by another party. For example, the mediator might say, "I don't know whether he will go to court, but he could, and that might hurt you." This phrasing uses negative coercion, creates doubt, and pressures the party to act without directly threatening the party.

Special Perceptual Problems

Perceptual problems are difficult issues for both negotiators and mediators. The two most difficult perceptual problems are probably those that deal with legitimacy and trustworthiness. I will now discuss mediator moves that assist parties in managing problems of legitimacy and trust.

Legitimacy. Legitimacy refers to a party's acceptance and recognition that an opponent, an opponent's issues or interests, and even an opponent's emotions are genuine and reasonable and conform to recognized principles or accepted rules or standards. Without a perception of legitimacy, negotiations often never begin.

A classic case in point is the perceptual change of farm owners in California in the late sixties and early seventies toward the representation of farm laborers by the United Farmworkers Union. Until the mid 1960s, growers refused to recognize the legitimacy of the union program that addressed workers' issues. Throughout the long conflict, which involved strikes, boycotts, and occasional violent confrontations, the growers' perceptions and acceptance of both union legitimacy and workers' interests changed, so that the United Farmworkers Union was finally able to negotiate and sign one of the first comprehensive agreements in the U.S. between growers and agricultural laborers.

How did this change of perception occur? Perceptual changes in this instance appeared to occur because of (1) pro-

tracted interaction, (2) stubbornness of farm workers in struggling for recognition of their rights, and (3) mobilization of
power to force agricultural interests to recognize the legitimacy
of workers' interests. This chapter is most concerned with persuasive, rather than coercive, means of perceptual change and
with encouraging parties to accept the legitimacy of the other
party's issues, interests, and emotions. I will explore the use of
coercion in Chapter Fifteen. Here I will explore each of the
areas of legitimacy—party, issues, interests, and emotions—and
how disputants shift their perceptions by means of persuasion.

   Legitimacy of Person or Party. A party recognizes another party as legitimate when the other party is willing to
talk with him or her. Negotiations often fail because one
party fails to perceive another as the legitimate spokesperson or bargaining agent for an opposing view. This can be the
case in family disputes, union disputes, or international relations. The refusal of the U.S. and Israel to recognize the Palestine Liberation Organization as the legitimate bargaining agent
for Palestinians has hindered peace talks in the Middle East for
years. The failure of one natural parent to recognize the legitimacy of a stepparent to participate in negotiations may hinder
or block post-divorce negotiations between natural parents.

   Changing perceptions about the legitimacy of a person or
party as the genuine bargaining agent for one side of an issue
can be accomplished in several ways. First, if the unacceptabil-
ity or illegitimacy of the negotiator is due to misperception,
clarification of communication and accurate perception may remove barriers to legitimacy.

   Second, if the problem with legitimacy results from the
procedure by which negotiators were selected to represent a
conflict group, the procedure can be explained or the mediator
can assist the parties in developing a procedure acceptable to all
parties. Acceptable procedures ensuring that a negotiator genuinely represents and can ensure the commitment of a constituency often removes barriers to the recognition of a party's
legitimacy. Mediators can and should assist the parties in making these moves.

   Third, if a particular person's legitimacy is questioned,

perceptions about that individual can be changed or another negotiator can be substituted. Perceptions about a particular negotiator can often be changed by direct discussion about images and perceptions. Blake, Mouton, and Sloma (1961) have succeeded with this approach in labor management disputes. Mediators can assist parties in changing their personnel and thus changing an opponent's perceptions.

Some parties may not be persuaded to change legitimacy perceptions, and coercion may be the only way to obtain recognition. When this perceptual deadlock occurs, mediators occasionally discuss with the party whose legitimacy is questioned coercive means likely to have the best effect on the other party and the least damage to the relationship of the parties.

Legitimacy of Issues and Interests. Legitimacy of issues and interests can be created in a variety of ways. Fisher (1964), drawing from his observations of international negotiations and mediation, suggests that a party can change the wording of the issue, redefine the issue in terms that are more favorable or acceptable to the other party, ask that another person with authority recognize the legitimacy of an interest, have another person advocate an interest, ask for a focus on another issue that has greater chance of being recognized as legitimate, be more specific, or be more general. Mediators can assist parties in making all the above moves by either indirect or direct suggestions.

Legitimacy of Emotions. Legitimacy of emotions refers to the acceptance of a party's right to possess emotions, not to whether another party legitimizes them (Gordon, 1978). As long as a dispute persists about whether the substantive issues or behavior of an opponent objectively merits a particular emotion, the possibility of productive negotiations will remain low. The mediator should try to translate the emotions and explain why the emotions are of a particular type. He or she should also inform the party that is denying legitimacy that it is not necessary to agree with the emotions to grant legitimacy. All that the party must do is accept that they exist and acknowledge that, for whatever reason, an opponent does feel a particular way.

Once emotions are acknowledged and accepted, the party

expressing the emotion frequently is encouraged to move on to substantive issues. This perceptual change is often crucial to productive problem solving.

Perception of Trust

Conciliation involves not only minimizing the impact of negative emotions and perceptions but enhancing positive feelings and perceptions. The importance of trust in conducting productive negotiations has been identified by numerous researchers and practitioners (Deutsch, 1958, 1960; Rapoport and Chammah, 1965; Zartman and Berman, 1982). *Trust* usually refers to a person's capacity to depend on or place confidence in the truthfulness or accuracy of another's statements or behavior.

The perception of trust in negotiations is very closely related to the mask-mirage images of disputants. "To believe everything the other person says is to place one's fate in his hands and to jeopardize full satisfaction of one's own interests. . . . On the other hand, to believe nothing the other says is to eliminate the possibility of accepting any arrangement with him" (Kelly, 1966, p. 60). At the start of negotiations, when the mask-mirage dynamic is strongest, the parties and the mediator face the problem of how to create the perception, if not actual behavior, that induces trust between disputants.

Base of Trust. Perceptions of trust are based on the experiences of the negotiators with past negotiations, the similarity of current issues to those in past negotiations, past experience with a particular opponent's behavior, rumors about a current adversary's trustworthiness, and the opponent's current statements or actions. Mediators often must respond to all these variables in the process of building minimal trust between the parties.

The past experience of a negotiator, his or her personality, and his or her needs, beliefs, values, and predispositions toward other parties will strongly affect his or her ability and willingness to trust another party. Mediators usually do not make any efforts to change or modify a negotiator's psychological makeup based on past experience with other negotiators. However, the mediator may attempt through careful questioning to modify and clarify a negotiator's perceptions of the current negotiation and may assist him or her in identifying similarities and differences between the present situation and the past. Since mediation is future oriented, in that the goal is to establish a new relationship or define future terms of agreement, the mediator often pushes parties to defer judgment about a present situation or party and to limit the intrusion of past judgments or biases on the current case until they are proved to be valid.

A negotiator's past interaction with an opponent can provide a base for either trust or distrust. Mediators negotiating with parties who have a history of negotiations between them may begin the trust-building process by asking questions that assess whether a positive or negative trusting relationship has been built over time. If the parties have a positive trust relationship, have been able to depend on the other party's veracity and count on the other party to follow through with established behavior, the mediator's task becomes simpler. In this case, the mediator may merely remind the parties of their positive and productive history, or may ask them to recount transactions in which trust in each other has been rewarded. This latter technique may often be used effectively even when little trust exists between the parties but the mediator has been able to identify a past positive interaction. For example, in difficult divorce mediation cases, mediators have asked spouses for specific examples in which they have been in conflict, have trusted each other, and have found the other spouse to be trustworthy in order to identify when the other has responded to cooperative gestures with reciprocation rather than exploitation. By affirming that disputants have been able to trust one another, the mediator may be able to enhance the positive aspects of their relationship.

If, however, the mediator discovers that parties have a negative relationship and that past trust has not been reciprocated, the intervenor has two options. First, he or she can assist the parties in determining if the breach of trust has been misinterpreted or is due to an unintentional misunderstanding. If so, accurate communication may remove the perceptual barriers to a new trusting relationship. If, however, the trust of one party was misplaced on another, and if intentional exploitation rather than reciprocity resulted, the mediator must pursue a second strategy and start from a point of no or little trust to build a positive relationship between the parties.

Mediator-Negotiator Moves to Build Trust. Trust in relationships is usually built incrementally over time. Through increasing the number of promises and congruent actions that reinforce the belief that the commitment will be carried out, negotiators gradually build a relationship of trust. Mediators may assist negotiators in incrementally building a trusting relationship by encouraging them to make a variety of moves oriented toward increasing credibility. Some of these moves include

1. Encouraging negotiators to make consistently congruent statements that are clear and do not contradict a previous statement (Creighton, 1972).
2. Encouraging negotiators to make symbolic actions that demonstrate bargaining in good faith (Fisher, 1978). Actions include providing for an adversary's physical comfort, negotiating at a time or place that is convenient for another party, making a minor concession that indicates a willingness to negotiate, and so forth.
3. Encouraging negotiators to place themselves in a subservient position to another party so that they incur a minor risk. This demonstrates trust since it places a party's well-being in the hands of an opponent (Pruitt, 1981).
4. Encouraging negotiators to ask for help, thus acknowledging the need for assistance from another participant (Fisher, 1978).
5. Encouraging negotiators to demonstrate a genuine concern to help other participants reach their objectives while retaining the ability to reach their own objectives (Zartman and Berman, 1982).
6. Encouraging negotiators to demonstrate that there will be

an earlier return of benefits to the agreeing party than had been previously expected (Zartman and Berman, 1982).

7. Encouraging negotiators to demonstrate that they are willing to undergo punishment or incur costs if they do not follow through on their promises (Zartman and Berman, 1982).

8. Discouraging negotiators from threatening an opponent or making promises that are unbelievable or unrealistic (Zartman and Berman, 1982).

9. Encouraging negotiators to make incremental agreements in which success can be measured along the way (Fisher, 1978; Zartman and Berman, 1982).

10. Encouraging negotiators to demonstrate an understanding of the other side's concerns, even if the party does not agree with the concerns.

All the above moves should be carried out by the parties. The mediator, however, can be a catalyst for these moves.

Mediators can also make specific interventions that will build trust between parties and change their perceptions. Some of these moves include creating situations in which the parties must perform a joint task, translating one party's perceptions to another, vocally identifying commonalities, verbally rewarding parties for cooperation and trust, and facilitating a discussion of their perceptions of each other (Fisher, 1978).

Communication and Conciliation

Communication is certainly a central component in negotiation. The amount, form, and quality of communication as well as who participates in the exchange usually strongly influence the outcome of negotiations.

The common assumption that "if parties are talking they will work out their differences" is not necessarily true. Deutsch (1969, p. 12) describes the communication of people in conflict: "Typically a competitive process tends to produce the following effects: communication between the conflicting parties is unreliable and impoverished. The available communication channels and opportunities are not utilized or they are used in an attempt to mislead or intimidate the other. Little confidence is placed in information that is obtained directly from the other; espionage and other circuitous means of obtaining information are relied upon. The poor communication enhances the possibility of error and misinformation of the sort which is likely to reinforce the pre-existing orientations and expectations toward the other."

Unproductive communication can lead to a breakdown of interaction between the parties or the inability to start negotiations at all. Mediators often assist parties in structuring or themselves structure communication. Mediator moves to modify communication involve controlling or assisting the parties in:

1. Determining what is communicated.
2. Determining how a message—both syntax and means of transmission—is communicated.
3. Determining by whom the message is communicated.
4. Determining to whom the message is delivered.
5. Determining when a message is delivered.
6. Determining where a message is delivered.
7. Improving the ability of the parties to receive messages.

I will examine each one of these points in detail.

Managing What Is Said to Another Party. The content of a message that a speaker conveys to a listener can be substantive information such as data regarding issues, interests, or positions; procedural information referring to the way that a negotiator does or does not want an activity to be conducted; or information about the negotiator's emotional state.

Mediators manage what negotiators say in several ways. First, the mediator may meet with the party before joint sessions or during caucuses to assist him or her in determining what information should or should not be shared with other disputants. The mediator's knowledge of likes and dislikes of other parties often assists him or her in making suggestions about what should be said in joint meetings that will best meet the needs of all parties. The coaching role of the mediator is often important.

Second, the mediator can influence what is said by a party in joint session by translating it into language that is both understandable and acceptable to another party. This process, often called reframing, will be discussed in more detail in Chapter Nine.

Third, the mediator can shift what is being said by structuring communications channels so that parties are allowed to make only limited and managed statements (Young, 1972). For example, the mediator may allow parties to talk only on particular subjects, may interrupt parties making statements that another party will not positively receive, or may even prevent direct communication by keeping the parties in a caucus. If a caucus is used, the mediator may filter information that flows between the parties to allow only content that builds toward an agreement to be communicated (Maggiolo, 1972).

Managing How Messages Are Communicated. Mediators may also help determine how a message is communicated. *How* in this sense refers not only to the medium—written, verbal (in person or by phone), and so forth (Cohen, 1980)—but also to the sender's syntax.

By managing how parties communicate, the mediator can vary both substantive and emotional content of a message. For example, written messages eliminate unproductive nonverbal communication and may be more explicit. It also takes more time both to initiate and to respond, thus allowing parties more time for deliberation on the messages sent and received.

Verbal communication in person may be good for some negotiations and poor for others. In some cases the mediator may want to deliver the message because the party may accept him or her more than the other party. This also allows the mediator to control and formulate what is to be communicated.

Managing Who Communicates. Mediators often take the initiative to manage who communicates in negotiations. In some disputes a negotiator may deem a message more or less acceptable depending on who sends it. If, for example, a mediator discovers that one group is disconcerted by a member of another group, the intervenor may advise the initiating group as to who will best represent it so that its message will be well received by the other group.

Managing to Whom the Communication Is Delivered. Communication may be accepted or rejected based on the recipient's identity. Because the mediator is aware of the structure of negotiating teams or their constituents, he or she may be able to suggest to whom a communication should be addressed. Variables that mediators should consider are: (1) Who has the power to decide? (2) Who is psychologically ready to hear the message? (3) Who are the moderates in the group? (4) To whom in the bureaucratic hierarchy should the message be addressed? and (5) What is the protocol for delivering messages?

Managing When a Message Is Delivered. Timing of communication is often important. Often *when* something is said is more important than *what* is said. In one case a manufacturer entered contract negotiations with his work force. After careful analysis, he determined what wage increases the union wanted and decided to comply. In his opening offer, he proposed to meet the union's demands. The union rejected the offer not on the grounds that it did not meet their expectations but because it was offered too soon. The union expected to fight for the increase. The offer's timing led to a strike that damaged both labor and management.

Mediators can often control communication timing by either encouraging or inhibiting discussion of one party until the other party or parties are most receptive. This encouragement or delay may be either directly or indirectly initiated. For example, a labor mediator kept parties apart in caucus and delayed joint meetings until their private discussions had progressed so that they would be able to agree in joint session (Shapiro, 1970).

Managing Where a Message Is Delivered. Where a message is delivered may also be important. An extreme demand made in joint session when a negotiator's entire group is present may meet with a stronger objection than if the proposal had been made in a private and more informal setting. A psychologically relaxing setting may induce a party to settle in some situations, while in others an uncomfortable setting may induce a resolution. For example, mediators occasionally conduct all-night negotiating sessions in unfamiliar settings. Representative Timothy Wirth used this strategy in his efforts to induce agreement by the Denver Water Board, the Environmental Protection Agency, and environmental groups on the siting of the Foothills water treatment facility in Denver, Colorado (Burgess, 1980). Time and setting can be used to influence recalcitrant negotiators. Mediators can often manage the negotiation and communication settings to enhance productivity.

Improving Ability to Receive Messages. Mediators can also help recipients of messages manage how messages are received. Under specific circumstances, mediators may wish either to clarify or to obscure a message's content.

Clarification includes moves that ensure that a listener fully understands a message's content and implications. I discussed active listening, one means of message clarification, earlier in this chapter, and I will discuss other clarification techniques in Chapter Ten. It is enough to say here that clarification usually includes restatement. If the message has been restated in one of a variety of forms, the speaker, whether negotiator or mediator, can determine if it has been accurately received. Restatement allows for corrections and modification to ensure accurate communication. Clarification can also directly involve the mediator, who can interpret messages and add or filter information.

Obscuring or de-emphasizing information may also be appropriate mediator behavior in certain disputes. Mediators can emphasize points that will lead to agreement, can encourage parties to ignore emotionally destructive remarks, or can abandon issues that do not seem important to the parties or that might hinder agreement. In the extreme, obscuring communication involves isolating the parties in a caucus or using shuttle diplomacy. By these devices, the mediator can allow only information that will produce a decision to be directly exchanged.

Nonverbal Communication

Nonverbal communication—gestures, use of space, and manipulation of objects—may be intentional or unintentional, but it still conveys messages. Henley (1977) argues that nonverbal communication may be the principal way that people communicate dominance, authority, and status. If a mediator is to assist parties in effective nonverbal communication, he or she must be aware of its various forms and how it can be channeled to the benefit of all parties.

   Gestures, Eye Contact, and Demeanor. Nonverbal gestures clearly can communicate a tremendous amount of information about a disputant's attitude and data about the power relationship between disputants. Hinde (1972) reported that people often communicate superior attitudes toward others with unsmiling or disdainful facial expressions, erect posture, and staring. People may communicate anxiety, on the other hand, by tense, rigid posture and wringing hands.

   Gestures are often difficult for parties—and mediators—to control. They frequently are initiated by the subconscious and are not consciously planned. Mediators can control nonverbal communication either directly or indirectly. Mediators may control directly by asking parties (1) to face or look at each other when they are speaking (if strategically or culturally appropriate), (2) to look at and speak only to the mediator to avoid eye contact with an opponent, (3) to stop tapping feet or fingers when they are frustrated, and (4) to adjust their body positions so that they sit in postures that are more likely to induce cooperation rather than competition. Encouraging handshakes to conclude negotiations is one way to nonverbally affirm an agreement.

   Caucuses can be used to control gestures and their possible effects in extreme cases. This entirely excludes nonverbal signals between disputants, since the mediator conveys written or oral messages.

   While controlling gestures and eye contact of disputants may be difficult, the mediator may initiate nonverbal communication that conveys particular messages to the parties. The mediator can use eye contact, handshakes, and body language to convey either engagement and approval or disengagement and disapproval to disputants.

   In one case, a contractor and a homeowner were engaged in an intense conflict over compensation for a fault in a house's construction. They became verbally abusive and pointed and shook fingers at each other, and one disputant began to pound the table. The mediator stood up very slowly, took off his glasses, and began to slowly pace around the room. He suggested that the parties look at the issue another way. He stopped and pointed to a chart on the wall that listed information about the house in question. The mediator's movements and gestures, because they were more active and interesting than those of either of the disputants, attracted their attention and focused them away from each other and onto the mediator. The mediator's manner—calm, deliberate, rational, serious, and focused—also changed the emotional tone of the disputants and encouraged them to seek a more rational approach to their problem.

In conclusion, mediators can manage the gestures of disputants by direct requests or separation, or by means of indirect signals initiated by the mediator's own gestures or eye contact. There is a caveat, however. Nonverbal communication is often culturally or racially bound; signals take on different meanings among different cultures or races (Kochman, 1981; Van Zandt, 1970). Mediators should take great care to adhere to cultural norms when they attempt to modify their own gestures or eye contact or those of disputants. Such violation can lead to a deterioration or breakdown in communication between disputants or between disputants and the mediator.

Use of Nonverbal Communication and Space. Mediators also initiate moves that control the environment in which parties negotiate. *Environment* refers not only to physical distance between the parties or between the parties and the mediator, but also to the way people's bodies are positioned in relation to each other.

In a seminal work on nonverbal communication, Hall (1966) observes that Americans have norms regarding acceptable proximity or distance between people for particular types of interactions. He identifies four general categories of relationships: intimate, personal, social, and public. The first three are relevant to negotiations. A distance of zero to six inches indicates extremely intimate interaction. It often includes body contact and may result in playful wrestling, affectionate touching, or gestures that comfort or protect. A distance of one-and-one-half to two-and-one-half feet is the acceptable proximity for people who have a close personal relationship, and is characteristic of parents and children or close friends. Henley (1977) notes that this is the limit of physical domination. Social distance—four through seven feet—is the normal distance for working colleagues. It is a distance for more formal settings in which people do not engage in intimate or personal relationships.

Although these zones are culturally based, mediators must be familiar with them because they establish norms that if violated may establish changes in the dynamics of disputes. Parties tend to become uncomfortable if acceptable distances are violated and will usually initiate behavior to re-establish a spatial norm or may even become hostile.

A case illustrates the role of physical space and settlement. Two co-mediators were talking with a party in caucus. One of the mediators stressed the negative impacts of not settling the case and crowded the physical space of the party by leaning toward him. There was no room for retreat, since the party was literally up against the wall. The party refused to budge from his position. The other co-mediator suggested a break to allow time for considering the proposal. During the recess this co-mediator suggested that the other mediator allow the party more physical space. The other mediator agreed, and when the caucus was resumed, the party began to move around, leaned forward, and accepted the proposal.

Mediators often take the initiative to maintain spatial norms in order to prevent conflict escalation. They may allow parties enough room in the negotiating setting that they are not crowded, may ensure that there is enough space between disputants so that they cannot harm each other, or may even position the mediator equally between the parties to provide a physical buffer between disputants and to physically demonstrate the intervenor's impartial position. Occasionally, however, a mediator may violate spatial norms for negotiations in order to destabilize parties.

Physical arrangement of space and the location's degree of formality are both closely related to physical distance between negotiators or between negotiators and the mediator. Seating arrangements have been discussed earlier so I will not repeat them here.

Some mediators manage the degree of formality to promote more cooperative negotiation or to emphasize the seriousness of the issues. Some court-related mediation programs may tend to reinforce a quasi-judicial perception of the mediation process by negotiating in a courtroom or judicial building, a lawyer's office, or a police station and maintaining a highly formal setting: sparse furnishings, few personal items, institutional furniture, and so forth. This environment seems to reinforce formality, seriousness, and a businesslike approach to negotiation. A setting of this type to manage behavior may subliminally suggest the seriousness of the dispute, and may psychologically reinforce commitment to the agreement later.

Other mediators, however, prefer informal settings such as their personal offices, a neutral and uninvolved third party's home, a restaurant, or a relaxing public setting such as a resort or retreat center. Mediators assume that informal settings will encourage parties to be more relaxed, comfortable, and not forced to manage an alien environment as well as controversial issues.

Mediators often take the initiative to either increase or decrease the formality of the negotiating setting to affect the psychological climate of the negotiators. These moves, of course, are contingent on the situation.

Nonverbal Communication and Objects. People use physical objects to convey messages in negotiation. Objects may include clothing, sunglasses, handkerchiefs, documents or reports, briefcases, or even firearms. Mediators manage objects to enhance conciliation with one of two categories of moves: (1) activities that promote or inhibit the use of objects by negotiators that influence settlement or (2) activities of the mediator that use objects to influence disputants toward settlement.

The most important objects that negotiators use to influence other parties are often their clothing. Clothing can produce either affinity or alienation between negotiators. Mediators may suggest to parties appropriate attire that may encourage another party to settle. In cross-cultural disputes, personal attire may often be a barrier to a party's consideration of another's trustworthiness or seriousness.

Clothing can also influence the mediator's acceptability and credibility with a party. Several years ago a group of professionals asked me to intervene in an interracial high school dispute. I wore jeans and a work shirt to the interview with conflicting students. My attire reduced the differences between myself and the students. The same attire, however, caused a controversy when I returned after speaking to the students to discuss the intervention with the professionals. They did not equate professional mediation services with my informal attire.

Mediators also may request that the parties bring particular objects to sessions that may enhance psychological cooperation—financial records or contested objects (televisions, radios, clothing, and so forth)—so that parties can refer directly to the objects. Mediators must also occasionally discourage the use of objects that have negative effects on negotiation. For example, certain negotiation projects require that all firearms be left at home or checked on arrival.

EIGHT

Beginning the Mediation Session

In this stage of intervention, the mediator will assist the negotiators in beginning a productive exchange of information about issues in dispute. If the parties have been meeting before the mediator's entry, he or she may abbreviate some of the component moves of this stage. Nevertheless, most of these moves will appear near the start of the first joint meeting held in the mediator's presence. This discussion of the various moves and strategies mediators use in this stage will assume that the parties have not yet held a joint meeting.

The mediator's major tasks in this phase of intervention parallel those of the negotiators. The mediator wants to

1. Begin establishing a positive tone of trust and common concern.
2. Externally provide or assist the parties in developing a procedure that encourages emotional expression but prevents destructive venting.
3. Externally provide or assist the parties in developing a structure for mutual education about issues they would like to discuss.
4. Provide a structure that enhances the possibility of accurate communication.

In Chapter Six, I discussed the general strategy or concep-

153

tual plan that mediators pursue when opening negotiations. I will now examine implementation of the strategy in more detail.

Opening Statements

Disputants usually enter negotiations in various states of emotional stress. Argyris (1970) notes that people are more likely to accept change—and negotiation means change—voluntarily if the negotiating climate enhances self-acceptance, confirmation of personal worth, feelings of essentiality, and a psychological sense of success. Maslow (1968) identifies that an individual's safety needs must be met before considering other higher needs.

The mediator's first moves in this phase of intervention should create a positive tone and meet the basic need of safety. A mediator accomplishes this nonverbally by physical arrangement of the parties in the room and verbally by his or her opening statement. The opening statement usually contains approximately eleven points. These include:

1. Introduction of the mediator and, if appropriate, the parties
2. Commendation of the willingness of the parties to cooperate and seek a solution to their problems
3. Definition of mediation and the mediator's role
4. Statement of impartiality and neutrality
5. Description of mediation procedures
6. Explanation of the concept of the caucus
7. Definition of the parameters of confidentiality
8. Description of logistics
9. Suggestions for behavioral guidelines
10. Answering questions posed by the parties
11. Joint commitment to begin

In Chapter Six, I discussed the general content of the mediator's opening statement. I will now explain how it is presented in practice.

Mediator Introduction. First, the mediator introduces

himself or herself and the parties (if applicable), and explains how he or she became the mediator in this negotiation. "Good morning, my name is —— and I have been asked to be your mediator and to assist you in discussing the issues that have brought you to mediation. I work as a mediator for the Center for Dispute Resolution and have a background in helping people work out their own solutions to situations they would like to change." The mediator, in referring to himself or herself with a social or professional title such as Mr., Mrs., Ms., or in using only his or her first name, sets the tone for the degree of formality in mediation.

Affirmation of Willingness to Cooperate. Second, the mediator should commend the willingness of the parties to cooperate and to try mediation to settle their differences. "I would like to congratulate you both for coming here today and trying to negotiate your own agreement to some issues which may have been hard in the past to discuss. It is an affirmative indication on your part that you want to take responsibility for making your own decisions."

The mediator may want to ask people how they feel, ascertain their emotions through their verbal or nonverbal messages, and acknowledge their emotional condition. The mediator may also acknowledge or restate what he or she sees or hears to test perceptual accuracy and demonstrate that he or she understands the emotions of the disputants. The point of recognizing emotions here is not to make a therapeutic intervention, but to release stress by talking about emotions. Early acknowledgment that disputants are uncomfortable often helps them dissipate tension so that they can relax and focus on the substance of negotiations.

Definition of Mediation and the Mediator's Role. Third, the mediator should define mediation and the mediator's role in dispute resolution. The mediator may have discussed this with each party in prenegotiation interviews, but it is psychologically important for all parties to hear the same information from the mediator in the presence of other disputants. This ensures that everyone has the same information and minimizes different interpretations of what the mediator may have previously said.

If the parties are extremely tense at the start of negotiations they may not be able to hear or retain all the mediator's comments. Although this is a drawback to presenting the information at this time, the mediator should still explain to the parties why he or she is there and what he or she proposes to do. This can protect the mediator from later charges that he or she brought the parties together under false pretenses, and outlines precisely what they can expect from the intervenor. An explanation of mediation and the mediator's role now may also give the mediator leverage later in negotiation, when he or she can refer to the role definition as explained at the start of the session.

Mediators in the community sector and in interpersonal disputes usually try to explain mediation and the mediator's role in the most informal language possible. Explanations vary considerably, but they usually cover (1) a brief description of what the parties will do during the next period of time, (2) what a mediator is, (3) what the mediator can do for the parties, and (4) the potential outcome of mediation. A sample explanation follows: "During the next (specified period of time) you will be engaging in negotiations and searching for a joint solution that will meet your needs and satisfy your interests. My role as mediator will be to help you identify problems or issues that you want to talk about, help you clarify needs that must be met by a solution, assist you in developing a problem-solving process that will enable you to reach your goals, and keep you focused and on the right track."

Next, the mediator should describe his or her authority relationship with the disputants. "As I told each of you previously, mediation is a voluntary process. You are here because you want to see if you can find solutions to issues that divide you. My role is to assist you in doing this. I do not have the power to, nor will I attempt to, make decisions for you. I will step out of the discussion of substance or content. My role is to advise you on procedure, and on how you might best negotiate. If you reach an agreement, we (or I) will write it down in the form of a memorandum of understanding. This agreement can become legally binding if it involves issues covered by law, or it may be left as an informal agreement. If you want to make your agreement legally binding, you may want to consult a lawyer at the end of mediation. He or she can draft the agreement and put it into the form of a contract. If you do not reach a settlement, you are free to pursue other means of dispute resolution that you feel are appropriate. You do not lose any rights to go to court if you use mediation and are unable to reach an agreement."

Statement of Impartiality and Neutrality. The mediator should explain that he or she is impartial in his or her views and neutral in his or her relationship to the parties. "Before proceeding, I would like to clarify both my position on the issues at hand and what my relationship has been with both of you. During this mediation, I will be impartial toward the substance of issues. I do not have any preconceived biases toward any one solution or toward one of you over the other. My relationship with each of you has consisted of (our preconference meetings, business association, a previous advisory role, and so forth). I do not believe that this relationship will jeopardize my capacity to act as an impartial assistant to you in resolving this dispute. If at any time you feel that I am acting in an unneutral manner, please call me on my behavior. I will try to change it. If at any time you feel that I am not able to remain impartial and am unable to assist you, you may cease negotiations, find another mediator, or pursue another means of settlement."

In claiming impartiality and neutrality toward issues and the parties, a mediator should disclose any relationship with one or more disputants that might bias his or her behavior or raise a question in the minds of the disputants as to whether the mediator can in fact remain impartial while assisting in discussions of these particular issues. If disputants feel uncomfortable about the mediator's relationship with one or more parties, the mediator's past experience with similar issues, or a known aspect of the mediator's private life (political activity, professional or economic relations, or social affiliations that might jeopardize neutrality), they should have the opportunity to question, obtain clear answers, and select a replacement mediator if necessary.

Disputants may not initially believe a claim of impartiality and neutrality in a highly polarized conflict. There is a tendency to see the dispute in bipolar terms: "you are either for us or against us," and anyone not taking a vocal position toward one side or another is suspect. Naturally, the parties will have to see neutral behavior before they believe that a mediator is impartial in attitude. The goal of the mediator at this point is to gain nominal approval from the parties to proceed with negotiations.

Description of Mediation Procedures. Next, the mediator should describe the procedures to be followed. If he or she has worked these out with the disputants in the prenegotiation interview, this description is no more than a reiteration of previous agreements. If, however, the mediator has taken the initiative to design negotiation procedures independently of the parties, he or she should present the proposal in a way that the parties are most likely to accept. The strategy, of course, must be adjusted to meet the idiosyncrasies of the particular parties. A common description of negotiation procedures follows:

"At this time, I would like to briefly describe the process that I propose you follow to begin the session. Both of you have a significant amount of information about the problems you are dealing with. Although I have spoken to you each briefly about this situation, I do not have the detailed understanding that each of you does. I suggest that we begin the discussion today with a brief description from each of you of how you see the situation that brought you to mediation. This will educate both you and me about the issues and give us a common perception of the problem. Each of you will have a chance, roughly (specify time) minutes, to present how you see the problem. I request that you not interrupt the other while he or she is explaining a viewpoint, and that you hold your questions until the end of the presentation. A pencil and a pad have been provided for each of you to note observations or questions so that they do not get lost prior to the question-and-answer time.

"During your presentations, I may ask some clarifying questions or probe your description so that I can gain a greater understanding of how you perceive the situation. My probing is not to put you on the spot, but rather to broaden the general understanding of the problem. At the end of each of your presentations, there will be a time for the other party (or parties, or give name) to ask questions of clarification. This is not a time to debate the issues, but to clarify issues and perceptions about the problem(s) at hand.

"At the end of the presentation and questions we will turn to the other (or next) person (or party) to repeat the process until a representative of each view has had an opportunity to speak. At this point, we will clearly identify the issues that you would like to discuss in more depth, identify the interests that you would like to have satisfied, generate some potential solutions, and assess whether one or more of these alternatives will meet your needs."

The mediator should clearly explain the stages of the problem-solving process and should take care not to appear as an authority figure toward the disputants. It is their process, not the mediator's. The process description is a procedural suggestion, not an order. The mediator may feign an incomplete understanding of the details of the dispute so that the parties can educate him or her, and in the process educate the other party, about the issues in dispute. The mediator also may initiate a proposal to control interruptions—writing pads and pencils, for instance.

Explanation of Caucus. Next, the mediator should explain the concept of the caucus with each party:

"There may be a need, at some time in the course of our meetings, for each of you to take some time out and meet with other members of your group (if it is a group dispute) or meet with me as a mediator. The need for this type of break or meeting is not unusual. It allows you time to reflect on alternatives or proposals, gather your facts to develop new settlement options, or reach a consensus within your group (if applicable). At times, I may call such a meeting, but you may initiate them also. If I call a separate meeting, it is not to make a deal, but to explore options that might be more comfortable for you to discuss in private. What is discussed in these separate meetings will be considered by me to be confidential. I will not reveal what we have talked about with the other party (or parties) unless you instruct me to do so."

Little more is said about caucuses at this time because the thought of private meetings often makes disputants uncomfortable. Disputants often fear clandestine deals. I will explain the uses of caucuses in more detail in Chapter Fifteen.

Defining the Parameters of Confidentiality. At this point, the mediator should describe his or her understanding of the confidential nature of the negotiation session. Confidentiality, although usually considered to be both an important aspect and, in fact, a functional necessity of mediation, is not universally guaranteed. Some states provide legal guarantees for confidentiality between disputants and mediator (Comeau, 1982; Folberg and Taylor, 1984). Other states do not allow for confidentiality between disputants and mediators and may, on occasion, request data or subpoena mediators to testify in postmediation court proceedings. Mediators should describe the limits of confidentiality as it is provided for in their state or agency so that disputants know their limits to privacy.

"These sessions will be considered by me to be confidential in that I will not discuss them publicly with any person not involved in this dispute. I will attempt to maintain this confidentiality to the best of my ability. On occasion, I may want to discuss this problem with a colleague so that I may gain greater insight into the conflict. I request that you grant me this privilege in that it will better enable me to assist you in reaching an agreement."

Some mediators at this point ask parties to sign a confidentiality statement or waiver and consent form designed to protect the mediator from a future court action to subpoena either his or her person or notes as evidence in a legal case (see Resource C). This document affirms that parties will not take such action against a mediator.

Description of Logistics. The mediator should now describe any relevant logistics: time schedule for the entire process, length of sessions, and note taking. The mediator often describes how much time he or she estimates will be necessary to settle the dispute. Parties need to know this in order to assess the cost and benefits of mediated negotiations. An initial commitment should also be gained from the parties for a specific period of time for the first session. Later meeting dates and times can be established as needed. Some mediators in complicated cases have gained a time commitment for several sessions, since it takes longer for data collection and education of the parties about issues in dispute if the conflict is complex. It may also take several sessions before any substantive progress is made or psychological barriers to settlement are lowered.

The mediator should gain permission from the parties to take notes and should explain that the notes are for the mediator's own reference, and that they will remain confidential. The notes are not an official transcript of the meeting, but might at a later time be used to construct a written memorandum of understanding or a settlement document.

Suggestions for Behavioral Guidelines. At this time the mediator should shift his or her focus to behavioral guidelines that will facilitate an orderly discussion. Guidelines that mediators may suggest include procedures to handle interruptions, agreements about the role of witnesses and relationships with the press, conditions for smoking, with whom disputants may discuss negotiations, the quantity of information that can or should be disclosed by the parties, and so forth.

"At this point, I would like to suggest several procedural guidelines that other negotiators have found helpful in their discussions. I would like to suggest that each of you have some uninterrupted time to talk. If one of you has a question about what is said, I request that you hold it until the question period. If you agree to this procedure, I request your permission to hold you to it. Is this acceptable? Do you have other guidelines that might help you discuss issues more productively?"

Some mediators who wish to establish behavioral guidelines for negotiations list the rules under which they will work and are inflexible on changing them, while others ask the disputants to identify and generate their own guidelines to aid them in holding productive discussions. This latter strategy is a first step toward making mutual procedural decisions and developing habits of agreement.

There is clearly no one way to establish behavioral guidelines. In tense situations, disputants may need the mediator to be more directive, while in less polarized disputes the parties themselves may be in total control. Mediators, in establishing behavioral guidelines, should be careful not to use authoritarian or command-ridden language. Terms such as *rules* or *terms for negotiation* or even *behavioral guidelines* that imply regulations that are being forced on the group should be avoided. Noncommanding terms such as *guidelines* or *suggestions for procedure* are often more acceptable to the parties and avoid putting the mediator in an authoritarian position. Once guidelines are established, the mediator should gain an agreement that he or she will be empowered to enforce or call disputants to be responsible to the agreed terms or procedure.

Answering Questions. The mediator is now nearing the end of his or her opening statement. At this point, he or she should answer any questions that the parties may have about the procedure to be followed. Questions should be answered to the satisfaction of the disputants before proceeding further. Lack of understanding by a disputant or dissatisfaction with an answer by a mediator may lead to a decreased commitment to the process or later resistance by a disputant.

Gaining a Commitment to Begin. Gaining a commitment to begin is the mediator's last move before turning the session over to the parties. The mediator's concluding remarks should outline what has been discussed, should set the information-sharing process in motion in a positive way, and should motivate the parties to begin discussing their issues. A sample commitment and consent statement follows:

"If there are no more questions about the process, I suggest that we are ready to move on to discuss the issues at hand. It is my understanding that you are both (or all) here to work hard and bargain in good faith to achieve a settlement. Are you ready to begin?"

After gaining either verbal or nonverbal assent, the mediator should turn the session over to the disputants.

How Parties Begin Negotiating

People in dispute usually start with an opening statement of their own. The opening statement of the parties is usually designed to outline their substantive interests, establish a bargaining procedure, and build rapport with the other side.

Disputants enter negotiations with a variety of levels of information and knowledge about their own issues and preferred solutions, and those of other disputants. In some disputes, issues and outcome possibilities may be very clear, and negotiators will have to spend little time exploring details of contested issues. In other conflicts, the parties may lack information on a number of dimensions.

Young (1972, p. 57) notes that at the beginning of negotiations, one negotiator may be unclear about (1) "the basic issue(s) at stake," (2) the "range of alternative choices or strategies" available, (3) the solutions that will best meet his or her interests or needs, (4) the number and identity of people who should be involved in the negotiations (or who will be affected by them), or (5) the way that other negotiators will make decisions. Knowledge at the start of negotiations may vary from very ill-defined relationships to situations in which strategies, issues, options, and potential outcomes are well known to all negotiators. Parties use opening statements to present and test their views and assumptions at the onset of negotiations.

Mediators should be familiar with the variety of ways in which parties make opening statements so that they are ready to respond. Parties may open negotiations by focusing on either substantive issues, procedures used to negotiate, or moves designed to improve the psychological conditions of disputants.

Opening Focused on Substance. The most common, but not necessarily the most effective, way to open negotiations is to focus immediately on the substantive issues of the dispute. In this approach, the negotiator usually selects several variables—the history of the problem, why there is a need for change, the issues, and possibly interests or positions—and orders them in a combination that will have the maximum positive effect on the opposing party or parties. Moore (1982b) and Lincoln (1981) list possible combinations:

1. *Focus on history, need, and position.* This combination is the most traditional. The negotiator reviews the background of the dispute, outlines how the status quo has

caused damage, tells why change is needed, and then proceeds to detail an opening position that he or she feels would solve the problem. This type of opening frequently forces the parties into hard positional bargaining.

2. *Focus on issues.* The negotiator may dispense with the history of the problem and proceed directly to a discussion of the issues. The issues may be presented in several ways:

    a. They may be left to each side to identify from the presentation of the history of the dispute.

    b. They may be outlined by the negotiator in an order that presents the most important issues first, indicating which items deserve the most attention.

    c. They may be outlined by each negotiator in an order that places simple and small issues first.

    d. The issues may be presented in a random order so that the parties may later jointly organize them.

    e. They may be presented in an exhaustive manner that includes the stated or expected issues of the other side, in order to demonstrate an interest in their viewpoint.

3. *Focus on merit.* In this approach the negotiator tries to educate the other party about the need for change without disclosing or proposing a position. The major assumption behind this strategy is that if a party can convince an opponent that his or her situation is intolerable and that change is needed, it will be easier to reach an agreement later on a particular solution.

4. *Focus on interests.* In this strategy, the negotiator discusses the interests or needs he or she would like to have satisfied through negotiations. By focusing on interests instead of positions, the groundwork is prepared, but not guaranteed, for possible interest-based negotiations.

5. *Focus on nonnegotiable position.* In cases in which parties are extremely polarized or feel that they have little room for bargaining, the negotiator may dispense with the history of a conflict or the issues involved, and present an extreme position instead. This position may or may not be reasonable or negotiable. This tactic will often stalemate negotiations and may force parties to pursue other means of dispute resolution such as litigation or direct action.

Opening Focused on Procedure. Another way of opening negotiations, which is not as common as substantive openings, is to focus on the negotiation procedure. With this strategy, the time in which the disputants focus on behavioral guidelines is expanded into an extended discussion of procedural steps that disputing parties will take to resolve their dispute. As discussed in Moore (1982b) and Lincoln (1981), advantages to pursuing a tactic for opening negotiations focusing on procedure are that such a focus

- Provides a jointly developed sequence for the negotiation to which all parties are committed.
- Allows the parties to practice making decisions as a team.
- Provides information about the behavior, attitudes, and trustworthiness of other parties.
- Allows parties to practice making agreements on problems that are neither substantively important nor as emotionally charged as the issues in dispute.
- Provides an opportunity to build "habits" of agreement.
- Demonstrates that agreement is possible and that the situation is not hopeless.

Central areas of procedure in which parties may make agreements include the following (Moore, 1982b; Lincoln, 1981):

- How an agenda will be developed.
- The negotiation procedure to be followed.
- The time frame and schedule for sessions, including beginning and ending times.
- How information will be shared among disputants.
- How legal rights or administrative mandates will be recognized and protected.
- Parties' relationships with lawyers.
- Acceptable behavior regarding personal attacks, attribution of motivation, respect for values, emotional displays, and attitudes toward win/lose solutions.
- How commitment to the procedure and potential agreements will be maintained.

- Determination of who should be at the table.
- The role of substitutes and observers.
- The role of task forces or small work groups.
- How knowledge gained at the table should or should not be shared with constituents or parties who are not at the table.
- The size of negotiating teams.
- The location of meeting sites.
- Determining how meeting records will be kept and by whom.
- How the media will or will not be informed.
- How procedural and substantive agreements will be enforced.

Mediators sometimes encourage negotiators implicitly or explicitly to focus on procedural agreements before delving into substance if the intervenor feels that parties need to build trust or experience working with one another, or would benefit from a more extensive set of procedural guidelines. Parties occasionally begin with this type of opening on their own.

Opening Focused on Psychological Conditions of Disputants. This form of opening is not as common as substantive or procedural openings to formal negotiations. It is more frequently observed in a form of third-party consultation practiced by organization development specialists and a few social scientists working in international peacemaking (Burton, 1969; Fisher, 1982; Walton, 1969).

This approach aims to improve the relationship of the disputants before focusing on substantive issues or discussing procedure. In its most casual form, some of the conciliation techniques mentioned in Chapter Seven may be initiated, or the process may be conducted more formally through structured experiences in which disputants may engage in general personal-sharing groups (Dubois and Mew Soong Li, 1963), focused-topic discussion groups (Levinson, 1954; Levinson and Soher-merhorn, 1951), intergroup training laboratories (Blake and Mouton, 1961; Blake and others, 1965), or the performance of common tasks unrelated to the issues in dispute (Fisher, 1978). In mediation of a public policy dispute, the mediators arranged for all parties to meet the night before the sessions were to begin for a casual dinner. The negotiators rode a double-decker bus to a Mexican restaurant where they ate, drank, and came to know each other as individuals and not representatives of an interest group. In another dispute involving timber cutting on national forest land the parties spent a weekend retreat in which they hiked on the land from which a proposed timber harvest would be taken. The hike built interpersonal relationships and raised awareness of the land in question.

Mediators in marital disputes occasionally spend time before formal bargaining over divorce issues discussing and processing the development and decline of the marriage (Milne, 1981). It is argued that this procedure helps the couple adjust to the fact that they are divorcing.

Mediators often initiate informal moves to promote conciliation between the parties, rather than focusing on formal measures that build more flexible and open attitudes in disputants. These moves include such activities as active listening, affirmation of some attitude of a party that is not related to issues in conflict, providing a communication structure that promotes safety, or focusing on feelings.

Choosing an Opening to Negotiations

The choice to focus on substance, process, or psychological condition of the disputants depends on (1) the type of dispute, (2) the abilities of the disputants to focus on substantive issues, (3) the level of emotional intensity of disputants, (4) the degree of control the disputants have given to the mediator to design and regulate the process of the meeting, and (5) the internal and external pressures that are on the negotiators to settle promptly. The mediator should try to focus the parties on the opening process that will be most successful for them. If the internal or external pressures to reach agreement are high or moderate and emotional tensions are high, the mediator will usually pursue procedural or psychological openings. Parties will often accept these delays if they can be convinced that such moves will later enhance the possibility of reaching a substantive settlement. Parties may also be more docile and willing to give the lead to a mediator at the start of negotiations if they are not used to participating in formal negotiations. This gives mediators added flexibility in designing opening strategy and the information-sharing process.

Turning the Negotiation Session Over to Disputants

The mediator shifts from the opening statement to a focus on the disputants with a transition statement. A sample transition statement in which the mediator proposes a focus on substance is as follows:

"At this time I propose that we move into a discussion of the situation that brought you to mediation. (The mediator turns to the party that he or she has previously decided should begin presenting first.) Will you please begin by describing the situation as you see it? Please include some of the historical background of the problem, the issues that you would like to discuss, and the interests or needs you want to have satisfied. At this point, it will be helpful not to identify specific solutions but to merely focus on defining the problem."

The mediator now turns the session over to the first party, who begins a presentation of his or her opening statement. Since the most critical task for disputants at this stage of negotiation is to begin an accurate transmission of information, the intermediary may play a valuable function by facilitating communication. The mediator can either assist in a verbatim exchange of information or may modify the way that it is transmitted so as to make it more palatable to the other party (Stevens, 1963).

Facilitating Communication and Information Exchange

At this stage of mediation, the intervenor is usually concerned with maximizing accurate information exchange. Negotiators may be hindered in achieving this task by excessive posturing, extreme demands designed to signal how intensely the parties feel about the issues or how much they want the other party or parties to move, jumbled or unstructured communication, inaccurate listening, intense emotional outbursts, or total dysfunction of one or more parties.

The mediator's main task therefore is to help the parties communicate about substantive issues in dispute and minimize the psychological damage resulting from emotional exchanges. To facilitate this communication, mediators use a variety of communication techniques, some of which were described in Chapters Five and Seven. Additional communication techniques that may be used include

1. *Restatement.* The mediator listens to what has been said and feeds back the content to the party in the party's own words.
2. *Paraphrase.* The mediator listens to what has been said and restates the content back to the party using different words that have the same meaning as the original statement. This is often called *translation.*
3. *Active Listening.* The mediator decodes a spoken message and then feeds back to the speaker the emotions of the message. This is commonly used in conciliation.
4. *Summarization.* The mediator condenses the message of a speaker.
5. *Expansion.* The mediator receives a message, expands and elaborates on it, feeds it back to the listener, and then checks to verify accurate perception.
6. *Ordering.* The mediator helps a speaker order ideas into some form of sequence (historical, size, importance, amount, and so forth).
7. *Grouping.* The mediator helps a speaker identify common ideas or issues and combine them into logical units.
8. *Structuring.* The mediator assists a speaker to organize and arrange his or her thoughts and speech into a coherent message.
9. *Separation or fractionating.* The mediator divides an idea or an issue into smaller component parts.
10. *Generalization.* The mediator identifies general points or principles in a speaker's presentation.

11. *Probing questions.* The mediator asks questions to encourage a speaker to elaborate on an idea.
12. *Questions of clarification.* The mediator asks questions to encourage the speaker to give further information about a point in question.

Mediators use these communication skills to help parties communicate more accurately with each other. The parties ideally also use these skills. The mediator can enhance communication between disputants by encouraging disputants to use communication skills, by teaching disputants how to use them, and by reinforcing their use by commending parties who utilize them.

Establishing a Positive Emotional Climate

In addition to facilitating communication, the mediator often must create an emotional climate conducive to clear communication and joint problem solving. Interventions related to promoting a positive emotional climate include

- Preventing interruptions or verbal attacks.
- Encouraging parties to focus on the problem and not each other.
- Translating value-laden or judgmental language of disputants into less emotionally charged terms.
- Affirming clear descriptions or statements, procedural suggestions, or gestures of good faith while not taking sides on substantive issues.
- Accepting the expression of feelings and being empathic while not taking sides.
- Reminding parties about behavioral guidelines that they have established.
- Diffusing threats by restating specific threats in terms of general pressure to change.
- Intervening to prevent conflict escalation.

If the parties and the mediator have communicated successfully at the end of the early mediation stage, all participants will understand the general boundaries of topic areas around which future negotiations will focus. This stage terminates as soon as the parties or the mediator focus on a particular issue or sphere of discussion and the parties move to discuss it in depth.

NINE

Defining Issues and Setting an Agenda

For parties to move toward a settlement of their differences, they must shift procedurally from interaction that is highly contentious to negotiated moves that are more cooperatively coordinated. The three critical tasks negotiators and mediators must accomplish in this stage are (1) identification of broad topic areas of concern to the parties, (2) agreement on what subtopics or issues should be discussed, and (3) determination of the sequence for discussion of the topics or issues. Coordinated activity by negotiators at this point in the process does not mean that they agree substantively. *Coordination* refers solely to an agreement on the procedure that will be used to handle the topic areas or issues.

Variables that influence how rapidly and how easily this stage in negotiations can be accomplished include

- The number and complexity of issues involved.
- The negotiator's understanding of the conflict's substantive matter.
- The clarity of presentation by the negotiators of each topic or issue.
- The capacity of the negotiators to recognize a distinct topic area or issue when it is presented.
- The degree of persuasion negotiators have mobilized to en-

courage other negotiators to accept a topic or issue for inclusion in the agenda
- The degree of psychological resistance or barriers to collaboration exhibited by one or more parties.

Mediators who enter a dispute before topic and issue
identification and agenda formation can help the parties complete this stage of negotiation. At this stage the mediator and
negotiators have parallel procedural goals.

Topic Areas and Issues

The content of negotiations varies considerably in terms
of the degree of specificity or conceptual boundaries of topics
under discussion. For example, in a community dispute involving a group of neighbors and a social service organization
that plans to site a health clinic for low-income clients in a
middle-class neighborhood, the parties may have the following
conceptual boundaries of the dispute. The neighbors oppose siting the clinic in the neighborhood, and define the boundaries of
the discussion as whether the facility should be sited there at
all. The clinic staff, on the other hand, are not concerned with
discussing *whether* the facility should be sited in the neighborhood. They want to discuss *how* a building can be leased and
what resistance they will encounter in locating their facility. If
a representative of each group were asked to identify what the
context and range of the negotiations should be, each of them
would answer differently. The neighbors would cite a general
topic area: whether the clinic should be built. The clinic staff,
however, would focus the discussion on issues related to how
the clinic can be located in the neighborhood and still have
community concerns or interests taken into consideration.

The degree of specificity of topic areas or issues that the
parties want to discuss varies, of course, from dispute to dispute. Some conflicts begin with a disagreement over a particular point and then move from the specific issue to a more general level of contention, while others begin with very general

topics of disagreement and gradually become more specific. More will be said about these two dynamics in Chapter Eleven when we consider what problem-solving technique should be applied to handle the dispute.

Aside from the level of specificity of the dispute, a second kind of distinction can be made. Issues can be classified according to whether they are consensual (interest-based) or dissensual (value-based) (Aubert, 1963).

Consensual or Interest-Based Conflict. Conflicts of interest usually exist in conditions of perceived or actual scarcity in which one or more parties believes that gains for one party may mean a loss for another. Conflicts of interest are often referred to as competitive cooperation, in that the disputants are collaborating to compete for the same set of goods or benefits.

Because there are numerous types of interests that any given party may have in a dispute, there is often great latitude in trading one set of interests for another so that all parties can be satisfied in a settlement.

Dissensual or Value-Based Conflict. In contrast to conflicts of interest in which a consensus exists between parties about competition for the desired end result or in which enough different interests exist to facilitate a trading process to minimize loss on all sides, dissensual conflicts are based on differences in values. Value disputes focus on such issues as guilt and innocence, what norms should prevail in a social relationship, what facts should be considered valid, what beliefs are correct, who merits what, or what principles should guide decision makers. Disputes of whether to build a housing development, whether to cut down a forest, whether divorcing parents should allow new lovers over when the children live at home, or whether a party should be punished (as opposed to making restitution) for committing a theft are all disputes over values.

Before discussing how parties and mediators identify topic areas and issues for negotiation, I reiterate that there is a third type of issue that was discussed in relation to conciliation in Chapter Seven—unnecessary issues caused by strong emotions, misperception, or poor communication. These issues in disputes are caused by neither conflict of interest nor values. I have discussed means to handle these "unnecessary" conflicts in Chapter Thirteen.

Identifying and Framing Issues

In the process of defining parameters of the dispute, the parties and the mediator engage in the preliminary definition of topic areas and issues that will be the focus of future negotiations. This process has been referred to variously as framing or reframing (Watzlawick, 1978), characterizing (Stulberg, 1981a), reconceptualizing, or redefining (Boulding, 1962; Sawyer and Guetzkow, 1965) the issues in dispute. Before exploring the moves of framing or reframing a situation, I will briefly explain how parties arrive at their viewpoint of the conflict.

Each disputant comes to the conflict with his or her own individual picture or subjective reality of what issues are in dispute and what the basis of conflict is (Berger and Luckmann, 1967). Watzlawick (1978, p. 119) describes the individual's condition: "Let us remember: We never deal with reality *per se,* but rather with *images* of reality—that is, with interpretations. While the number of potentially possible interpretations is very large, our world image usually permits us to see only one—and this *one* therefore appears to be the only possible, reasonable, permitted view. Furthermore, this one interpretation also suggests only one possible, reasonable, and permitted solution."

An example of how a situation is framed is the joke about how one distinguishes between an optimist and a pessimist: "The optimist says of a bottle that it is half full; the pessimist sees it as half empty. The same bottle and the same quantity of wine—in other words, the same first-order reality— but two very different world images, creating two very different (second-order) realities" (Watzlawick, 1978, p. 119).

More in line with our focus is the classic dispute in child custody over which parent will receive legal custody of the child. Both parents want to ensure that they will have a high level of involvement in their child's life. They, and in many cases the judicial system, have defined the resolution procedure as a court decision determining who can legally possess the child. There are, however, alternative ways that this parent-parent/parent-child relationship can be framed. If, for example, the struggle over legal custody is defined in terms of maximizing the parent-child relationship, and the concept of legal custody or ownership of the child is reframed into terms of parental rights and responsibilities toward their offspring, the bipolar struggle with only a win-lose outcome is transformed into a more complex issue with multiple variables that may be traded off one against another (Haynes, 1981; Ricci, 1980). By reframing how a dispute is seen and defined by the parties, the mediator can open the door to more collaborative and mutually satisfactory solutions.

Variables in Framing and Reframing Issues

When negotiators frame issues in a productive, problem-solving format, the mediator may be merely an interested observer. However, some disputes become deadlocked because disputants have not discovered a mutually acceptable definition or framing of the issues that will allow them to cooperate. At this point, the mediator's intervention can be invaluable. The mediator may either frame the issues before the parties restrict themselves with a particular definition, or may reframe the issues by moving the parties away from an unproductive definition toward one that will lead to successful problem solving.

When reframing the definition of issues in dispute from terms put forth by one or more parties to new terms that are subjectively acceptable to all disputants, the mediator should consider (1) the process for reframing interest-related issues, (2) techniques for reframing value-related issues, (3) the explicitness and timing of reframing, and (4) the appropriate language or syntax used in the redefinition of the situation.

Reframing Interest-Related Issues. The act of reframing itself raises some important questions regarding the mediator's neutrality. The general assumption of mediators when reframing an issue is that they are making such a move "based on some conception (implicit or explicit) of a more constructive or desirable relationship for the original players than the one that they see themselves engaging in at the outset of the interaction. And in this context, the terms 'constructive' and 'desirable' inevitably carry normative content. Be this as it may, mediators constantly redefine the context of disputes in ways that disputants find to be extremely helpful to avoid or overcome impasse" (Young, 1972, p. 59).

In general, reframing interest disputes is easier than reframing value conflicts resulting from dissensus over such issues as guilt, rights, or facts. In reframing interest disputes, mediators often use a technique that expands issues to provide the parties with more bargaining power. For example, in a labor-management dispute, the union and management are bargaining to a deadlock over a wage increase. The union negotiators must bring to their constituents some tangible benefits from the negotiations. They have selected salary increases as their goal. The mediator can reframe the issue from the problem of wage increase to the problem of how the union can obtain benefits that its constituents will see are the result of the negotiations. This reframing of the situation allows the negotiator to look for other means of meeting union needs than solely emphasizing wages.

Reframing interest disputes requires a careful analysis of position statements put forth by the parties and the interests represented by the position. Shifting from specific interests to more general ones may widen the number of settlement options available.

Reframing issues and interests in narrower terms is also occasionally effective. For example, consider the case in which several people agreed to purchase a piece of property together that was to be used for cooperative housing. Several months after the purchase, the relationships among the owners deteriorated and several of the people decided that they wanted their money back. However, this would only be possible by revising the financial contract all the owners had agreed on. The initial issue, stated in the form of a demand, was "I want my money back." The problem as the disputants framed it was that one person wanted his money back and was withdrawing from the contract, but the others felt that they could not reimburse him without selling the property. Sale of the property was not acceptable to the other owners. From this either/or situation, the mediator and the parties mutually reframed the issue into smaller, more manageable subissues: How much money? When? In what form? With interest? and so forth. The parties were then able to reach agreement on trade-offs for these subissues.

Reframing Value-Related Issues. Reframing conflicts over values is much more difficult than redefining interest-related issues. This seems to be because value issues have a strong tendency to become bipolar, with one side representing right and the other side wrong. Disputants place great emphasis on normative judgment, which often makes it difficult to compromise and trade as in interest-related issues. Even proposing such solutions may provoke escalation. People will claim that their "ideas are not for sale" or that one "can't bargain with the truth" (Aubert, 1963).

Mediators accomplish identification and framing of value-based issues by (1) translating value disputes into interest disputes, (2) identifying superordinate goals, and (3) avoidance. I will discuss each approach in turn.

Pure dissensus in conflicts over values and facts is relatively rare. Usually, value disputes are mixed disputes in that participants also have some common interests. Mediators who work with value disputes often try to translate values into interests so that the parties have more tangible issues. For example, if a value dispute over authority can be translated into a conflict over the division of power, there are some possibilities for compromise based on a formula for the division of power. In one case, two employees are rivals for promotion in their organization. There is only one position available at the next grade above their current rank. Both employees want the job and claim to be the best person for the job. If it is in the company's interest to satisfy both employees, those responsible may explore how the tasks, authority, and status of the job could be divided between the two equally qualified employees. Thus, a struggle over who is best becomes moot as each employee is rewarded based on interest.

In another dispute, an association of single-family home-owners were in dispute with a planning department over the construction of multifamily dwellings on the edge of their neighborhood. The single-family homeowners charged that the new construction would change the neighborhood's ambiance and that it would mean an entire shift in life-style. On careful examination, life-style values were translated into interests—limited noise, no abrupt transitions from single-family to multifamily homes, minimizing height of new construction to preserve views, and maintaining privacy by avoiding building complexes that overlook single-family home backyards. Given the interests of all parties, a mutually satisfactory development plan was negotiated that met most of the needs described above.

A second approach to reframing value disputes is to identify larger superordinate goals with which all parties can identify (Sherif and others, 1961). For example, in a dispute over a dam's location, one party may argue that the proposed construction site damages a pristine wilderness area, while the other party argues that it has a mandate to provide water to a nearby city and that the dam allows the party to fulfill contractual obligations. The mediator looks for a superordinate goal to join the parties in a cooperative effort. In this instance, the mediator might gain consensus that the topic to be discussed is (1) an agreement that the city needs a certain amount of water and (2) that the wilderness is to be protected. The parties can then participate in a joint search for potential sources of water.

The third strategy for managing and identifying value-based issues is to avoid identifying or responding to them directly, or to reframe the situation so that parties agree to disagree. Since it is difficult to mediate guilt or innocence, right or wrong, respect or lack of respect, and so forth, the mediator may want to avoid these questions entirely and focus only on the dispute's components that can be turned toward interest-based bargaining. If enough issues can be solved with interest-based bargaining, the importance of value differences will fade and will be dropped from a list of demands or topics for discussion.

Explicit-Implicit Reframing and Timing

To resolve disputes over interests or values, parties often must be explicit about the topic areas that divide them, the issues that need to be discussed, and the points on which they must conduct bargaining or negotiation. The degree of explicitness, however, may vary over time due to the dynamics of the negotiation process itself or to conscious strategies of the negotiators or the mediator. The mediator should manage the timing of issue identification so that the parties will be most receptive to the way the issue is framed. Parties are often vague at the start of negotiations about the specifics of issues in dispute. Only through a process of discussion and mutual education can the parties jointly define and make explicit the concrete issues that must be resolved.

One party will often name an issue precisely only to have another party repeatedly reject it. After several rounds of proposal rejection and exploration, the parties may finally be able to agree to discuss the issue. The final framing of the issues by the parties, or reframing by the mediator, may be identical to the earlier characterization of the problem. The final acceptance of the framing is a result of timing and the psychological readiness of the parties to accept the definition of the situation. This psychological shift often occurs after dialogue or when the neutral intervenor states the framing. There is research evidence that parties are often willing and able to hear and accept statements worded by the mediator when they are not able to hear or accept the identical statement from another disputant (Rubin and Brown, 1975).

Appropriate Language or Syntax

One remaining point needs to be covered regarding framing the issues: the mediator's language or syntax. *Syntax* refers to the order and manner in which words are put together to form phrases or express a thought. Disputants use language that is judgmental, positional, and biased toward their subjective view. In joint session, mediators usually try to translate the language of the disputants into neutral terms to remove bias, positions, or judgment. Thus, when one party says, "That fat slob hasn't paid his rent money for the past two months," the mediator translates this to: "You are upset that you have not received money that you feel is due to you according to the terms of your rental agreement with Mr. Brown." In this case, the judgmental statement that Brown is a slob is dropped and the "you message," the portion of the communication directed at Brown for nonpayment, is also shifted to focus on the landlord's feelings of deprivation and need for reimbursement. This, after all, is what concerns the landlord. Reframing the problem in this way also makes Brown feel more comfortable with the issue. The focus is no longer on his character but the landlord's need to be paid.

In identifying and framing issues, mediators should be careful to state the problem clearly in a manner that favors neither side nor makes one party blameworthy. Ideally, the mediator should depersonalize the issues and put them outside the relationship between the disputants. The parties can then focus on the topic in a more objective manner (Filley, 1975). Stulberg (1981a) notes that mediators should take great care to avoid "trigger" words or statements that parties may interpret as mediator bias or preconceived judgments as to who is wrong. Mediators occasionally avoid any adversarial language, referring to conflicts as *problems,* positions as *viewpoints,* parties as *your group,* and negotiations as *discussions* in order to depolarize and neutralize value-laden and conflict-oriented terminology.

There are times, however, when entirely neutral terminology may not be as effective as more partisan language. If, for example, the parties cannot reach an agreement on issues in joint session, the mediator may call a caucus to discuss the problem of issue identification. The mediator may use language more biased toward the interests or values of a particular party in the caucus to influence their decision making. The mediator may use the same terminology, syntax, and emotion as one party to encourage identification by the party with the mediator and to progress toward agreement on issues with another disputant. Usually, however, mediators should take care that the way they speak in a caucus is not drastically different from their manner in joint session so that parties neither are confused nor feel double-crossed by the shift to more neutral language when they return to joint session.

Determining an Agenda

The agenda the mediator designs before negotiations, as discussed in Chapter Six, is a rough draft to which new information is added from the opening statements of the parties. The negotiating agenda that disputants ultimately follow should be developed and approved either by the parties alone, by the parties in conjunction with the mediator, or by the mediator alone (with the consent of the parties). Once issues have been identified, they must be placed in an order for discussion.

There are at least eight different approaches to agenda development in negotiations: (1) ad hoc, (2) simple agenda, (3) alternating choices of items, (4) ranking according to importance, (5) the principled agenda, (6) less difficult items first, (7) building-block or contingent agenda, and (8) trade-offs or packaging.

Ad Hoc Development. With ad hoc sequencing, one party proposes that the negotiators discuss an item, the other party or parties concur, and the item is discussed in its entirety until a conclusion has been reached. The parties then mutually agree on another item, and the process is repeated. The parties move through all items, ordering their agenda as they proceed. This model allows for flexibility, but also allows and promotes manipulation between parties for placement of agenda items at particularly opportune moments.

Simple Agenda Approach. Gulliver (1979, p. 143) describes the simple agenda method and some of its drawbacks: "Issues in a dispute are merely taken, one at a time, in the order already prescribed by the agenda [that is, given or presented by one or more parties], and treated and settled separately. Although this may commonly succeed for decision making in committees and conferences, it can rarely work in negotiations.

The chief reason is that it attempts to ignore the essential problems of multiple criteria: that issues are often interconnected in the social life of negotiations and that, in any event, they are necessarily interconnected within the specific context of the negotiations in progress. Parties are aware of this and are unwilling to forfeit advantages that might be gained by getting better terms on one issue through concession (or refusal of it) on another. They wish to explore interconnections without the rigidity of a fixed agenda order."

The simple agenda approach encourages stalling and manipulative tactics in order to gain leverage on items that will come up later on the agenda. Gulliver notes that this procedure tends to subvert the ordering almost immediately.

Alternating Choices of Items. A third model for agenda construction is the alternating issue approach. In this method, the parties alternate who chooses the topic of discussion. This structural solution allows the parties to proceed and often inhibits the development of deadlocks. Gulliver (1979) says that this process rarely works for long, however, since one or more parties invariably insist on breaking the order.

Ranking According to Importance. A fourth model of agenda design is for the parties to pick the one or two most important items for each of them and place them at the head of the agenda (Gulliver, 1979). The assumption is that if they can agree on these items, the remainder of the less important items will follow suit. This procedure, of course, depends on the ability of the parties to agree on the most important issues and the order in which they will be approached. There is evidence that this approach is best utilized when no claims or counterclaims are made or no offense has been alleged, as when parties are attempting to establish a new relationship where no previous one has existed before.

The Principled Agenda. A fifth approach is to define issues in terms of principles or general levels of agreement that will guide the decisions on specific items. The parties jointly establish the principles and then work out the details of how these principles will be applied on specific agenda items later (Fisher and Ury, 1981). For example, in negotiations between telephone companies, a public utilities commission, and consumer groups over access charges on the use of intrastate phone lines, all parties agreed that the universal telephone service should be maintained. This agreement in principle became the basis for an agenda item in which the negotiators would discuss how universal service could be financed.

This procedure works only under conditions in which the parties are willing and able to negotiate at a high level of generalization or abstraction and in which they are willing to defer decision making on minor issues until later. This process of approaching a negotiation agenda will be discussed in more detail in Chapter Eleven.

Less Difficult Items First. A sixth method of agenda formation is to identify issues on which the parties will most likely reach agreement and that will probably not take long to discuss and settle. These issues are often small, self-contained, less emotion-laden, and not symbolic in comparison with other topics that might be discussed. These simple items are placed at the beginning of the agenda and alternated with more difficult items (1) to ensure agreement on some issues early in negotiations, (2) to promote a habit of agreement, (3) to provide for a backlog of agreements that the parties will be reluctant to lose as the result of an impasse later on, and (4) to provide agenda items that can be dropped or traded later as a demonstration of good faith.

Naturally, this strategy is contingent on the ability of the parties to mutually identify simple issues. This is usually accomplished by trial and error, or the mediator may ask parties to identify issues on which they feel ready agreement may be achieved with little effort.

Building-Block or Contingent Agenda. A seventh method of agenda construction is the building-block approach. In this process, a party or parties identify which agreements must be made first, based on which issues lay the groundwork or foundation for later decisions. Agenda sequencing is coordinated according to which agreements are contingent on previous ones. Contingency may be based on principles, time, payment schedules, and so forth. This approach, while fairly complicated and dependent on a high degree of party coordination, does prevent deadlocks due to incorrect sequencing of issues. This procedure for approaching agenda formation will be discussed in more detail in Chapter Eleven.

Trade-offs or Packaging. The final approach to agenda formation is issue trading or packaging. Parties in dispute are sometimes reluctant to settle agenda items one at a time for fear that they will lose leverage on one item if they have settled another one earlier. To avoid this problem, parties link and formulate combinations of issues and offers in return for concessions from the other parties. This means that they negotiate more than one issue simultaneously. Issues may be traded one for another in such a way that equivalence of exchange is attained. Trading can also be conducted issue by issue so that issues are eliminated by one party in exchange for elimination of issues by another party.

Packaging proposals containing multiple-issue solutions has advantages as an agenda-setting tool. It (1) demonstrates a willingness to trade issues and meet the other party's needs, (2) may induce an opponent to generate alternative packages, (3) demonstrates that some concessions are possible if they are linked with specific gains, and (4) can eliminate some of the difficulty, at least for one party, in producing settlement options. However, packages do have drawbacks. They may be seen as a way of forcing an unfavorable settlement or denying a party the chance to participate in consensus or settlement building. A way to circumvent these drawbacks is to present a series of small packages that are not as comprehensive and are less likely to produce resistance.

Procedural Assistance from the Mediator

The above approaches can be initiated by either one or more disputing parties or the mediator. Reaching an agreement on an agenda requires coordination between parties that they may not be able to achieve on their own. The mediator may need to suggest a procedure that in his or her judgment will best facilitate the solution of a critical situation.

If the parties are progressing toward a procedure for agenda formation that the mediator feels will be unproductive, the intervenor should either (1) suggest an alternative method outlining why he or she feels it is superior to the one chosen by the parties or (2) remain quiet, allowing the parties to negotiate and reach an impasse, and then intervene when they are more motivated to use the mediator's services. Selecting the latter strategy must be carefully weighed against the damage inflicted on the relationship of the parties due to failure to bargain.

It is important that the mediator, in making procedural suggestions about the agenda, avoid being maneuvered into the position of forcing a process on the parties (Fisch, Weakland, and Segal, 1982). This situation can only result in loss of credibility, decreased acceptability, more disputant resistance, and less effective later interventions.

TEN

Uncovering Hidden Interests of the Disputing Parties

People negotiate because of interests they want to have satisfied. The negotiation process may be considered to be a game (Cross, 1977) in which one or more parties engage in an educational process, a decoding process, and a bargaining process to present and discover interests and trade promises to meet those interests.

Difficulties in Identifying Interests

Parties in dispute rarely identify in a clear or direct fashion what their interests are. This lack of clarity occurs because parties (1) often do not know what their genuine interests are, (2) are pursuing a strategy of hiding their interests on the assumption that they will gain more from a settlement if their genuine goals are obscured from the scrutiny of other parties, (3) have adhered so strongly to a particular position that meets their interests that the interest itself becomes obscured and equated with the position and can no longer be seen as a separate entity, or (4) are unaware of procedures for exploring interests. I will discuss each of these obstacles to identifying interests.

Lack of Awareness of Interests. Parties often negotiate

under misperceptions about what their interests really are. Misperception may result from external factors, such as law, tradition, or advice from friends, that describe how the negotiation game is to be played and completed, or from internal confusion of the negotiators themsélves. In Chapter Nine, I illustrated the case in which two parents are struggling over the question of who should have legal custody of their child after a divorce. Both parents are excellent child rearers and nurturers and are equally qualified to raise the child. They are fighting over a specific solution, sole legal custody, and in the process are damaging their relationship and indirectly harming the child. They each see their interest, and that of the other parent, defined as gaining legal custody of the child. Each parent views settlement outcomes narrowly because of advice from attorneys and relatives and traditional ideas about custody settlement arrangements. In reality, their interests are having time with the child, having the opportunity to be involved in making decisions about how the child is to be raised, having the chance to go on vacation with the child, and so forth. The struggle is over a position—which parent will gain legal custody of the child—not over how to meet the real substantive, procedural, and psychological interests of each parent. Unless genuine interests are addressed, the parents will remain caught, negotiating over positions that can result only in a win-lose outcome.

Intentional Hiding of Interests. A second reason that interests are difficult to identify is that negotiators often intentionally obscure them. This strategy is designed to maximize gains or outcomes in negotiations. Parties often see interests, and the degree to which they are met, in terms of positions along a continuum of options. Particular outcomes are more satisfactory or meet more needs than others. Each party obscures his or her real interests on the continuum of possible settlement options and through a series of feints. Parties try to convince the other party to modify offers so as to better satisfy their interests. Neither party wants to publicly present his or her interests, or the particular point on the bargaining continuum at which he or she is willing to settle, for fear that that point would be less advantageous.

Equating Interests with Positions. A third reason that interests are difficult to identify is that they are often equated with particular positions. Parties engaged in heated conflict occasionally begin to gradually equate the satisfaction of an interest with a particular position. Separation of the interest from a specific solution becomes difficult. The tendency for interests to become caught in particular positions poses a difficult problem for negotiators who are attempting to back off hard-line positions and seek mutually acceptable solutions.

Lack of Awareness of Procedures to Explore Interests. The final reason that parties often do not directly explore interests is that people are not used to thinking in terms of interests. Parties are not aware of procedures to discover and discuss them. This procedural barrier to the identification of interests often proves to be an insurmountable obstacle in high-tension negotiations.

These four barriers—lack of awareness of interests, intentional obscuring of interests, equating interests with positions, and lack of awareness of procedural approaches to interest discovery—are often significant blocks to progress in negotiations. Because of this critical situation, parties often reach a deadlock and can no longer progress.

Procedures for Identifying Interests

Negotiators and, if necessary, mediators use two general procedures to identify the interests of disputing parties: indirect, low-profile procedures and direct, high-profile procedures.

Indirect procedures are used when parties (1) use a positional bargaining approach to negotiations, (2) try to obscure interests by adhering to rigid positions, or (3) seem unsure of their interests, and the trust level is not high enough to merit direct exploration of their needs.

Mediators use direct procedures either to pre-empt (Saposnek, 1983) or to prevent parties from engaging in positional bargaining or to move them toward interest-based bargaining once positional negotiations have begun. Direct procedures are used in the first case when parties (1) are not caught in the process of positional bargaining, (2) are not committed to absolute positions, (3) are aware of the need to separate the identification of interests from the adherence to particular positions, (4) are willing to explore their interests explicitly because the trust level is high enough for mutual exploration, or (5) have delegated to the mediator the authority to design a structured interest exploration and identification procedure. Direct procedures are used when parties are engaged in positional bargaining to (1) identify interests when less directive methods have failed, (2) prevent parties from hardening their adherence to positions, or (3) manage a large number of parties or issues that are making negotiations cumbersome.

Before exploring direct or indirect moves to identify and explore interests, it is important to note attitudes that lead to a productive exploration of interests.

Productive Attitudes

Regardless of whether positional or interest-based bargaining is being used, an understanding of interests on the part of negotiators can promote more productive outcomes. Identification of interests is facilitated by the development of open attitudes toward interest exploration. These attitudes include:

1. A belief that all parties have interests and needs that are important and valid to them.
2. A belief that a solution to the problem should meet the maximum number of interests of each party.
3. A belief that interests can be traded to achieve the most satisfactory combination.
4. A belief that there is probably more than one acceptable solution to a problem.
5. A belief that any conflict involves compatible interests as well as conflicting ones.

Negotiators who hold such attitudes or beliefs about negotiation will be able to make the transition to a focus on interests more easily than disputants who have become engaged in positional bargaining.

The critical situation negotiators face at this stage is how to gain an understanding of each other's interests. The first step to overcoming this block is an awareness that interests are important. Most negotiators do not distinguish between a solution or position and the specific interest it is designed to satisfy. This linkage prevents creative problem solving.

A mediator may assist parties in handling this critical situation. Before beginning actual interest exploration, mediators can work with parties to change their attitudes and awareness, and to encourage acceptance of diverse interests. This can be accomplished through a variety of indirect and direct moves. Indirect moves include modeling behavior that promotes desired attitude change. A mediator may state that "all needs and interests of parties are important and valid to them," "we are looking for a solution that allows everyone to have as many needs met as possible," or "there is probably more than one solution that will meet the needs of all parties" to increase awareness of the importance of interests. Mediators may make even lower levels of intervention by modeling an attitude of expectancy and hope (Freire, 1970). The mediator's expressed attitude often encourages a more conciliatory climate.

Mediators can also confront the need for attitude change more directly. They may explicitly spell out the differences between issues, positions, interests, and settlement options for the parties. They may also state that if a solution cannot be found that meets at least some of the interests of all parties, there will be no settlement. Usually, the more explicit the mediator is about the need for attitudinal change or increase in awareness, the greater the possibility of confrontation between the intervenor and disputants. Most mediators prefer low-level indirect interventions at this point to explicit and direct confrontation over attitudes.

Indirect Moves for Discovering Interests

I have discussed several indirect and direct moves to induce attitudinal change in negotiators in interest identification and exploration. I now turn to an examination of procedures for discovering interests.

Mediators may use many of the communication skills outlined in Chapters Seven, Eight, and Nine to identify interests. Particularly helpful skills are active listening, restatement, paraphrase, summarization, generalization, fractionation, and reframing. When used alone or in combination, these skills help disputants and the mediator to decode and uncover interests that are intentionally or unintentionally obscured by negotiators.

One particularly common combination of these skills is the process of *testing* (Moore, 1982b). Testing requires a negotiator or mediator to listen carefully to another negotiator's statements and then to feed back the interest that he or she hears expressed. Through trial and error, the listener can gradually gain an understanding and agreement about a negotiator's needs.

Another method to identify interests is *hypothetical modeling* (Pruitt and Lewis, 1977), in which the negotiator or mediator presents a series of hypothetical settlement options or proposals to another negotiator. The questioner does not ask for commitment or acceptance of any of the proposals, but merely an indication of whether the proposal is satisfactory. Repeated proposals that contain a variety of solutions to satisfy another's interests can increase a mediator's or negotiator's understanding of needs to be met without ever having to confront interest identification directly. This approach is often used when a party is hiding interests or when there is not enough trust to explicitly reveal interests.

Direct Moves for Discovering Interests

Fisher and Ury (1981) advocate direct *questioning* about interests. They suggest that when a disputant presents a position to another disputant, the presenting party should ask himself or herself, and ask the other party directly, why this position is important. Carefully worded questions that demonstrate genuine concern for understanding the other party's perception of the situation can be used to encourage revelation of important interests.

Since the intervenor has credibility as an impartial party, disputants may be more open to directly identifying and discussing their interests with the mediator than with another party. The mediator plays a valuable role in this situation because he or she can help the parties explore the substance and salience of a party's interests while minimizing the risks of full disclosure to an adversary. These conversations are often held during a caucus.

Another common procedure is the *interest-oriented discussion.* The mediator in this process should request that disputants refrain from discussing issues or positions and focus on the general interests or elements that would make a settlement satisfactory. Through careful questioning, the mediator moves the parties from a discussion of general interests to more concrete and explicit interests.

Brainstorming is a process in which items are rapidly generated by a group. Brainstorming separates the generation process from evaluation procedures so that the group has multiple options to consider. (See Chapter Eleven for instructions on how to conduct a brainstorming session.) Brainstorming can be conducted by negotiators in joint session or in caucus. This procedure is probably the most common direct move to identify interests.

Brainstorming was used to identify the interests of parties in a complicated dispute over water supply to an urban area. The mediators carefully divided the thirty-two negotiators into groups of eight. Each group had members who represented diverse views on the questions of water supply. Each group had at least one water supplier, one consumer, one environmentalist, and one person from the agricultural or rural community. The groups were instructed to list without evaluation the various interests that would have to be met if an agreement were to be reached. A mediator and a recorder worked with each small group to record the interests on a wall chart that everyone could see. These lists were compiled and presented to the entire group to educate all negotiators about the general interests that would have to be addressed for a settlement to be reached.

Positions, Interests, and Bluffs

A mediator's involvement does not mean that parties will be candid about their interests. Parties may engage in bluffing activity. "A party to negotiation is engaged in bluff when he asserts or implies that he will do what he does not intend to do at the time the assertion is made" (Stevens, 1963). Bluffs may also involve a party's misrepresentation of interests to convince another disputant that only a settlement with certain criteria will meet the party's needs. In ideal negotiation situations, bluffing is not possible because all disputants have accurate knowledge of the interests, settlement options, power, and preferences for behavior of the other parties. In reality, however, these variables are not known, and bluffing is common. This seems to be the case especially when there is no external deadline or factors that force the parties to be candid and to come to terms with their differences.

To work, bluffs must be credible. One party must be perceived by another to have the authority, capacity, and will to carry out a threatened activity to satisfy a particular interest. Mediators should probe and question parties in joint session, but more often in a caucus, to determine if a threat or a position is a genuine stance that the party believes will best meet his or her interests or is a bluff to mislead an opponent. If the latter is true, the mediator should assess with the bluffing party (1) the long-term effect a bluff will have on the relationship of the parties, (2) the potential cost to the negotiators of letting the bluff go unchallenged by the mediator, and (3) the cost to the parties if the bluff becomes solidified into a position from which the bluffing party cannot retreat or extricate himself or herself. This last outcome can have drastic effects on negotiations if the parties reach an impasse based on a false claim.

If in the process of position and interest exploration a mediator discovers that a party has been bluffing and sending inaccurate messages about his or her interests, and this appears to be having detrimental effects on the negotiation process, the intervenor may decide to help the bluffing party shift from his or her artificial posture toward a more accurate presentation of his or her interests. Procedures used by mediators are persuasion and rationalization (Stevens, 1963). *Persuasion* refers to activities designed to influence or control the course of actions or operations of another negotiator, alter a party's preferences, or change how a party perceives the negotiation environment. A *rationalization* is a logical and plausible argument for a shift in position or approach. A rationalization for a change of position may be presented to a negotiator, to other parties, or to a negotiator's constituency as a means of explaining a shift in position or to stress the importance of heretofore undisclosed interests. The rationalization may be presented by the negotiator or by the mediator. Ideally the negotiator makes the presentation because it will increase his or her commitment to the move. However, in some disputes, the negotiator may need to save face (Brown, 1977). In this situation, the mediator may want to present the newly identified position, interest, or move to help explain or share the responsibility for the shift.

Regulatory negotiations between industry groups, a public utility commission, and consumer advocates provide an example of how mediators used persuasion and rationalization to help bargainers identify genuine interests and avoid impasse. One issue facing the negotiators was how they were to pay for mediation. Large-industry representatives believed that participants in the negotiations should "pay to play." They took the hard-line position that if interest groups did not contribute financially for mediation, then they should not be represented. The consumer advocate indicated that they could not afford to pay to participate, and intimated that if they were required to pay, they would boycott the negotiations and attack the proposed settlement later when it was presented to the public utility commission for consideration.

The mediators saw that each interest group was escalating its threats (and bluffs) to push the other party to accept its position. The mediators, in reflecting on the large-industry group's interests, asked whether they saw payment as a party's indication of commitment to the process and assurance that the group would not sabotage or delay settlement. The large-industry representatives replied that they did. The mediator asked the consumers why they believed they need not pay. The consumer advocates replied that since theirs was a nonprofit group, it did not have assets to fund the process, and that in principle advocacy groups should not have to fund alternative regulatory negotiations when they would normally have free access to the regulatory hearing process.

The mediators asked the industry group if it was reasonable or fair to ask groups that did not have funds to pay to participate, and asked the consumer groups if they could find a way other than a financial contribution that would indicate that they were committed to the process and were bargaining in good faith. The consumer group representative made a public statement that she was committed to the process and asked if in return the industry groups would allow a nonprofit group to have a place at the table. The rationalization that disconnected financial contribution from bargaining in good faith enabled the parties to reach agreement.

Interest Identification, Acceptance, and Agreement

Once the mediator and the negotiators have identified the interests of the parties, they will confront one or more of the following situations. Interests may be (1) *mutually exclusive* in that satisfaction of one party's needs prohibits the satisfaction of another's interests, (2) *mixed* in that the parties have some compatible and some competitive needs, or (3) *compatible* in that they have similar and nonexclusive needs. A particular case illustrates how the division of interests applies.

An author was working on a research organization staff to prepare a book describing the state of the art of practice in a human relations field. The author had worked for many months on the project and was pleased with the product. As the book neared completion, the organization's director distributed a memorandum informing the staff that in the future no individual authors' names would appear on publications produced by the agency. The author responded with a counter-memorandum that argued in favor of having the author's name on the book and pointing to a precedent in the agency that staff were identified on the cover of published works. In this dispute, it appeared that the positions of the parties were mutually exclusive. A careful examination of the interests, however, indicated room for cooperation. Both parties had *compatible interests* in that they wanted to see the book published and distributed. Publication would financially and professionally benefit both. The parties also had *mixed interests*. The research organization did not want the author to take all the credit for the work. The director wanted to build his agency's credibility and wanted the work to be seen as an agency product. He was not willing to give away all the credit but was willing to share it. He also wanted the staff to enjoy working for the agency.

The author wanted to take credit but was not willing to push the issue so far that he risked losing his job. There was clearly a mixed set of interests that allowed for competition and cooperation. Both parties believed that incompatible or exclusive interests predominated in the dispute. The director wanted the agency's name on the cover and wanted to have the work identified as a team project. The author wanted only his name on the cover. It seemed like a win-lose dispute. Both parties agreed to negotiate on the issue of identification of authorship. They agreed that they had a common interest in publishing and distributing the book as soon as possible. The author acknowledged that the agency should get credit for sponsoring the research as long as he was given credit for producing it. The director acknowledged that the author was the primary researcher for the book but wanted the team that had performed some of the preliminary work to be given credit also. The author agreed that this was fair and proposed to include this point in an acknowledgments section at the beginning of the book. This proposal was accepted.

The process of deciding what was to go on the cover was more difficult. Both parties acknowledged that they wanted a particular name on the cover. A variety of options were explored. The final decision was that both the agency and author should be credited on the cover. The agency's name was to be in larger type and the author was to be identified by his title in the agency. By this solution, both parties agreed that their interests were satisfied.

This case study illustrates several approaches that mediators can use to work with the interests of the disputing parties. First, the mediator should work with the parties to jointly identify interests. A party's willingness to identify and explore his or her interests and those of others does not necessarily mean that he or she agrees with the needs of other disputants. Creighton (1972, p. II–8) makes explicit the difference between acceptance of information (emotions, in this case) and agreement. "You express acceptance when you say: 'I understand that you feel such-and-such a way about this topic.' You express agreement when you say: 'You couldn't be more right, I feel that way too.' In the first you accept that the other person feels the way he does, but in agreement you *ally* yourself with the other person."

At this stage the mediator should be more concerned that negotiators accept information about interests than with obtaining agreement. While agreement with the interests of other parties greatly facilitates a party's progress through later negotiation stages, agreement at this point is not mandatory. Parties can accept that others have interests that are different from theirs and still search for mutually acceptable solutions.

Next, the mediator should identify and make explicit compatible or complementary interests. This enables the parties to change their assumptions about the conflict's purity, builds a habit of agreement, and promotes cooperation. Finally, the mediator should focus on mixed and mutually exclusive interests. I will discuss measures to handle these needs in later chapters. Using a process of interest-based bargaining, trade-offs, and compromise, the mediator can assist parties to progress and agree on even the most difficult of incompatible interests.

ELEVEN

Generating Options
for Settlement

By this stage the parties have defined the parameters of the dispute, clarified issues, developed an agenda, and through joint education and questioning, identified common and conflicting interests. The central task of negotiators and mediators in the generating options stage is to develop mutually acceptable settlement solutions.

Mediators and parties progress to a process of generating settlement options either because initial positions put forth by one or more parties in the opening statements are unacceptable, or because the parties have focused only on identifying issues and interests and have not explored any concrete settlement options at all.

To develop alternative settlement options, the parties must be aware of the need for alernatives from which to choose, be flexible enough in their adherence to any stated positions that they can disconnect themselves from unacceptable proposals to explore new ones, and be aware of procedures to develop alternative settlement options. In this chapter I will discuss (1) how negotiators and mediators approach the problem of awareness, (2) how to disengage parties from adherence to unacceptable positions, (3) strategies of option generation, (4) procedures to develop options, and (5) types of settlement options.

199

Developing an Awareness of the Need for Options

Awareness of the need for multiple settlement options from which to select the best solution is not an inherent characteristic of negotiators engaged in intense disputes. Disputants often enter negotiations with a preconceived belief that they have already discovered the best solution for all concerned and all that remains is to persuade, or coerce if necessary, the other party into agreement or submission. For another negotiator or the mediator even to suggest that other solutions are available or desirable may be abhorrent to a negotiator committed to a particular solution. Only after persuasion and pressure fail to convince other parties of the merits of the position can an entrenched negotiator be persuaded to consider other options.

Negotiators and mediators begin their search for settlement options with the development of an awareness that multiple choices are needed from which to select the ultimate solution. The mediator may elicit awareness, or it may be induced by actions of other negotiators. In the latter case, awareness of the need for alernatives may result from a response to an opening statement or position.

Opening statements are often an expression of a party's maximal position and often do not take others' needs and interests into consideration. They are put forth to educate other parties about how strongly a party feels about an issue or to express how far a party wants an opponent to yield. For these reasons, opening statements and the positions expressed therein are rarely accepted as representations of legitimate interests by other disputants, who both understand and expect parties to adhere to the practice of making a large initial demand. Once a proposal is rejected, one or more parties usually take the initiative to propose another solution or counterposition.

Occasionally, however, the party who initiated a proposal or position does not recognize the categorical rejection of his or her alternative, and doggedly adheres to the original position. The party ignores the need for alternative proposals, assuming that if the right persuasive technique is used or the correct influence is exerted, the other party will concede. This posture often results in a deadlock.

At this point, other negotiators or the mediator must convince the intransigent negotiator that his or her perception that the other parties will accept the current position as a solution for the problem is inaccurate, and that there is a need for other alternatives.

Disengaging Parties from Adherence to Unacceptable Positions. Parties commit themselves to a position for diverse reasons:

- It meets intangible psychological needs.
- They feel it is the best solution.
- They believe other parties do not know what is best for them.
- They believe they can weaken resistance if they continue to argue their position.
- They believe they have the power or influence to force their solution on the other parties.

Negotiators and mediators faced with an intransigent party need to assess why a party adheres so strongly to his or her position and determine the moves they can initiate to encourage the party to explore other options. Negotiators and mediators use a variety of strategies to persuade a party to reverse commitment to a previous position.

Psychological Means to Reduce Commitment. Most psychological approaches to reducing *positional* commitment begin with identification of the psychological needs of a recalcitrant party through active listening, restatement, and summarization. A disputant or the mediator can verbally identify the psychological needs of the party.

The second step is to gain a commitment from all parties to explore settlement options that will meet those needs. This does not mean that the parties agree that the need will be satisfied in the way demanded, but that they are willing to examine other solutions to meet the need. If a disputant can be convinced that his or her need has been heard and will at least be considered in alternative solutions, he or she will often agree to abandon an intransigent position.

It is often the mediator's task to persuade other parties to consider the need of a recalcitrant negotiator. Parties may be very reluctant to respect and consider a psychological need that they believe to be irrationally founded. Mediators may have to assist parties in assessing the cost of failure to consider another's need, in determining if the parties actually have a choice, and in deciding what the costs of impasse will be.

Procedural Means to Reduce Commitment. Procedural methods to reduce commitment refer to processes or steps that encourage the likelihood of finding a solution to meet needs and satisfy interests. Parties often adhere to positions because they see no other ways of developing new ones. Introducing a logical or acceptable problem-solving process may allow a party to abandon a position. The party will do so because he or she likes the proposed process and considers it fair. I will examine procedural means of reducing commitment later in this chapter.

Leverage to Reduce Commitment. Parties do not always respond to psychological moves or procedural proposals to satisfy needs. Negotiators may have to resort to leverage or means of influence to shift an intransigent party from a hard-line position. There are four ways to reduce commitment to an unacceptable position:

1. One negotiator can convince another that the latter has overestimated the cost to the first party of maintaining his or her position or advocating his or her interests.

> Employee to former employer: "I know that you think that the cost of going to court will deter me from filing this affirmative action suit. Well, it won't. In fact I've asked my brother who is a lawyer to represent me and he said he would do it for free. It won't cost me anything but time to fight this, and I've got a lot of that these days!"

2. One negotiator can convince another that the latter has underestimated the costs involved in maintaining the latter's position.

> Public interest group representative to a developer: "Look, if you won't put up a performance bond that will assure us that the mine land will be reclaimed as you promised, we will oppose your permit. We are prepared to go to court if necessary. Are you prepared for a delay of several years while we fight this out in the legal system? If time is money to you, it will cost you a lot more if you don't settle soon."

3. One negotiator can convince another that the first party's position or interests are more important that the latter had initially realized.

> Homeowner selling her home to prospective buyer: "I realize that when you look at this home, what you see is a nice Victorian house. To me, it's much more than that. It's my family legacy. It was built by my grandfather and willed to me. That is why I'm unwilling to change the terms of the sale."

4. One negotiator may convince another that the latter's interests or position is not as important as he or she originally believed and that his or her needs can be met satisfactorily in another way.

> Wife to husband in child custody negotiations: "You say you want legal custody of Jamie so that you can be involved in decisions about his religious upbringing. What happens if I agree that that arena of his life is for you to decide? Isn't the religious training issue more important to you than legal custody?"

These four means of persuasion are essentially maps for a logical argument to persuade a party to abandon a position. The mediator can aid one or more parties in exerting the means of leverage listed above. In addition, the mediator may use other motivational tactics that will be discussed in detail in Chapter Fifteen.

Strategies for Option Generation

Once parties are aware of the need for alternative settlement options from which to choose, they must select a specific issue to discuss and choose a strategy to generate possible solutions.

The focus of the option generation procedure depends on the way the issue is defined, the type of solution desired, and the way alternative generation fits into the overall strategy of reaching an agreement. Settlement options can be generated (1) on a specific issue that is merely a component of a larger issue or (2) on a general principle level. These two basic strategies are similar to the building-block approach and the agreement in principle or formula approach (Fisher and Ury, 1981; Zartman and Berman, 1982) to agenda formulation discussed earlier. The approaches can be used independently or in combination within any given negotiation session or on a particular issue. I will discuss these two overall strategies and then proceed to explore specific procedural moves mediators and negotiators use to develop settlement options.

The Building-Block Approach to Settlement. The *building-block approach* requires disputants to divide an issue into subissues or component parts. Fisher (1964) refers to this procedure as *fractionation.* Ideally, these smaller components are more manageable units for problem solving. Each of these subissues is sequentially resolved and combined with the settlements of previous issues. When combined in a building-block approach, these agreements allow the parties to develop an elaborate and complete settlement. Procedurally the parties move from the settlement of specific subissues toward a total package which settles the dispute. The parties may agree to accept as final agreements on each subissue, or may delay final settlement until agreement can be reached on all the issues in dispute.

Problems or issues are divided into smaller components

because (1) disputants may see and understand smaller issues more easily than those that are complex and many-faceted, (2) dividing issues into components prevents moves to join or link unrelated subjects that block agreement, and (3) dividing issues into components may depoliticize or isolate issues that prevent settlement.

There are two ways to divide issues into smaller components. First, the mediator may suggest that the definition of what is being discussed be narrowed. Second, the mediator or a negotiator may ask parties to look at an issue and ask them to divide it into component subissues. Obtaining the involvement of the parties in subissue definition can create greater commitment to the process.

Negotiation over how privacy could be maintained for single-family homeowners if condominiums were built close to their residences illustrates fractionation and the building-block approach. The mediators and the parties divided the problem of privacy into several subissues: visual privacy, auditory privacy, and congestion. To accomplish visual privacy, the parties generated solutions that (1) reduced building height so that second-floor dwellers could not see into the backyards or windows of the single-family homes, (2) provided for berms and fences to shield single-family homes from views of the condominiums, (3) graduated building heights so that condominiums close to single-family homes were one story in height and those further away were gradually increased to two or three stories, and (4) shielded lights in the condominium parking lot to prevent the light from entering single-family home windows. Similar solutions were generated to handle auditory and congestion problems. By dividing the problem or issue into smaller pieces and solving the component parts, the parties were ultimately able to forge a comprehensive settlement.

Agreement in Principle Approach to Settlement. The second major strategy for defining issues and progressing toward a settlement is the *agreement in principle* or *formula* approach. This procedure requires negotiators to create or identify a bargaining formula or set of general principles that will guide the shape of the final settlement. This approach is the polar opposite of the building-block approach in that it requires negotiators to reach a general level of agreement and then initiate steps to define the specifics. This approach is often appropriate when underlying values of the disputants are similar or when superordinate goals can be identified.

The agreement in principle or formula approach to settlement is often not as familiar to disputants as the building-block approach. The mediator may have to be more directive in educating the parties about the procedure. The mediator may either directly reframe the issue to be resolved in broader terms and then encourage the parties to generate general principles of agreement, or may explain the philosophy behind the strategic approach and turn the implementation over to the negotiators.

An example of the agreement in principle approach occurred in the Metropolitan Water Roundtable negotiations in Denver, Colorado, among water suppliers, environmentalists, ranchers, and recreation interests. The parties were initially stalled over whether additional water was needed in the Denver area and over a proposal to construct a dam at a particular site.

After an intensive educational process, all the parties agreed that the water was needed and that a dam was needed somewhere on the eastern side of the Rocky Mountains. After agreeing on these two principles, the parties began to investigate how the water needs could be met using a variety of sources—conservation, groundwater, transmountain exchanges— and the location and size of a new dam. By reaching a series of agreements in principle on several different levels, the parties were able to progress toward agreement.

Procedures for Generating Options

Once parties have decided on the level of settlement option—general or specific—that is desired, mediators or negotiators need to devise a procedure to generate settlement options. There are two general approaches: (1) initiating counterpositions or counterproposals and (2) a collaborative search for options. These approaches reflect the basic assumptions, respectively, of positional bargaining and interest-based bargaining.

Positional Bargaining and Counterproposals. In positional bargaining, the parties assume that the way to present settlement options is to exchange proposals and counterproposals. If the conflict is a two-party dispute, the normal dynamic is for the parties to alternately offer possible solutions, proposals, and counterproposals so that no more than two proposals to resolve a given issue are considered at any given time. Ideally, each proposal brings the parties closer to a settlement or settlement range because of increased satisfaction of interests for both sides (Stevens, 1963). The settlement range refers to possible solutions, any one of which is preferable to a stalemate or no agreement.

There are several limiting characteristics to positional bargaining. First, only two proposals or positions are generally examined at one time. This two-sided view tends to limit the number of options explored by the parties. Second, an analysis of only two proposals or positions at a time inhibits the development of solutions to meet specific needs. The two-sided view inhibits the integration of ideas and encourages negotiators to view proposals as total packages or "yes or no" alternatives. Parties fail to realize that proposals can be combined or recombined to create new options.

Third, two-sided negotiations, with only two possible proposals, tend to produce win-lose or "right" and "wrong" attitudes toward concessions or counterproposals since a win for one party is viewed as a loss by the other. Parties conducting positional bargaining often commit themselves psychologically to their proposal and view acceptance of another's position as an abandonment of principles. Fourth, positional bargaining encourages evaluation of the proposals at the same time that the options are generated. Simultaneous evaluation and generation of only two options tend to hinder the development of a spectrum of settlement possibilities.

Because the proposal-counterproposal procedure places limits on the negotiating process, negotiators may wish to shift to an interest-based bargaining strategy. This shift is more difficult to accomplish in negotiations in which parties have already used positional bargaining, but the transition is not impossible.

The transition from positional bargaining to interest-based bargaining can be greatly facilitated by the presence and intervention of a mediator.

   Interest-Based Bargaining: Criteria and Transition. Interest-based negotiation, a procedure that promotes integrative bargaining in which the interests of all parties are combined and met by jointly developed solutions, is often superior to positional bargaining in generating settlement options. Interest-based bargaining works most effectively under certain specific conditions: (1) the resource or interests over which the parties are negotiating must be divisible or negotiable in a way that a gain for one party does not necessarily mean a loss for another, (2) there must be enough trust and spirit of cooperation so that the parties can develop a joint solution, (3) one party must not have, exhibit, or be willing to exercise overwhelming power or influence in the negotiations to force a decision in his or her favor, and (4) the parties must be aware of a procedure to develop options that all disputants will perceive as equitable and fair. I will examine each of these points in turn.

   Many negotiators, when entering a dispute, assume that the disputing parties have entirely conflicting interests and that the outcome will yield more benefits to one party than to another. They are prepared to play a win-lose game.

   Most conflicts, however, are not pure in that the relationship of the parties is not purely conflictual and all interests are not mutually exclusive. This mixed characteristic applies even to such apparently indivisible commodities as money. Some negotiators assume that money is indivisible and that an increase for one side inevitably means a loss for another. This assumption means that a compromise in which each party receives some but not all of what he or she desires is the only possible option. This type of dispute is often referred to as a *half-a-loaf dispute* (Warren, 1978). However, monetary disputes can be subdivided into issues of timing of payment, rate of payment, and form of payment so that a win-win outcome is possible.

   Negotiations over seemingly pure conflicts can in many cases be transformed into disputes in which all parties can win more than if they had merely divided available resources in some sort of compromise. Negotiators can accomplish this shift themselves, but often they are locked into the perception of issues and interests as pure conflicts. At this point the mediator can intervene and reframe the issue so that the parties see the issue in a new way.

Mediators use several techniques to produce win-win options. One important technique is *expansion of the resource* (Pruitt and Lewis, 1977) to be traded. Union-management negotiations, for example, have a history of deadlock when the parties negotiate solely on the wage increase issue. However, by adding issues such as cost-of-living benefits, insurance options, goodwill, working conditions, or increased productivity, the mediator may change a win-lose negotiation into a situation in which a mutually satisfactory outcome is a possibility.

Mediators also assist parties in *logrolling* (Pruitt and Lewis, 1977), trading components of differing importance. Logrolling was utilized in a case in which an employer hired a consultant and had not been explicit about contract termination. The consultant, who was working in good faith, worked more than the employer wished to pay for. The consultant felt that the employer owed additional pay, but the employer refused because she was not satisfied with the work. The consultant hired a collection agency, which contacted the employer and asked for compensation.

By this time the parties had developed an extremely antagonistic relationship and could not talk to one another. The employer, who did not want to deal with the collection agency, contacted a mediator. The employer realized that she would probably have to pay something to settle the dispute, but she did not want to pay the consultant for unsatisfactory work. The mediator discovered that the consultant was more concerned with the principle that the employer should pay her debts than with receiving the small sum due him.

The mediator, operating on the principle that payment of the debt was the important issue, asked the consultant whether having the employer pay the amount owed to the consultant to another party, such as a charity, might meet his needs. The consultant agreed. The mediator then discussed this solution with the employer, who was willing to pay as long as she could choose the charity. The parties ultimately agreed that the employer should pay the sum owed to the consultant to the charity of the employer's choice. By logrolling, trading components of differing importance to the negotiators, the mediator was able to assist the parties in meeting each other's strongest interests without compromising on principles.

A further technique is *alternation*. When there is no way to expand resources, the parties may alternate between the options each of them favors. In an alternating scheme, neither side forsakes his or her *preferred option,* but each is allowed to enjoy it at a different time. For example, to settle a domestic conflict over where to vacation, a couple might go to the mountains this year and to the seashore next year, thus meeting the wife's interest in beachcombing and the husband's interest in mountain climbing. Alternating schemes will be more integrative than simple compromise when the options sought cannot be divided into parts without excessive loss of value to the negotiators.

The final procedure for interest-based bargaining is *seeking integrative interest-based solutions.* This procedure involves seeking solutions in which the needs of all parties are met, but not at the expense of another's needs. The classic illustration of this type of solution, told by many mediators, is the conflict between two children who are fighting over the last orange left in the fruit bowl. Each child adamantly demands that he or she get the orange. The wise parent intervenes and offers to help the children decide who should get the orange. At first examination, it appears that each child has equal claim to the orange. What should the parent do? He or she could halve the orange and give each child a piece. He or she could even alternate who slices and who chooses which piece goes to whom to increase the children's perception of procedural fairness. The parent is, however, dissatisfied with this solution and pursues the discovery of each child's interests in more depth. After several minutes of discussion the parent discovers that one child wants to eat the fruit and the other wants the rind to prepare a cake icing. The parent helps the children agree to split the orange and satisfy all of each other's needs. Mediation, through careful data collection and alternative generation, can often help parties build solutions of this type, but it challenges parties to overcome apparent barriers to settlement that would require them to settle for less than they could attain if they produced a truly integrative solution.

Trust has already been discussed in great detail in Chapter Eight. Interest-based bargaining requires the development of at least a minimal level of trust. To accomplish this end, mediators should utilize techniques described in the earlier chapter.

Parties must have some means of influencing each other to even begin formal negotiations. The threat or exercise of power may, however, inhibit interest-based bargaining.

The mediator can intervene and reduce or prevent the effects of threats or exercises of power by (1) ignoring them and persuading the other parties to do the same, (2) minimizing them by translating the threat into nondetrimental terms, (3) educating the parties about the cost of perceived or actual threats, or (4) in extreme cases, helping another party to realize and exercise its power to counter the threat or display. This last strategy tends to maintain polarization and competition rather than promote cooperation. I will discuss contingent moves mediators initiate to respond to power problems in Chapter Fifteen.

Parties often remain locked in positional bargaining merely because they are not aware of alternative means. Mediators can assist people in shifting from positional to interest-based bargaining by suggesting means to accomplish cooperative option generation.

A mediator's procedural suggestions to achieve this transition may have several advantages over moves initiated by the disputants themselves. First, research shows that suggestions by an impartial third party may be more readily trusted and accepted by disputants than those suggested by a party with substantive concerns in the conflict's outcome (Rubin and Brown, 1975).

Second, the mediator's suggestions may, because of professional stature and experience, be accorded more credibility.

The parties may be more willing to try a procedure because they believe the mediator would not make a poor suggestion (Rubin and Brown, 1975; Brookmire and Sistrunk, 1980).

Third, the mediator can take some responsibility for the success or failure of a negotiation procedure (Stevens, 1963). Parties are often reluctant to initiate new methods because they might have to bear the ill will of other parties or their constituents if the procedure does not work. The mediator, by sharing the responsibility, takes the burden on himself or herself and removes the party from blame.

Finally, a mediator may be of assistance because he or she expends the time and energy to identify the appropriate procedure. Often, parties can develop a process that would suit their needs if given the necessary time and resources, but these are not always available. Mediators can accelerate the transition and avoid the accumulation of additional negative experiences that may result from a struggle over procedure by providing a viable process for alternative generation.

Option Generation Procedures

Parties in mediation have used numerous processes to generate settlement options. These procedures have several characteristics in common. First, they attempt to generate several options so that the parties can move from a bipolar view of solutions to a multipolar approach (Maier and Hoffman, 1960). Second, they attempt to separate the stage of generating options from the later evaluative or assessment stage. This separation ensures that the search process will be more comprehensive and complete and not inhibited by premature judgments. Third, they focus the effort of the negotiators on the issue or problem and not on the other party. The dispute is depersonalized so that the parties aim their attacks not at the people in the negotiations but at the issues that divide them (Chandler, 1945; Fisher and Ury, 1981; Walton and McKersie, 1965; Filley, 1975). I will now discuss six common procedures mediators or negotiators can initiate to generate settlement options.

Brainstorming. Brainstorming is a procedure in which a

group of people generate a variety of ideas or options for consideration. The mediator or a negotiator begins the process by framing an issue into a problem. A *problem* is a restatement of an issue into a "how-to" format. "How can enough resources be found to send a wife to school so that she can be self-supporting?" "How can an outstanding bill be paid by a company with limited assets?" "How can a popular recreation area be maintained while still allowing companies to explore for minerals?"

The parties are then instructed to speak one at a time and suggest as rapidly as possible a list of alternative solutions that might meet the needs of the parties. The mediator should instruct them to avoid stating purely self-serving options and should caution them against making verbal or nonverbal judgments of practicality or acceptability during the session. The mediator should inform them that assessment and evaluation of the options will be initiated after they have generated a substantial number of solutions, and he or she should encourage them to build and modify each other's ideas as long as the results incline them toward an option that might meet more of their interests. The mediator should record alternatives on a pad or wall chart, taking care to record accurately and keep the session going. When the parties have generated a number of options or have exhausted their resources, they may shift to an assessment procedure.

Brainstorming can be conducted (1) as a whole group activity, (2) individuals or teams, (3) within subgroups of a team, or (4) in subgroups composed of delegates or representatives of each of the parties. Brainstorming as individuals, teams, or team subgroups may be used when disputants do not trust other parties and are uncomfortable disclosing options publicly, but want to enlarge their settlement alternatives. The mediator may randomly assign subgroups with members from opposing parties when he or she or a negotiator wants to maximize participation and increase personal contact between disputants by using small groups. Brainstorming in a subgroup with specifically assigned membership may be used to group or more evenly distribute moderates from opposing negotiating teams. Moderate team members are more likely to come up with integrative solutions that will meet the needs of all parties than subgroups composed of hard-line negotiators.

Utilizing Nominal Group Process. Building on the basic small group process concept that individuals invent and groups evaluate, the nominal group process seeks to maximize individual creativity to help a group solve a problem (Delbecq, Vandeven, and Gustafson, 1975). In this process, the issue is stated in problem format to the participants. Individuals list independently within a specific time limit all possible alternatives that might resolve the group's differences. They then form small subgroups of about five members each. All ideas are shared and recorded within the small group, with each member offering one suggestion at a time. These ideas are then elaborated on, discussed, and assessed for merit.

Discussion Groups or Subgroups. People in conflict are often hindered from generating options because groups are too large in size to be manageable for problem solving, high-level interaction, or candor. This may be especially true for multiparty community disputes. Small, informal discussion groups are often helpful for alternative generation. In disputes with multiple parties, the entire group may delegate subissues or problems to small working groups or committees, charging them to propose an integrative solution that can be referred back to the main group for final decision.

Developing Hypothetical Plausible Scenarios. Parties may occasionally be encouraged to develop possible settlement options by engaging in hypothetical scenario development. The mediator describes the issue as a problem and then charges individuals or small groups to develop hypothetical scenarios, in narrative form, about how the problem can be overcome. Scenarios should describe procedural, substantive, and psychological outcomes and processes used to incline the parties from their present stance to the preferred result. This approach, when used in small groups of disputants from all parties, often produces greater commitment to cooperative solutions. Once the scenarios are developed, the groups may present each until the negotiators have heard all the possibilities. The parties then assess whole scenarios and individual components for relevant alternative solutions to their dispute.

Single Text Negotiating Document. Hypothetical plausible scenarios can often be developed into a single text negotiating document (Fisher and Ury, 1981). Either a party or the mediator may initiate this procedure. The first step is to identify the interests of all parties. The initiator should then develop a text or proposal that might satisfy the majority of the interests and resolve the dispute. This document becomes a draft settlement text that is circulated between the parties for comments and revision. Each party should have an opportunity to modify the text to better meet his or her needs. Gradual revision often results in a single text that is acceptable to all disputants.

President Carter used this procedure in 1978 to negotiate the Camp David accords between Israel and Egypt. A similar procedure was used in the Law of the Seas negotiations. The one-text approach is helpful for two-party disputes and almost a necessity for a multiparty dispute.

Using Outside Resources. Parties are often frustrated by a myopic view of the conflict when generating viable alternatives. This condition may result from proximity to or lack of objectivity toward issues in dispute. Disputants may also be limited by their own experiences or possess inadequate data. The use of outside resources, initiated by either the parties or the mediator, may be of great assistance to the negotiations. Often the mediator can enhance the acceptability of a move to obtain outside help because of his or her perceived neutrality.

Outside resources can take the form of specific information or experts in the topic under discussion. For example, in child custody disputes, mediators may want the couple to read *Mom's House, Dad's House* (Ricci, 1980) or *Joint Custody and Co-Parenting* (Galper, 1980) so that they may obtain ideas outside of mediation on how to establish a new parenting relationship. For companies trying to negotiate the structure of a new employee-management grievance procedure, representatives may want to consult books on organizational dispute resolution (Bazerman and Lewicki, 1983; Blake and Mouton, 1984).

Outside resource persons may be substantive or procedural experts on the issue. Lawyers, assessors, or accountants; other parties who have had similar conflicts and have resolved them, such as government officials, managers, or parents; or individuals from other disciplines or backgrounds may have data to contribute.

Types of Settlement Options

Settlement options must satisfy the substantive, procedural, and psychological interests of the parties if they are to be considered solutions to the conflict. The degree to which interests are met determines how strong the agreement will be. Negotiators and mediators formulate settlement options by varying a number of factors to form a package that meets an acceptable level of needs for all parties.

Fisher (1978) identified some of the variables that determine how strong an agreement will be.

Stronger Agreements Are:	*Weaker Agreements Are:*
Substantive. They define specific tangible exchanges (money, services, labor, and so forth) that will result from negotiations.	*Procedural.* They define the way or process by which a decision is to be made.
Comprehensive. They include a resolution of all issues in dispute.	*Partial.* They do not include a resolution of all issues in dispute.
Permanent. They resolve for all time issues in dispute.	*Provisional.* They may be temporary or trial decisions that may be subject to change in the future.
Final. They include all the details in their final form.	*In-principle.* They include general agreements, but the details remain to be worked out.
Nonconditional. They provide for the termination of the dispute without the requirement of future conditional performance.	*Contingent.* They state that the conclusion of the dispute is conditional upon additional information or future performance by one or more parties.

Stronger Agreements Are:	*Weaker Agreements Are:*
Binding. People agree to be bound and to adhere to the terms of settlement often to the extent that they identify consequences if a party does not follow through.	*Nonbinding.* The agreement is a recommendation or request to which none of the parties guarantees adherence.

Mediators generally want to help the parties to reach the strongest agreement possible, but it may not always be feasible to develop a settlement with all the characteristics listed in the left-hand column. For example, a mediator may not be able to obtain a substantive agreement on the value of a piece of property but may be able to establish a procedure for assessing the land's value that all parties will accept. The mediator in another case may not be able to obtain a permanent decision about where a child will live after his parents divorce, but may be able to reach settlement on a trial solution that will be periodically evaluated and changed if necessary.

A procedural solution that partially settles issues, is provisional, is contingent on future performance, elaborates general principles, and is nonbinding may be the strongest agreement possible and is preferable to no solution at all. The mediator, by experimenting with the form of settlement options, can assist the parties in negotiating the strongest agreement possible, while tailoring it to their specific needs and interests.

TWELVE

Assessing Options
for Settlement

The assessing options stage of mediation is procedurally similar to some of the processes identified in the prenegotiation stage of searching for a dispute resolution approach and arena.

Parties are engaged in (1) reviewing their interests; (2) assessing how these interests can be met by solutions developed through positional bargaining or interest-based generation procedures; (3) determining the costs and benefits of selecting or not selecting one of the solutions; (4) determining the best alternative to a negotiated settlement; and (5) beginning the process of modifying, integrating, combining, dropping, and trading alternatives to reach a final settlement.

The major differences between the assessment process at this stage and the earlier stage are that the amount of time invested in negotiation tends to push parties toward negotiated settlement, the parties may jointly assess options rather than conduct their evaluation in isolation from each other, and the focus of the parties is on the content of the negotiations rather than the negotiation procedure as was the case earlier.

The central task of the negotiators at this stage is to assess or evaluate how well their interests will be satisfied by any one or combination of solutions that have been generated collaboratively or offered by an opposing party. The mediator's task is to help the parties evaluate these options and to assist them in assessing the costs and benefits of acceptance or rejection.

218

Since assessment procedures have already been discussed in detail in Chapter Four, they will not be reexamined here. However, two concepts and related series of moves need to be explored further: the establishment of a settlement or bargaining range and the consideration of the best alternative to a negotiated agreement (Fisher and Ury, 1981).

The Settlement Range

The *settlement range* has been defined as a field of options, any one of which disputants would prefer to accepting the consequences of ceasing negotiations. The settlement range is often referred to as the *bargaining range* when applied to options generated by positional bargaining. I will examine how parties recognize when they have produced, by means of positional bargaining or cooperative problem solving, options that fall within the settlement range.

Creation and Identification of a Bargaining Range. Positional bargainers generally assume that they are negotiating about a fixed-sum resource: money, time, or tangible objects. Thus, the total value available to all parties cannot be increased. This assumption is not always valid, but I will consider it here as a hypothetical given. If parties are negotiating for fixed shares of a finite resource, a gain for one party must mean a loss for another. If parties are to reach an agreement on the division of the resource, they must reach a compromise position.

Possible outcomes in fixed-sum negotiations are plotted in Figure 8. In this figure, the vertical column represents gains for Party A and the horizontal line represents equivalent gains for Party B. If the parties are to divide a fixed-sum resource, the division will have to occur at some point along the diagonal line *xy*. Some of the settlement options are identified at points along the line, with point 5.5 considered an equal distribution of the resource. On this continuum of distribution, parties usually identify a point that is a preferred solution or target. This point becomes their goal in subsequent negotiations.

The *target point* is a particular manner for distributing the resources in which a particular party's compensation is considered satisfactory. It is also a point of aspiration. Negotiators

Figure 8. Possible Outcomes in Fixed-Sum Negotiations.

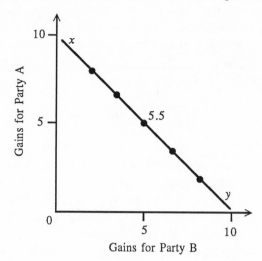

may develop their targets arbitrarily, or they may be the result of highly sophisticated calculations and analysis.

In addition to target points, negotiators may have upper or lower limits that are often called *resistance points*. The upper limit indicates a figure above which a party refuses to accept a settlement. The lower limit is the figure below which a party will cease negotiations due to unsatisfactory compensation.

Between the target point and the resistance point is the settlement or bargaining range—a field of options that, while satisfactory, provide different degrees of satisfaction for each negotiator. Since each party has a range of preferred options, the goal of each disputant is to (1) discover the other party's settlement range, (2) determine if there is an overlap with his or her own settlement range, and (3) maximize his or her own gains within the range of possible alternatives if there is an overlap.

In the best possible case, the disputing parties will have overlapping settlement ranges so that there are mutually satisfactory solutions or divisions of resources. Figure 9 illustrates how the options of two parties are compatible. Parties in positional bargaining, with or without the assistance of the mediator, will ideally be able to identify a mutually acceptable settle-

Figure 9. Positive Settlement Range.

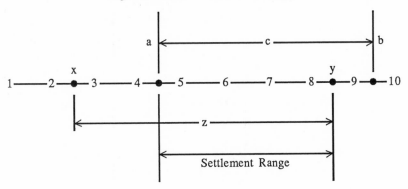

a = Party A's resistance point   x = Party B's target
b = Party A's target   y = Party B's resistance point
c = Acceptable options for Party A z = Acceptable options for Party B

ment range and make proposals between the boundaries established by their resistance points. When settlement ranges overlap, parties must decide how they will make a final decision on the distribution of the resource within their general area of agreement.

Occasionally, parties reach the assessment stage and discover that their settlement ranges on solutions to an issue do not overlap (see Figure 10). This condition is known as a *negative settlement range.*

When a party discovers that a negative settlement range exists, he or she has several procedural options: (1) continue to negotiate and make subsequent proposals in the hope that the other parties will shift their target and resistance points so that a positive settlement range is created, (2) change his or her own target point and resistance point and continue to offer new proposals that demand fewer concessions from other negotiators, (3) expand the number of issues to allow for trade-offs on other interests that will compensate for losses on the fixed-sum variable, or (4) cease negotiations. The mediator can assist the party in assessing the feasibility and desirability of pursuing any or all of these four options.

Figure 10. Negative Settlement Range.

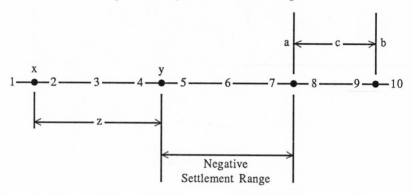

a = Party A's resistance point   x = Party B's target
b = Party A's target   y = Party B's resistance point
c = Acceptable options for Party A   z = Acceptable options for Party B

Settlement Range and Cooperative Problem Solving.
Reaching a settlement range when parties are engaged in interest-based bargaining is a somewhat different procedure than for positional bargaining. While the concept of the settlement range remains valid, the potential outcome options that the parties consider do not necessarily fall along a continuum in which one party gains values at the expense of another. Potential outcomes in interest-based bargaining result in a compromise only in a worst-case scenario. The norm appears to be solutions that are more satisfactory in the long run for all parties concerned. Figure 11 identifies the field in which this type of outcome can be found.

In Figure 11, the diagonal line *xy* represents a division of values in which parties reach some compromise in an apparently fixed-sum negotiation. The point 5.5 represents an equal division of the contested resources. The solutions sought by interest-based bargaining are those found in quadrant *C,* which represents maximum satisfaction of interests by settlement. In this field of settlement options any outcome is superior for all parties to a division of the resources along the *xy* range.

Figure 11. Cooperative Problem-Solving Settlement Range.

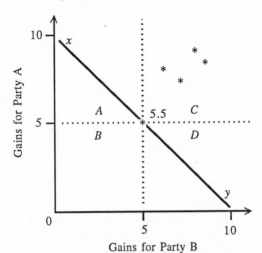

Gains for Party B

Note: Asterisks indicate cooperative problem-solving settlement options.

Recognizing the Settlement Range

In some negotiations, parties have little difficulty recognizing their arrival at a settlement range. Either through prenegotiation planning in which a range was established, or in the process of interaction, all parties may recognize that they have reached a field in which any settlement is preferable to no agreement.

Occasionally, however, parties have perceptual difficulties in recognizing a settlement range. This condition is due to (1) misperception of what is an acceptable field of settlement or (2) the existence of a negative settlement range. The mediator's intervention to prevent an impasse at this stage of negotiations may be crucial. I will discuss here how mediators respond to the first problem.

Identifying the Acceptable Field of Settlement. The problem of identification here is similar to perceptual or attitudinal problems identified earlier in negotiations—for instance, that it is necessary to be aware of the importance of interests and to recognize when a party should shift from an initial position to a new one. The mediator, through public and private discussions with the disputing parties, often has the most accurate perception of what the settlement range will be for all the negotiators. The problem for the intervenor is to communicate to disputants that a bargaining range has been reached without disclosing or determining the precise outcome of the dispute.

Mediators should attempt to raise the awareness the parties have that they have reached a settlement range by indirectly questioning individual parties about how well their interests or needs can be met by the available solutions. Mediators can also ask whether the party is willing to lose one of the available options as the result of an impasse. If the party responds that he or she is not willing to risk the impasse caused by rejection of a settlement option, the mediator knows that the party has reached a point equal to or better than his or her resistance point. The party has moved into an acceptable range of alternatives. The same procedure is then repeated with the other parties, generally in a caucus.

Once the mediator identifies that an acceptable settlement range has been reached, he or she may announce privately, or on occasion publicly, to the parties that the conditions for settlement do exist. Perhaps more commonly, the mediator may quietly lead the parties into the settlement procedures that will be described in Chapter Thirteen.

Moderating Parties with Inflated Expectations. So far I have discussed disputes in which the parties have been willing to acknowledge that they have moved into a settlement range. In some disputes, however, negotiation creates inflated expectations. Parties may raise their hopes and subsequently make unreasonable demands about expected outcomes. This behavior may prevent disputants from progressing into an acceptable settlement range. In order to avoid this, mediators should try to (1) convince the party with inflated expectations that his or her demand is out of line with what is attainable in reality or (2) convince the party that the other party has reached his or her bottom line and cannot offer any more. Both strategies are designed to raise the specter of impasse unless the unrealistic party modifies his or her position.

The mediator often accomplishes the first strategy, convincing a party that his or her demands are unrealistic, by asking one or more of the following questions:

- If you were in the other party's situation, would you offer more or accept the proposals that you are making now?
- Is the offer fair? Will those whom you respect, the community or the public, perceive it as such?
- Is the offer in line with community norms?
- Is the demand that you are making in line with other negotiated settlements or court decisions for similar issues or under similar conditions?
- Do you have the power to force the issue?
- What are the benefits to you of pursuing your present course? Are there any risks?

If the mediator cannot induce the party to decide to moderate inflated hopes or positions by careful questioning, he or she may have to use information about the other side as a lever of influence. Transmitting specific information about one party's position or means of influence is always problematic for mediators. The mediator may not have an accurate assessment of a party's position or influence, or may be the victim of a party's bluff tactics. Before telling a party that another party has reached his or her bottom line and cannot offer any more, the mediator should be certain that there are no additional offers to be made. The mediator should generally give the party to whom the request is being directed an opportunity to make additional offers before the mediator transmits the message of total commitment to the other party. Most of this activity occurs within a caucus. Once a mediator has gained permission to transmit a final offer, he or she may convey it to the party who has inflated expectations. The form in which a final offer is transmitted may vary according to specificity, timing (when it must be accepted), and implications for rejection (Fisher, 1978; Walton and McKersie, 1965).

Mediators should be cautious and use this tactic only as a last resort. If the party with inflated expectations does not shift position, an impasse occurs. Mediators should usually try to keep parties uncommitted to particular solutions for as long as possible so that the parties do not become entrenched in a position. However, if disclosure of a party's bottom line is successful, the intransigent party may deflate his or her demands and progress into the mutually acceptable settlement range.

Negative Settlement Range

Unfortunately, negotiations do not always result in a positive settlement range. I have discussed the moves that a mediator makes when there is a perceptual problem in recognizing an existent settlement range. I now turn to strategies when the problem is not perceptual; when the differences are real and there are no mutually acceptable solutions.

The major strategic move mediators initiate when a negative settlement range is present is assisting the parties in determining their "best alternative to a negotiated agreement" (BATNA) (Fisher and Ury, 1981). In defining the BATNA, the mediator returns to the process of selecting an approach and arena of conflict as outlined in Chapter Four. The mediator and the parties should, separately or jointly, discuss procedural options available to them should negotiations fail, and potential outcomes that might result from these different conflict resolution approaches. Parties may at this time decide either to terminate negotiations and move to other resolution approaches, or to reassess their positions and proposals and move toward an acceptable settlement. Often a careful and realistic assessment of each party's best alternative to a negotiated agreement brings all the disputants back to negotiation with a renewed commitment to reaching a mutually acceptable agreement.

THIRTEEN

Final Bargaining

Final bargaining involves moves disputing parties initiate late in negotiation to reduce the scope and number of differences between negotiators and to progress toward agreement and termination of the conflict. Gulliver (1979, pp. 161-162) identifies four situations in which negotiators find themselves in the final bargaining stage:

1. The bargaining range may have been so narrowed that the advantages to be gained from bargaining have become small, even trifling, given the agreement already achieved. . . . What remains to be done is a clearing up of minor details and a joint commitment to the culminating outcome.

2. The bargaining range may have been narrowed, or the bargaining formula may have already established much agreement in principle and orientation, but the details of terms need to be worked out.

3. In a third bargaining situation, although something like a viable bargaining range has been discovered, albeit roughly and with unclear limits, considerable differences may remain between the parties. In principle, any point within the range is mutually preferable to no agreement, yet considerable gain or loss of advantage

227

can still result from final agreement on a particular point.

4. No viable range has been discovered and it
may well not exist. Here although the parties
are deliberately working toward agreement
and are making "real" proposals for an outcome, their preference sets and expectations
are still not altogether clear.

Parties who find themselves in the first situation usually
reach agreement easily. Their relationship is cordial, the acceptable options are clear, and the procedural route to complete the
negotiations is uncomplicated and direct. The remaining situations, however, are more problematic for negotiators, and a
mediator's intervention may be needed to prevent impasse or
deadlock. I will focus the discussion on the procedures negotiators and mediators use to accomplish final bargaining in the
last three situations.

There appear to be four major patterns of moves negotiators use during the final stage of bargaining: (1) incremental
convergence (Gulliver, 1979; Walton and McKersie, 1965), (2)
a delay of agreement and then a final leap to a package settlement (Zartman and Berman, 1982), (3) development of a consensual formula, or (4) procedural means to reach agreements
(Fisher, 1978; Zartman and Berman, 1982). In this chapter I
will first explore these approaches to final settlement, and then
examine the crucial factor of timing to see how the mediator
uses deadlines to bring negotiations toward conclusion.

Incremental Convergence

In Chapter Twelve I explored the dynamics of incremental convergence. In this procedure the parties make gradual concessions within the bargaining range until they reach a mutually
satisfactory compromise position. Parties may isolate concession to a single issue or link issues to balance losses and benefits.

If parties have adhered to positional bargaining, the mediator's main task is to assist disputants in making offers that

will be acceptable to the other party and to prevent them from prematurely committing to a position that will be difficult to back off from later in negotiations.

Offers are the specific terms of a position that a party presents as a possible solution to an issue. An offer usually implies some form of concession or trade a party is willing to make in exchange for a counteroffer, concession, or agreement. Parties engaged in positional bargaining face several problems that may inhibit them from making offers. I will examine these blocks and observe how mediators assist parties in making offers that facilitate incremental convergence.

Reluctance to Overconcede or Reveal Bargaining Positions. At this point in negotiations parties may be reluctant to make subsequent offers, even if they have discovered an opponent's settlement range. This reluctance occurs because they do not want to concede more than necessary, nor do they want to indicate their bargaining positions within their own settlement range. This situation can result in endless avoidance behavior and a lack of commitment to a specific proposal.

Mediators should assist parties in developing tentative offers that can be used to test for potential agreement while not formally committing a party to a specific solution. Tentative or probing offers can be designed by a negotiator, the mediator, or both. These offers can vary in degree of specificity, resources exchanged, time of performance, and implications if the offer is accepted or rejected in a timely manner. This allows a party more flexibility in exploring the settlement range without prematurely committing to a position.

Fear of Being Perceived as Weak. A second factor that inhibits parties in initiating offers is the fear of being perceived as weak (Rubin and Brown, 1975). People in conflict often do not want others to see them being "forced" to make a concession. They fear that concession making will become, or will be perceived to be, a pattern, and that the opponent will hold out on later issues, waiting for similar compliant behavior. There is evidence in pure game theory that concession making may be perceived as a sign of weakness (Deutsch, 1974); however, in actual negotiations in which there is interpersonal interaction, making the first offer or concession can be turned into an asset rather than a liability. The classic case is Anwar Sadat's initiative in proposing to Menachem Begin that they begin discussions on a Middle East peace plan. Sadat's proposal to travel to Israel to talk was a potent first offer.

Mediators can aid a party in making a first offer by assisting the party in framing the offer in such a way that the concession becomes an initiative of strength, not weakness. Through framing, the party can make explicit the fact that they are making an offer or concession to demonstrate good faith, to show a willingness to take the other's needs into consideration, to encourage the other party or parties to make similar moves, or to establish a trading arrangement in which a concession is made on one issue in exchange for a concession on another. The mediator may prepare, coach, and assist the party in framing the offer so that the other party will perceive it favorably. The mediator may also prime the recipient so that the offer will be accepted or reciprocated.

Negative Transference. Parties often reject an offer not because of its substantive content but because of their attitude toward its initiator. The mediator can help negotiators avoid this pitfall by taking their ideas, often in private, and proposing them to the other party as his or her own ideas. This avoids the possibility that the other party will perceive offers as "partial, biased, or tainted more because of their source than because of their substantive content" (Young, 1972).

Fear of Rejection and Impasse. Parties are often discouraged from making offers because they fear rejection and stalemate. They may prefer to continue discussions rather than reach impasse. Mediators can assist parties in overcoming this obstacle by testing the ideas of the parties in private and bringing to the joint session only those points on which the parties can agree. The mediator can encourage the parties to make the offers or may make the offers for them. Whenever possible, it is preferable for the parties to make the offers because it increases their commitment to proposals and maintains the mediator's impartiality toward the substance of the negotiations.

Public Pressure on Negotiators. In cases in which negotiators represent a constituency, the parties may be constrained from making public offers because of possible personal repercussions from unpopular concessions. Here the mediator can make a proposal for agreement and become a negotiator's scapegoat. Negotiators can agree to the concession and later claim that they agreed because the mediator requested concurrence, not because they initiated it or the other party forced them to agree.

The Mediator as Coalition Former. Closely related to the scapegoat function of the mediator is the role of coalition former. The mediator's presence and his or her potential suggestions of offers can cause the disputants to reevaluate their relationship to each other and the issues that divide them. "What must always happen when a third party intervenes in a conflict between two, is that there arises a possibility of an alliance. . . . Instead of the stalemate one to one, it can now become two to one. One possibility is, of course, that the two original contestants both become antagonistic towards the third person and decide to agree so as not to let the newcomer influence the settlement" (Aubert, 1963, p. 35). The mediator can induce this situation by proposing one or more solutions that are more extreme than either party is willing to accept. They may be forced into a coalition to moderate the mediator's exaggerated position.

Loss of Face. Another block to parties initiating offers is the issue of "saving face" (Brown, 1977). Mediators can assist parties in making new offers by providing them with rationalizations for shifts in positions and reframing the situation so that an offer does not result in a loss of dignity. This strategy also aids parties in abandoning untenable postures.

The seven blocks listed above can all be impediments to negotiators who are initiating offers that lead to incremental convergence of positions. Appropriate mediator intervention, however, can minimize the negative effects and ease the decision-making process of positional bargaining.

Leap to Agreement

The leap to agreement approach to final bargaining is characterized by a strategy of opening with a high demand, offering few concessions, and then making a final leap toward a package that meets the negotiator's demands (Zartman and Berman, 1982). Leaps to agreement usually occur when (1) negotiators consciously pursue a hard-line strategy to educate an opponent about a principle, (2) negotiators want to use deadline pressure to force an agreement, or (3) all options are equally acceptable (or unacceptable) and no one proposal has superior merit.

The leap model of negotiation is often characterized by "package deals" or "yesable proposals" that attempt to incorporate the needs of all parties into one acceptable linked package (Fisher, 1969). Advantages to this approach are that (1) it prevents incremental concession making that may result in expectations of more concessions and allows a party to make a point about his or her commitment to an issue or principle; (2) by turning the task over to one party, it attempts to eliminate part of the difficult task of jointly drafting an agreement; (3) it demonstrates that trade-offs are possible; and (4) it may incline a party toward agreement when a deadline is close and there is no time to develop a counterproposal.

This approach does, however, have some drawbacks. Intransigence on a position and lack of progress early in a negotiation may cause the other party to adhere to its position and may also foster increasing hostility over the procedure used to resolve the dispute rather than over the issues themselves. Presenting a package late in negotiations may also cause problems because the opposing party may believe that he or she has not had an opportunity to participate in formulating the plan for the settlement. Rejection thus may be based upon procedural participatory factors rather than the proposal's substantive content.

Rejection may also be based on the lack of time to adequately assess the proposal. Parties often resent a new settlement option that is presented suddenly when there is insufficient time to assess the offer and make a response.

The Mediator and Leaps to Agreement. The leap to agreement approach may have both positive and negative benefits for negotiators. Mediators can either promote or inhibit the use of this procedure, depending on the dynamics of the particular negotiation session. If a mediator encounters a party that uses this approach in final bargaining, causing damage to negotiations, the intervenor can notify the party in caucus of the detrimental effect on the other party. If, on the other hand, the hard-line procedure of delaying commitment is educating the other party on a particular principle or point and the mediator has learned that the other party is progressing toward agreement, the mediator may encourage the process.

The mediator can also use the leap to agreement tactic by delaying a party's commitment to a solution until the mediator is certain that they will agree to a particular proposal. At that time the mediator can ask one of the parties to make the proposal, or he or she may even make it. With agreement assured, the parties can leap to a one-step settlement.

Formulas and Agreements in Principle

I have already discussed at some length the procedures used to reach a bargaining formula or an agreement in principle. This strategy is one of progressing from the most general level of agreement to more specific details of a settlement. The mediator may initiate this approach early in negotiations, even as early as the defining dispute parameters stage, or it may appear as late as final bargaining after more specific alternatives have been generated and assessed.

The procedures for reaching a formula settlement are somewhat like those used in constructing a puzzle. First, the outside boundary—the general agreement—is constructed. The outside pieces determine the overall boundaries of the settlement. The negotiators then construct various packages that will fit into this framework. The formula development process is conducted by consensus and usually involves modification, refinement, and synthesis of proposals or, occasionally, the exchange of small incremental pieces. The formula process often involves the creation of multiple levels of agreements with increasing specificity.

The Mediator and Formula Construction. Parties often begin building a formula or attempt to develop agreements in principle early in negotiations. This process usually starts during the stage of defining dispute parameters when the parties attempt to outline the boundaries, both conceptual and substantive, within which they will negotiate. The development of a formula or agreement in principle may later become much more explicit in the process of defining issues and interests.

Formula development or agreements in principle in final bargaining are primarily useful in preventing deadlocks. Formulas may be designed to define principles by which a limited resource within a bargaining range can be divided, or to set forth procedures for combining solutions that meet the needs of all parties. Mutual decision about a formula or agreement in principle "is desirable . . . because a formula or framework of principles helps give structure and coherence to an agreement on details, helps facilitate the search for solutions on component items, and helps create a positive, creative image of negotiation rather than an image of concession and compromise" (Zartman and Berman, 1982, p. 93).

Parties with extensive experience with or bias toward positional bargaining are often not aware of the merits of establishing a bargaining formula or agreements in principle to reach final settlement. Mediators can often assist parties by educating the parties about the approach and by identifying such a formula in much the same manner as the intervenor was able to help identify interests.

Zartman and Berman (1982) maintain that the recognition of a common formula depends on three elements: (1) a shared perception or definition of the conflict, (2) an understanding of the primary and underlying values or interests that give meaning to the issues under discussion, and (3) an applicable criterion of justice. By the final bargaining stage, the parties have hopefully developed a shared perception or definition of the conflict. If they have not, the mediator should refer them back to the previous stages of issue and interest identification. Interests and underlying values must be satisfied or be met by a settlement. The formula must contain provisions for responding to the primary and secondary interests of the disputants or it will be unacceptable.

The third component of a formula is a mutually accepted standard of justice. Zartman and Berman (1982) identify five types of justice: substantive, procedural, equitable, compensatory, and subtractive. *Substantive justice* refers to a concrete objective outcome that the parties believe is fair. *Procedural justice* refers to the process by which a solution is reached and the settlement is carried out. Most disputants expect the same procedure to be in effect for both parties, or if the procedure is to be different, the reasons for the difference should be mutually acceptable. *Equitable justice* refers to the "apportionment of shares on the basis of each party's particular characteristics" (Zartman and Berman, 1982, p. 104). The basis of equity will vary from dispute to dispute and may be based on need, power, historic precedent, size, or amount of resources available to divide.

Compensatory justice refers to payments that remedy an unequal distribution of resources. Compensatory justice usually occurs when one party has been deprived as a result of a previous relationship. For example, a husband may agree to pay spousal support and fund his ex-wife's school expenses so that she can earn an income and attain a standard of living equal to what she was accustomed to in the marriage. A developer may monetarily compensate the immediate neighbors of an unpopular new facility needed by the community, for potential damages to their lifestyle (O'Hare, Bacow, and Sanderson, 1983). *Subtractive justice* refers to equal denial to all parties of a resource so that no one wins. This component of a formula is used when parties have a higher priority of denying access to a resource to another than possessing it themselves. For example, if in a divorce property settlement the couple cannot decide which of them should take their antique brass bed, both may agree to sell it and deny possession to each other rather than agree that one of them should have it.

Procedural Means of Reaching Substantive Decisions

Occasionally, negotiators are unable to make a decision on a particular substantive issue, and the impasse delays the settlement of the entire conflict. Inability to agree may be based on psychological unwillingness to settle a dispute, reluctance to agree to a point for fear of constituency disapproval, multiple solutions that are mutually acceptable (or undesirable), and so on. Regardless of the reason that agreement cannot be reached, the parties may still be under pressure to find some solution to their impasse. To break the deadlock, parties may turn to a procedural solution to a substantive problem.

Procedural solutions are process decisions that parties make to resolve disputes without directly deciding the issue. There are four common types of procedural approaches to resolve substantive impasse: the procedural timeline approach, third-party decision makers, arbitrary decision-making procedures, and postponement or avoidance.

Procedural Timeline Approach. The procedural timeline approach requires negotiators to develop a process and timeline for when particular substantive agreements have to be reached and define specific advantages or consequences for parties reaching or failing to reach these deadlines. Time determines the substantive outcome. For example, if parties are negotiating payment, they may agree that if payment is received before a specific date, a certain amount is to be given. If payment is received after this date, a penalty charge will be imposed. A party then has a choice as to when payment is to be made. The amount is dependent on timing and is procedurally determined. The procedural timeline approach allows the parties to avoid reaching a specific substantive decision on issues in dispute and instead creates a procedural formula for how the decision will be made.

Third-Party Decision Makers. Parties who reach an impasse on a substantive question can turn the problem over to a third party other than the mediator for a decision. The most common form of third-party decision making is performed by a judge or jury. Disputants are legally bound by the decision of the impartial third party. Another third-party structure is arbitration, which was defined in Chapter One. Mediators often suggest referral of issues over which parties are deadlocked to an arbiter or judge.

Other third-party decision makers who can assist parties to break deadlocks include property appraisers, custody evaluators, and other technical experts. Parties can agree to engage the assistance of third parties and agree that they will abide by the recommendation supplied.

Arbitrary Decision-Making Procedures. Parties often wish to decide on issues in which there is an equal chance of winning or losing or in which the outcome is of little consequence to the disputants. Negotiators or mediators frequently resort to procedural mechanisms that automatically and arbitrarily result in a decision.

Parties may agree to share equally benefits and losses of a particular resource. This procedure is appropriate when the difference between the parties is not large and therefore the loss for either would not be great, or when the probability of reaching a decision by another means has an equal chance of loss or gain for one of the parties. Parties split the *difference* in order to maximize their rewards and minimize their losses.

Negotiators may also choose to alternate choices, or to use games of chances such as flipping coins or drawing lots or straws. These arbitrary procedures provide each disputant with an equal chance to win rewards. The process, not the disputants, decides the outcome. The mediator may impartially supervise the process to ensure fairness.

Postponement, Avoidance, and Abandoning Issues. Parties may also reach a decision on an item by postponing, avoiding, or abandoning a decision or issue. Postponement may mean delaying making a decision until the other party is more psychologically disposed toward an issue, to a time when the opponent has changed his or her opinion or a new person represents the opposing party, when new proposals or arguments can be raised, when more power has been mobilized, or when external structural variables or influences on the conflict have changed.

Postponement may also be used in conjunction with third-party decision making. In cases in which parties cannot reach agreement on a particular issue and in which failure to agree may result in total impasse, negotiators may decide to agree in general and defer decision making on the particular point until the specific conflict arises at a later date. They may designate one component of a dispute to be referred to an arbiter or judge for final resolution. This approach avoids deadlock and allows agreement to be reached without attaining a full consensus on all issues.

At the start of negotiations, parties raise a number of issues or demands that they want addressed. Each issue can be ranked according to its importance in terms of the overall settlement. It is not unusual for negotiators to include one or more bogus or throw-away issues that are made to appear important and that are used for educational or trading value in final negotiations. A party uses throw-away issues as part of an initial large demand to educate his or her opponents about how many concessions will have to be made for a settlement to be reached. Throw-away issues are used in final bargaining as bargaining chips that are traded for desirable concessions. They are valuable only if the other party believes that they are genuine. If this illusion can be maintained throughout negotiations, a bargainer may truly have a tradable commodity.

The manner in which throw-away issues are used varies. They may be used as an early concession to demonstrate goodwill or may be used later in exchange for the removal of another negotiator's demand from the table. Negotiators will often mutually agree to abandon issues in an "I'll get rid of mine if you'll get rid of yours" manner.

On occasion the mediator can best manage arrangements to abandon issues. The intervenor should determine with the parties in caucus whether the parties require joint acknowledgment to abandon the demands or issues, or whether they prefer merely to not mention them. If they prefer acknowledgment, the mediator can help establish the conditions for the abandonment of issues or demands.

Parties often develop arbitrary decision-making procedures or decide to abandon issues on their own. However, if disputants find themselves in a situation in which one of the means listed above might be appropriate and they are not able to identify a procedure, the mediator may suggest one or more procedural methods to avoid impasse.

Deadlines

Timing is a critical component in final bargaining and settlement. Cross (1969, p. 13) notes, "If it did not matter *when* the parties agreed, it would not matter whether they agreed at all." Time is both an important motivational factor for negotiators and a variable that helps determine how well their interests will be met. Time and timing in final bargaining refer primarily to the management of time in order to induce a settlement. The most common form of time management in this stage is the deadline.

Deadlines are limits that delineate the period of time in which an agreement must be reached. Deadlines perform an important function in the settlement of a variety of issues. "Of the 85,420 federal civil cases that were filed in the United States in 1975, only 9 percent were disposed of by trial" (Shallert, 1982, p. 255). Lawyers often settle legal cases in a limited number of days or hours before the court date. Much of the impetus for out-of-court settlement before the court date comes from the unpredictable outcome of court proceedings and the potential for negative consequences if the parties engage in direct litigation. The deadline of a court date motivates parties to settle.

Just as in the settlement of legal cases, deadlines play an important function in prompting labor-management dispute settlement. The eleventh-hour settlement before a strike deadline is well known. The same dynamics are common in nearly all other types of negotiations. Stevens (1963, p. 200) argues: "An approaching deadline puts pressure on the parties to state their true positions and thus does much to squeeze elements of bluff out of the later steps of negotiation. However, an approaching deadline does much more. . . . It brings pressures to bear which actually change the least favorable terms upon which each party is willing to settle; thus, it operates as a force tending to bring about conditions necessary for agreement."

An understanding of deadlines and how they can be used is an invaluable tool for negotiators and mediators. It is beneficial to discuss several characteristics and variables of deadlines that affect their utility in negotiations.

Internally and Externally Established Deadlines. A party can establish his or her own deadline, or outside forces may determine when negotiation ceases. A contract deadline, an ultimatum imposed by an outside agency, and an impending court date are examples of externally imposed constraints.

External deadlines are often important to negotiation strategies. Shapiro (1970, p. 44), in referring to negotiations in which one party represents a constituent group, observes that "any settlement made without the pressure of a last minute crisis leaves the negotiators open to attack by the people they represent, who may feel that they could have gotten a more favorable contract if only their negotiators had bluffed the other side right down to the final moment."

Coordinated and Uncoordinated Deadlines. Deadlines can be symmetrical or asymmetrical in that the parties may have either the same time limits or different ones. For some parties, a delay in decision making may result in increased benefits, while for others a rapid decision may be essential (Lake, 1980).

Actual and Artificial Deadlines. Parties may be constrained by deadlines that correspond to particular events beyond which they have little control, or they may be influenced by artificial time constraints that are almost arbitarily established by one or more parties.

An example of an artificial deadline occurred in 1982 during negotiations between environmentalists and industry representatives regarding environmental restrictions on oil and gas development on federal lands. The environmentalists stated that if they did not note progress in the talks within six weeks, they would cease negotiation. They arbitrarily set a deadline in order to encourage industry and government representatives to reach an agreement.

Rigid and Flexible Deadlines. The rigidity/flexibility variable is closely related to actual and artificial deadlines. Although rigid deadlines are usually viewed as the stronger impetus for settlement because they provide fixed time boundaries beyond which the parties dare not transgress, more flexible deadlines, at least at the eleventh hour, may allow the parties necessary latitude to effect a decision. Parties often need additional time to reconsider a last-minute proposal or to gain constituent or bureaucratic approval to reach a final settlement. Mutually determined extensions of deadlines may be a prerequisite for a settlement.

Deadlines with and Without Consequences. Deadlines promote settlements primarily because they usually imply negative consequences if the time limit is transgressed. Consequences may include a termination of negotiations, a stalemate, a loss of gains already achieved, a withdrawal of an offer, acceptance of another party's offer, a court suit, a strike, or other undesirable outcomes. While a deadline does not have to imply dire consequences such as threat or actual imposition of negative sanctions, it must offer the possibility of a worse option than if settlement was reached. Negotiators and mediators often manipulate the explicit or implicit consequences of not settling before a deadline because known or unknown consequences may incline another party toward agreement.

Explicit or Vague Deadlines. Deadlines may be explicitly defined or may remain vague. The appropriate strategy depends on the particular negotiation. Explicit deadlines tend to create a definite point for termination of negotiations and a temporal point at which settlement must be reached. While providing a positive benefit in creating motivation for settlement, explicit deadlines may also create resistance because of a perceived threat of negative consequences, may promote unwise decisions because there is not enough time to consider all options, or may encourage an overwillingness to settle at the sacrifice of principle. Negotiators usually argue for explicit deadlines only when all parties will bear the negative consequences of a failure to reach agreement within the prescribed time. An example of this situation is a strike in which both labor and management stand to lose if a new contract is not negotiated.

Vague deadlines, on the other hand, imply that the negotiator is willing to talk as long as necessary to reach an acceptable settlement. Vague deadlines can be used to the advantage of negotiators who know that an opponent is under pressure to settle by a certain time. The appearance of unlimited time for discussion may motivate an opponent to settle early to decrease rising costs that result from delay. Even if time is an important factor for negotiators, however, a negotiator may gain more in the end by concealing his or her deadlines. Cohen (1980), a business negotiator, describes a drastic case in which he lost thousands of dollars because he was not vague about his time constraints and his opponent discovered his settlement deadline. His opponent was willing to talk for a longer period of time than was available to Cohen.

Mediators and Deadline Management

Mediators can significantly assist negotiators in managing deadlines by making the parties aware of internal or external deadlines or assisting parties in setting deadlines when none exist. When appropriate, mediators may also make rigid deadlines more flexible, assist the parties in avoiding negative moves related to time, and enhance the usefulness of deadlines.

Making Parties Aware of Deadlines. Parties are often not aware of the existence or consequences of deadlines. This is especially the case when the deadlines are externally imposed or implicitly assumed. Mediators often function in final bargaining to remind negotiators that the deadline approaches and that negative consequences may result from failure to settle. This function of the mediator should not be construed to mean that a mediator should reveal a hidden time deadline that is crucial for a party to meet his or her interests. Mediators should take great care not to reveal confidential information about time constraints lest they unduly influence the settlement and create an imbalance in the power relationship between the parties. The mediator should, however, bring to the consciousness of the negotiators the explicit time parameters that affect final bargaining.

Assisting Parties in Establishing a Deadline. The presence of a deadline often enhances a negotiation's outcome. Deadlines can be created by disputing parties who have the influence to harm other disputants who do not adhere to established time parameters or reward them if they do. Deadlines can also be established by external constituencies—bureaucratic authorities or collectives of interested parties—or by external events. Finally, the mediator's moves can establish deadlines. I will examine each of these means of defining time boundaries to negotiation and the mediator's role in influencing them.

The mediator, if he or she deems it advisable or necessary, may encourage one or more parties in a dispute to establish a deadline. This move may be conducted in caucus or in joint session and may be developed unilaterally or multilaterally. There may be some situations in which it is advisable for the mediator to suggest that only one party set a deadline, while in other situations a cooperatively established time limit may be necessary to motivate all disputants to reach agreement. A mediator's suggestion in a caucus that only one party set a deadline may mean a loss of neutrality, undue manipulation of the negotiation process, or the risk of exposure in joint session. This step is taken only with great care.

If a jointly established deadline is desirable, the mediator can assist the parties in deciding the criteria to be used in determining the deadline. Relevant factors may include time needed to learn about or study the issue; time for ratification of an agreement by a constituency; later availability of additional data; and structural constraints such as court dates, business schedules, or even change of seasons.

Persons or events external to negotiations may also establish deadlines. Mediators often help parties negotiate with superiors or constituencies not directly involved in mediation regarding the establishment of time parameters and deadlines for negotiations. Such externally imposed boundaries that are beyond direct control of the negotiators are often needed to motivate other parties to settle.

Although mediators rarely control external events that impose deadlines on negotiations, they can translate the consequences of these events to the parties to encourage them to settle within an agreed period of time. For example, if economic forces allow an offer to be made for only a limited period of time, the mediator may inform the parties of this factor. Raising awareness about an imminent court date that cannot be changed is another means of deadline leverage.

The mediator can also create his or her own deadline if such a move appears to be the only means of settlement. The mediator can accomplish this in several ways. First, the mediator can make all parties aware that a settlement is possible and that he or she thinks this can be accomplished within a specific period of time. The mediator can request that parties reach agreement within these proposed time parameters. Imposed deadlines may encourage the parties to negotiate within the intervenor's time frame. Some divorce mediators who have a structured and limited number of sessions within which the parties must agree or cease mediation may use this approach.

Second, the mediator can announce that he or she will make a public statement after a certain date that the parties are not negotiating in a timely and serious manner. Finally, a mediator may threaten to abandon the negotiators at a certain time unless the parties agree to honor a deadline (Kolb, 1983). This threat creates a functional deadline to which the parties must respond if they want to retain the mediator's services.

Mediators can only impose deadlines on parties if (1) the mediator's threat is credible, (2) the parties are willing to agree to the mediator's request or demand, or (3) the services of the mediator are genuinely needed or desired. The mediator's expendability or his or her failure to carry out a threat will lead to either a loss of credibility or the mediator's dismissal.

Lack of a deadline may not be the problem in a dispute. Parties may believe they are locked into a deadline so that the time parameter itself raises the specter of deadlock. The mediator's task in this situation is to create a more flexible deadline, which can be accomplished by several different methods.

First, the mediator may find ways to actually extend the time available for negotiation. Specific procedural agreements may be proposed to postpone the deadline so that parties have more time to make a decision. A suggestion by the mediator rather than one of the parties often makes the proposal more palatable to the disputants, and also avoids the appearance that if the deadline is extended one party will make a concession. Another mediator tactic is to "stop the clock." In this maneuver, the mediator obtains agreement to continue negotiations and to temporarily ignore the passage of time and the deadline. Negotiation time is extended without publicly disavowing that a deadline exists. A third move mediators can use to create more flexibility in deadlines is to delay the time or date by which a specific component of a decision is to be made or is to go into effect. This allows the parties more time to work out controversial details of a particular problem and still reach general agreement.

Avoiding Deadline Dangers. There are several dangerous but common moves that negotiators may apply in conjunction with deadlines. Among these are exposure of another party's deadline, games of "chicken," threats of dire consequences if agreement is not reached before the deadline, unrealistically quick agreements because of a false momentum toward the deadline, and manipulation of embarrassment to force an agreement. Mediators help parties avoid pitfalls in each of these situations.

"Chicken" is a strategy in which each party delays making concessions until the deadline is imminent. The tension of intransigence will supposedly force another negotiator's will to fail so that he or she will make concessions rather than risk deadlock or negative costs if the deadline passes. Unfortunately, no party may be willing to break the cycle of resistance, and then all parties are forced to carry out threats and endure unintended consequences that no one wanted. Mediators may help parties avoid playing "chicken" with deadlines by (1) publicly labeling the strategy, (2) privately working with each party to assess the costs of pursuing such a tactic, and (3) figuring ways that parties can abandon extreme positions and make offers that will allow them to maintain their dignity.

Threats seem to be especially common when parties experience intransigence from other negotiators and the deadline approaches. Mediators should discourage parties from making threats and encourage them to make positive offers to induce agreement as a positive and less risky tactic.

A deadline's presence occasionally forces parties to reach unrealistic and unimplementable agreements. Parties begin a process of agreeing and become so involved in the dynamic of settlement that they formulate impractical agreements. When a mediator recognizes this dynamic, he or she should temper the enthusiasm of the disputants by utilizing reality testing, asking questions that raise doubts, encouraging the parties to seek more information, or physically separating parties into caucuses so that they can more realistically assess the settlement under less pressure and without the stress of the presence of other negotiators.

Kheel, a labor mediator, has used this delaying tactic both to avoid untenable agreements and to psychologically encourage settlement (Shapiro, 1970). Kheel separates parties with assurances that they are "not ready to settle" until they virtually demand to return to joint session to make an agreement. After the delay, in which the real merits of the settlement are analyzed, the parties are ready to make a solid and realistic settlement.

Parties are often embarrassed if they ask to delay settlement until they can be more certain of a proposal's merits. Other negotiators can manipulate such embarrassment to force an untimely agreement. Mediators can legitimize delay and prevent the manipulation of embarrassment by publicly calling for more time to reasonably consider a proposal. As an impartial intervenor, the mediator may even claim a personal lack of understanding of the settlement to delay a decision and provide the parties with more time for deliberation.

Enhancing the Usefulness of Deadlines

Mediators can assist parties in enhancing the positive use of deadlines in two ways. First, mediators can assist parties in designing offers that contain fading opportunities. They can also create artificial deadlines or mileposts before the ultimate deadline. Each milepost marks a certain amount of benefits that an opponent will receive if he or she settles at that time. The longer the settlement is delayed, the fewer benefits are offered.

An example of this negotiation strategy occurred at a recent dinner party. Parents of several children told them that they had had enough hors d'oeuvres for the evening. As the party continued, more firewood was needed to heat the room. The children were offered an exchange of more food if they would each bring in one log. They protested, started delaying tactics, and made several counteroffers. One of the guests clarified the offer by saying that if the children did not bring in the wood in five minutes, he would do so; thus the offer would not be available to the children. The children decided that it was a worthwhile exchange and carried in the wood before the adult could do so.

Second, mediators can help parties structure their pre-deadline offers to contain more positive benefits than could be achieved once the deadline passes. By stressing the positive advantages of settlement versus the negative costs of passing the deadline, the offering party and mediator may be able to induce negotiators to settle.

FOURTEEN

Achieving Formal Settlement

The final stage of mediation requires disputants to design an implementation and monitoring procedure and to formalize the settlement. Success in this final stage assures both an immediate settlement and an agreement that will hold over time.

Implementing the Settlement

Implementation refers to procedural steps that disputants or mediators take to operationalize an agreement and to terminate a dispute (Coser, 1967). Implementation is discussed here as a specific phase of negotiation and separate set of mediator interventions because it poses critical problems that must be overcome if the agreement is to endure. The process may occur before, during, or after reaching a substantive settlement.

The success of a substantive agreement frequently depends on the implementation plan's strength. Parties may fail to reach substantive agreement because they cannot conceive how it could be implemented. Later, parties may fail to adhere to a poorly conceived plan. Insufficient consideration of implementation may result in settlements that create devastating precedents that may result in reluctance to negotiate in the future; damaged interpersonal relationships; and financial, time, or resource losses. For these reasons, mediators may need to carefully assist parties in devising reasonable, efficient, and effective implementation procedures.

There are two types of procedures for executing agreements: "A self-executing agreement is one which is either: (1) carried out in its entirety at the time it is accepted, or (2) formulated in such a way that the extent to which the players adhere to its terms will be self-evident. A nonself-executing agreement, on the other hand, is one which requires from the parties continuing performance which may be difficult to measure in the absence of special monitoring arrangements" (Young, 1972, p. 58).

An example of a self-executing agreement was the mediated settlement of a dispute over the amount of legal fees a client was to pay a lawyer. Once the parties agreed on the amount, the client wrote the lawyer a check for the amount owed. The payment immediately terminated the dispute.

The negotiated settlement of visitation terms for the child of a divorcing couple illustrates a nonself-executing agreement. Since visitation will occur over many years, the agreement will not be carried out in its entirety when the negotiation terminates. The parents will need to cooperate over time to ensure that the spirit as well as the specific terms of the agreement is carried out. Frequent conflicts over visitation rights illustrate the difficulties of interpretating and complying with nonself-executing agreements.

A self-executing agreement is clearly a stronger and more effective means of ensuring that a settlement will be managed according to the negotiated terms. Compliance is tangible and immediate, and chances of violation are minimized. Mediators can often significantly assist parties in designing self-executing implementation plans so that the conflict can be terminated rapidly and to prevent settlement from being extended over time.

However, not all conflicts can be terminated or settlements completed in a self-executing and immediate manner. Certain settlements may inherently or structurally require continued performance over a long period of time. Child or spousal support payments, house or car payments, environmental performance standards monitoring, and compliance with agreements about ongoing work relationships illustrate cases that require ongoing performance.

Compliance is difficult to measure in nonself-executing agreements, and this type of agreement often results in later discord due to differing interpretations. In disputes in which parties cannot reach a self-enforcing agreement, they often prefer not to settle at all or to use other settlement procedures rather than negotiate an agreement that may not be implemented or in which compliance is difficult to determine. In these cases, disputants may fail to agree not because they are unable to reach a substantive settlement on issues in dispute, but because they do not trust each other to perform according to the plan over time (Schelling, 1956).

Mediators and negotiators consider eight factors in implementing a settlement:

1. A consensual agreement about the criteria used to measure successful compliance.
2. The general and specific steps required to implement the decision.
3. Identification of the people who have the power to influence the necessary changes.
4. An organizational structure (if applicable) to implement the alternatives.
5. Provisions that will accommodate either future changes in agreement terms or changes in disputing parties.
6. Procedures to manage unintended or unexpected problems or violations of the settlement that may arise during implementation.
7. Methods to monitor compliance, and identity of monitor(s).
8. Determination of the monitor's role (for example, whistleblower or enforcer).

Criteria for Compliance and Implementation Steps

The probability of noncompliance by one or more parties may increase according to (1) the larger the number and complexity of issues in dispute, (2) the greater the number of parties involved, (3) the higher the level of psychological tension and distrust, and (4) the longer the terms of the agreement must be performed. This does not mean that the parties will intentionally violate the agreement, but that structural variables make violation more likely. Negotiated or mediated agreements are not inherently more prone to noncompliance than other forms of dispute resolution processes. In fact, research indicates that mediated agreements have a high compliance rate (Cook, Rochl, and Shepard, 1980; Pearson, 1984; Bingham, 1984). However, because negotiated settlements are often conducted on an ad hoc basis, they are more susceptible to violation than conflict resolution approaches with strictly defined implementation procedures such as judicial or legislative decisions.

Mediators encourage disputants to strictly define both the criteria and the steps to be used in implementing their decisions to mitigate this inherent weakness. Mediators usually assume that the degree to which compliance criteria and steps are defined determines how well substantive or procedural disputes due to misinterpretation of agreements can be avoided. Implementation steps clearly can be so strictly defined that they hinder more than help, and parties can use highly defined agreements to create problems for each other. Minor infractions can escalate into another full-scale conflict or to claims of compliance in bad faith, but this does not appear to be the norm.

Criteria for evaluating the success of implementation steps are similar to those used to evaluate a substantive settlement's effectiveness. Implementation steps should be (1) cost-efficient; (2) simple enough to be easily understood, yet detailed enough to prevent loopholes that cause later procedural disputes; (3) realistic in their demands on or expectations of parties; and (4) able to withstand public scrutiny, if necessary, of standards of fairness.

Monitoring the Performance of Agreements

Agreements that must be performed over time often have self-contained evaluation procedures and structures. Parties often strictly define standards and schedules of performance, and periodic meetings are designated to review compliance.

The performance agreement may be monitored by the parties themselves; by a joint committee composed of party representatives in complex multiparty disputes; or by a third party who is usually not the mediator (Straus, Clark, and Suskind, n.d.).

For example, in a complex dispute involving seventy city government employees, the parties established an ongoing monitoring committee to ensure that all participants complied with tasks, responsibilities, and a work schedule that had been established. An annual facilitation meeting was established in which all the parties were to report on their progress and reach additional decisions as new issues developed.

If a third party is to conduct monitoring effectively, the monitoring body must be composed of an individual or group that the disputants respect and trust. Its membership may vary according to the type of dispute. Community disputes may call for a large committee. Straus, Clark, and Suskind (n.d.) urge that "a committee of this type should include prominent community leaders, agency representatives, and technical advisors committed to the consensus that has been reached and to implementing the terms of the bargain. The membership of such a committee should be approved by all parties to the negotiation (and might include some of them)" (p. V-55).

In small interpersonal disputes or in intraorganizational conflicts, the monitor may be one or two individuals who are trusted by the disputing parties. For example, a divorcing couple designated relatives to monitor compliance with visitation terms.

Parties should clearly define the performance standards by which compliance is measured, the role of the monitors, and the limits of the third party's authority for monitoring to be effective. Careful definition of these variables minimizes problems with the monitoring committee's or individual's functioning at a later time.

Monitoring committees or individuals assigned to oversee an agreement's implementation may be given a degree of responsibility according to their function. Monitors may merely review progress and confirm or deny that compliance has occurred, or they may actually oversee implementation of the agreement.

A third role for monitors is to activate a grievance procedure conducted by the parties themselves or by a third party. A grievance procedure is a process disputants identify to manage disagreements that arise during or as a result of the settlement's implementation phase. The establishment of a grievance procedure is often a functional prerequisite for initial settlement. Parties often believe that a grievance procedure gives them a way to redress new problems, to modify agreement if necessary, and to avoid abandoning the entire settlement because of difficulty implementing a small component of the settlement.

Grievance procedures vary in form and process. The grievance procedure may be no more than a general agreement to reopen negotiations or return to mediation before pursuing other options such as litigation, or it may specifically define the method of settling a new conflict. Many labor-management, commercial, and interpersonal contracts provide for either renegotiation or binding arbitration to resolve a dispute. Courts are including or requiring similar procedures in some mediated settlements involving child custody.

Formalizing Settlement

The final steps of negotiating or mediating a dispute focus on formalizing the settlement. This depends on (1) the implementation of commitment-inducing procedures to enhance the probability of adherence and (2) some form of symbolic conflict termination activity.

Commitment-Inducing Procedures. Negotiated settlements endure not only because their implementation plans are effectively structured and meet the interests of the parties, but because parties are psychologically and structurally committed to the agreement. Negotiators and mediators should be particularly concerned in this last phase of negotiations with building in psychological and structural factors that will bind the parties to the negotiated settlement. Commitment-inducing procedures can be voluntary and self-executing practices or measures executed by an external party.

Self-Executing Commitment Procedures. Self-executing commitment procedures are activities initiated by the mediator

or the negotiators that enhance the probability that the disputants will comply with the settlement. Specific measures include

- Private oral exchange of promises between disputants in the
  mediator's presence.
- Private oral exchange of promises between disputants in the
  presence of authority figures or parties from whom the disputants would not like disapproval should they violate the
  agreement (relatives, workplace superiors, mentors, religious
  leaders, and so forth).
- Public oral exchange of promises (press release or press conference).
- Symbolic exchange of gifts, tokens of affection, first payments, early payment (Fisher, 1969), and so forth as an indication of bargaining in good faith and willingness to fulfill
  commitments.
- Symbolic gesture of friendship that demonstrates a willingness to take personal risk in order to implement the negotiated settlement.
- Informal written agreements (memorandums of understanding).
- Formal written agreements (contrasts, covenants, and so
  forth).

Self-executing activities to enhance commitment should
not be underestimated as means of ensuring compliance. Cook,
Rochl, and Shepard (1980, p. 56), in a study measuring agreement stability among mediated cases in neighborhood justice
centers with informal or unenforced commitment procedures,
found that of 315 respondents, between 81 and 95 percent of
all initiators stated that they had honored all the terms of the
agreement. Between 52.4 and 74.1 percent of a sample of 286
respondents in the same study agreed that the other party or
parties had honored all the terms of the agreement. Labor-
management settlements have much higher rates of compliance.
These data indicate that there is significant voluntary adherence to the terms of negotiated settlements.

Externally Executed Commitment Procedures. There are,

however, problems with voluntary compliance. Negotiators and mediators attempt to overcome these weaknesses with structural and external enforcement provisions that enhance commitment to agreements.

Parties often initiate mutually binding commitment procedures that, once established, are structural assurances that the settlement will be maintained. These structural assurances determine that performance of established settlements will be enforced and that the parties will not rely on promises of good faith or unpredictable pressures of public opinion. There are a variety of structural means of inducing commitment.

Legal Contracts. The most common way of assuring commitment to an agreement is to turn the settlement into a legal contract, an agreement between two or more parties that is judicially enforceable. Contracts are characterized by an exchange of consideration, a promise, or an act that one party agrees to perform in return for promises or acts from another. For example, several therapists wanted to establish a private group practice. One of their prospective partners was better known and earned a larger income. They wanted to resolve how they were to invest capital in the practice and the terms for payment of each partner. They hired a mediator to help resolve their differences over financial arrangements and to draft a memorandum of understanding that they would later ask a lawyer to formalize as a contract. All parties wanted to have their financial rights protected by a formal contract.

Legal contracts provide parties with judicial recourse should one or more parties fail to honor promises. Parties who have suffered what they consider a breach of contract can sue another party for redress of grievances. If the suit is successful, the plaintiff or party initiating the suit can receive one of three possible types of remedies (Straus, Clark, and Suskind, n.d., pp. V-58-59):

- Damages—financial compensation for the consequences of the defendant's breach.
- Recision of the contract—the court voids the contract and releases the plaintiff from his or her contractual obligations.

- Specific performance—the court orders the defendant to comply with the terms of the contract.

Negotiated agreements do not automatically become contracts enforceable under law. The enforceability of contracts depends both on the laws and rules of the legal jurisdiction in which they are promulgated and the forms that the contracts take.

Although a verbal agreement may be considered a legal contract, especially if conducted in the presence of witnesses, a written document is safer. Written documents that are to become contracts must contain at minimum (1) the *name* (or kind of contract); (2) the *parties,* including date and place of agreement; (3) *recitals* that detail the relationship of the parties and describe the contract's function; (4) the *promise clause,* which describes the exchanges the parties are to make; and (5) *closing* and *signatures* (Brown, 1955).

In addition to the contents of agreements listed above, the way that the settlement is written can make a difference in its acceptability and later compliance. Saposnek (1983, p. 102) identifies four additional factors to consider in drafting agreements: (1) "the clarity of the clauses," (2) "the degree of detail in the clauses," (3) "the balance of . . . concessions," and (4) "the attitude and perspective connoted."

Clarity of clauses refers to writing that details the agreement in such a way that diverse interpretations or misinterpretations are not possible. Mediators should work with the parties to clarify their intentions and then draft the memorandum of understanding, which will later become a contract, so that loopholes are eliminated. The mediator should ask himself or herself and the parties where later interpretation problems might exist and try to eliminate them in the initial draft.

Degree of detail in the clauses refers to the degree of specificity in the agreement. Usually, the more precise the terms of settlement, the less likely that interpretation conflicts will arise. In disputes in which the parties are highly emotional and in which there is little trust, strictly worded agreements that specify all details may be crucial in terminating the dispute.

In disputes in which the parties have a positive relationship, however, detail can, on occasion, be viewed as a disadvan-

tage. The detailed agreement may indicate lack of trust or inability to solve new problems that may arise in the future. One
party may also use the detailed agreement to harass the other so
that the terms are honored to an excessive degree. Fanatical adherence to an agreement's details can cause another party to
resist compliance and thus promote additional discord. The mediator, in drafting an agreement, must clearly consider the abilities of the parties to negotiate later details if they are specifically defined in the agreement, the degree of trust of the parties, and the tendency of the parties to use an agreement as a
weapon against their opponents. Specificity can either encourage or discourage future conflict.

Balance of concessions refers to the equity of exchanges
the parties conduct. The written agreement should clearly identify what is to be exchanged and written so that the settlement
does not appear one-sided. The document may alternate parties
from one exchange clause to the next to maintain the perception of balance. The exchanges need not be equal in number,
but the importance of the interests satisfied must be equivalent
to avoid renewed conflict. The mediator will often have to
search for the terms that will facilitate exchange.

On occasion, a psychological concession such as "John
acknowledges that Philip was proceeding in good faith" can be
traded for a specific substantive exchange. Equality of exchange
can also be maintained by mentioning both parties in the clause.
For instance: "Neither Paul nor Mary will make disparaging remarks about the other parent in the presence of the children."
By treating both equally, an acceptable exchange may be made.

A positive attitude and perspective are the final consideration in drafting an agreement. A settlement document is an affirmation of the willingness and ability of the parties to cooperate. The document should note and encourage cooperative attitudes and behaviors. In the recitals, the preamble to the section
that details precise exchanges, the mediator may include a
statement about the willingness of the parties to end the dispute, their commitment to bargaining in good faith, their dedi-
cation to complying with the agreement, and their commitment
to cooperative problem solving.

In a business relationship, the statement may read, "After

a period of bargaining in good faith, labor and management have agreed to the following terms that both expect to result in mutual benefit." In a custody case, the parents may affirm that "both of us love our children very much and want to arrange for a living situation that will provide them with stability and continuity with both parents, their extended families, their neighborhood, and friends. We make the following agreements because we believe that they are the best possible arrangements for the children and for each of us."

Judicial supervision is a second structural means to bind parties to agreements. In this instance, the disputing parties may have reached a negotiated settlement while they were in the midst of the judicial process. They have already filed to contest a case in court, but they reach an agreement before the judicial hearing. The parties then stipulate to the court the terms of their agreement and the court includes these terms in the final decree. This is common practice, for example, in mediated settlements of divorce. The court must legally mandate the separation, but the parties can negotiate and stipulate the terms of the divorce providing that they are not unconscionable. In this model of implementation, the parties take their agreement to their respective lawyers, who may change the wording to comply with legal standards and practice and then submit the document to the court as a stipulated settlement.

A second example of judicial supervision of negotiated settlements is in the selection of representatives to negotiations that will affect classes of people in complex disputes. Straus, Clark, and Suskind (n.d., pp. V-61-62) suggest that legislation could be passed that would establish "a process whereby a court supervises the selection of representatives to act as agents of recognized diffuse interests. This is precisely the procedure currently employed to appoint representatives in class action suits." A similar procedure has been used to appoint the guardian *ad litem* to represent a child's interests in mediated disputes involving termination of parental rights (Mayer, 1985).

Some negotiated settlements ultimately result in legislative action. Legislative bodies inherently use negotiation procedures in their daily operations, but in this case I refer to extraparliamentary negotiations.

Negotiated settlements that concern policy content have occasionally been recommended for inclusion in legislative bills. The National Coal Policy Project and the Air Quality Dialogues produced recommendations that were sent to Congress as the basis for subsequent bills (Murray, 1978; Carpenter and Kennedy, 1980). A negotiated settlement that is drafted into a bill and passed by a legislature attains status as a law. This law can be enforced by appointed officials, thus binding the parties to the terms of the negotiated settlement.

In some instances, negotiated settlements can be formalized and parties bound to adhere to agreements by executive action. This is especially the case when negotiations are sponsored by an elected or appointed executive. The negotiated settlement on flood control of the Snoqualmie River in Washington State and the negotiated environmental protection measures for the issuance of dredge and fill permits on Sanibel Island in Florida were both negotiated under the auspices of an executive office—the governor and the U.S. Army Corps of Engineers, respectively—and were subsequently approved by executives or the regulatory agency.

Parties can be structurally bound to implement settlement agreements by devising economic incentives or constraints that encourage adherence. Two economic approaches are common: agreeing on indemnification and performance bonds (Straus, Clark, and Suskind, n.d.).

Agreement on indemnification refers to a commitment by the parties to the amount and form compensation will take if one or more parties fail to comply with the terms of the agreement. Agreement on indemnification pressures the parties to adhere to the agreement because the costs of not doing so are specified before the breach of contract occurs. However, this succeeds only when conditions of violation are easily identified or measured. An example of agreement on indemnification occurred in the terms of settlement between a shopping center developer and residents of the surrounding neighborhood who might be adversely affected by the mall's presence. The developer agreed to protect land values of residential property owners by guaranteeing a sale of the property at a fair market price to be determined by an appraisal before the mall's construction.

The developer agreed to buy the properties or pay the difference between the actual selling price and the appraised value if the former price was lower. This offer was to be in effect for five years after the mall's construction (Baldwin, 1978).

Performance bonds are one step beyond agreements on indemnification in that they require a party to post a bond or reserve a specific sum of money to ensure that assets are available to pay for noncompliance. The use of performance bonds is an ancient method of ensuring adherence to agreements. Fifteenth- and sixteenth-century Japanese warlords required performance bonds in the form of relatives of their subordinates; the warlords held these relatives captive in their capital cities. If a functionary did not perform the established duties, his relatives would be put to death.

Performance bonds are usually funds held in escrow by a financial institution. The release of the bond is effected by an appointed neutral party who establishes if the terms of the settlement have been violated. This third party may be a monitoring committee established by the parties themselves or an independent, publicly recognized authority.

In the case described above, the shopping center developer agreed to construct a fourteen-foot-high landscaped berm as a boundary between the development and the residential neighborhood. A $100,000 letter of credit was deposited at a local bank to guarantee construction funds.

Symbolic Conflict Termination Activities. While some social processes have definite beginnings and endings, others have no precise points at which they may be said to have started or terminated. Coser (1967, p. 47) observes that social conflicts "follow a law of social inertia insofar as they continue to operate if no explicit provision for stopping their course is made by the participants. Whereas in a game, for example, the rules for the process include rules for its ending, in social conflict explicit provisions for its termination must be made by the contenders."

Whereas lower animals have devised regularized communication patterns to symbolize when a conflict should or has in fact ceased, human beings have not. Failure to define when a conflict has ended or when a negotiated settlement has been reached can result in extended unnecessary conflict. The forms that symbolic conflict termination activities take clearly depend on the context in which the dispute occurs and the degree of common acceptance of the symbols.

Negotiators and mediators often try to create activities that symbolically indicate termination of a conflict. Handshaking, formal signing procedures, toasts, and celebratory meals are common ways of jointly affirming the termination of a dispute. One mediator provided a divorcing couple with a bottle of champagne to acknowledge the end of a successful child custody negotiation. In a large community dispute over county land use, the participants celebrated successful completion of negotiations with a banquet that all parties attended.

Although negotiators themselves may identify and initiate some ritual act or behavior that terminates a conflict or negotiation, persisting antagonism or lack of innovative skills may inhibit their acceptance. Mediators can often help the parties to plan or structure termination ceremonies. Naturally, the mediator's initiative depends on the situation, what is appropriate for the parties, and the authority the parties have vested in him or her to design termination activities.

FIFTEEN

Strategies for Dealing with Special Situations

The previous chapters have focused for the most part on noncontingent mediator strategies. These interactions between the mediator and a single party or between the mediator and multiple disputants are always performed regardless of the type of dispute, the number or variety of issues, or the number of parties.

I now turn to contingent strategies and activities—interventions a mediator initiates to respond to specific or unusual problems posed by disputants, or to conditions that are not present in every negotiation. In examining contingent activities I will discuss interventions that are applicable to two-party conflicts and disputes involving negotiation teams and their constituents.

It is impossible to identify and describe all of the contingent strategies and activities mediators initiate to respond to specific situations. The most comprehensive listings to date of contingent strategies are those developed by Fisher (1978), Maggiolo (1972), and Wall (1981). There are, however, five categories of contingent strategies and activities that are more common: (1) the caucus technique, (2) responses to power discrepancies between the parties and forms of mediator influence, (3) mediator activities with multiperson negotiation teams, (4) techniques for working with teams when wider constituencies are involved, and (5) procedures for payment of the mediator.

Caucuses

In a caucus, the disputants are physically separated from each other and direct communication between parties is intentionally restricted. Caucuses are initiated in response to external forces that affect the negotiators or the general conflict situation, or to problems with issues, events, or dynamics between the parties in the joint session.

Factors That May Necessitate a Caucus. External forces—political, economic, and social and cultural pressures—can all create changes during negotiations. Internal dynamics or pressures present between negotiators that may require a caucus are more easily catalogued. There are three general categories of internal dynamics: (1) problems with the *relationship* of the parties or a team, (2) problems with the *negotiation process,* and (3) problems with *substantive issues* under discussion.

Numerous problems in the relationships between team members or opponents may encourage a party to initiate a caucus. The parties or the mediator may initiate a caucus to allow intense emotions to be vented in a setting that does not escalate differences between the parties, to clarify perceptions or misperceptions, to change unproductive or repetitive negative behavior, or to diminish and limit unhelpful communications.

Procedural problems may also call for a caucus. The parties or the mediator may initiate a private meeting to clarify or assess the negotiation procedure used by a party or jointly by disputants, to design new procedures for either negotiations within a group or joint negotiations, or to break the flow of negative procedures. Caucuses can also be called by parties or the mediator to explore substantive issues such as definition of interests, clarification of positions, identification of new offers, or weighing of another party's proposals.

In addition, mediators can use a caucus to

• Provide the parties (or the mediator) with a pause when the pressure to progress in joint session is too intense and is not promoting productive exchange.

• Refocus the motivation of the parties on why a settlement is important and what alternatives exist to negotiated settlement.

- Conduct reality testing of a party's proposals.
- Encourage a party in doubt whether he or she can satisfy his or her wants by pursuing present unsatisfactory tactics.
- Act as a sounding board for a party.
- Uncover confidential information that may not be revealed in joint session.
- Control communication between parties so that they focus exclusively on substance and eliminate all emotional communication as conveyed by speech or nonverbal signals.
- Educate an inexperienced disputant about negotiation procedures or dynamics.
- Prevent a party's premature concessions or commitment in joint session or to prevent adherence to an untenable or gard-line position.
- Develop a single-text negotiating document when parties are too numerous, issues too complex, or emotions too heated for face-to-face encounters.
- Develop settlement alternatives in an environment that separates the process of option generation from evaluation.
- Determine if an acceptable bargaining range has been established (or create one).
- Design proposals or offers that will later be brought to joint session.
- Test the acceptability of one party's proposal with another by presenting the offer as an option they have generated.
- Make appeals to common principles or superordinate goals.
- Express their perceptions of the situation and possibly make settlement option suggestions.

Timing. Caucuses can be initiated at almost any time in negotiations. Those initiated early in negotiations are usually called to vent emotions, design negotiating procedures, or identify issues. Caucuses held in the midst of negotiations usually focus on preventing premature commitment to a position, identifying interests, generating alternatives, and testing bargaining ranges. Caucuses held at the end of negotiations usually are designed to break deadlocks, develop or assess proposals, develop a settlement formula, or achieve a psychological settlement. Clearly there is no correct time to call a caucus because its necessity is highly dependent on the needs and skills of the individual negotiators and mediator. In some disputes there may be numerous caucuses while in other conflicts no caucuses may be used at all.

Mediators should take care not to schedule caucuses prematurely when parties are still capable of working productively in joint session, nor too late after unproductive hostile exchanges or behavior has hardened their positions.

Location. For caucuses to be most effective, they need to provide a genuine separation of the parties. This usually means separate rooms where parties neither see nor hear each other and where they feel safe to discuss issues or problems candidly. Mediators engaged in selecting the negotiation site should provide facilities that have spaces for caucuses. Inadequate sites may necessitate returning to a party's headquarters or to neutral ground where confidentiality can be assured.

Protocol. Although the caucus is a common technique mediators use to facilitate productive negotiations, there are few common standards for implementation that apply to all situations. Strategic factors faced by mediators who initiate a caucus include: (1) educating the parties about the technique, (2) overcoming resistance of the parties to separate meetings, (3) making the transition to the caucus, (4) deciding which party to caucus with first, (5) determining the duration of the caucus, (6) determining what is said in the caucus, and (7) facilitating the return to joint session.

Although the caucus is familiar to the experienced negotiator, novices may not be aware of its usefulness to negotiations. Mediators should explain at the start of negotiation and in their opening statements that caucuses may be held at some time during mediation, and that either the parties or the mediator may initiate such meetings.

Parties occasionally resist caucusing with a mediator. This fear may be associated with problems of confidentiality regarding information shared in caucus, fear of coalition formation between the mediator and the other party (Simmel, 1955), or political problems with constituencies that can result from private meetings (Maggiolo, 1972). The mediator does not want to create unnecessary barriers between himself or herself and one or more parties by pushing disputants to use an unacceptable technique. Mediators should explain in abstract reasons for the caucus before using the technique, and then allow disputants to later decide whether they will meet in private. If the parties do not consider a caucus necessary, the mediator should accede to their decision. However, if the mediator believes that failure to caucus will eventually lead to a breakdown in negotiations, he or she may refuse to mediate unless the parties meet separately.

Progress from joint session to caucus must be conducted smoothly so the flow of negotiations is not interrupted. Parties may initiate caucuses by formally calling for a time to meet privately or by asking for informal breaks. Mediators use the same procedures. When caucuses are formally called, a specific time duration for separate meetings is often jointly established. To make this transition, the mediator can say, "You have been discussing this issue together for quite a while. I believe that it might be helpful to take a break so that you can reflect on the available options in private. During this time I would like to speak to each of you privately and explore whether there is any additional room for movement. I estimate that I will talk to each of you for about ten minutes."

Mediators can use several informal guidelines to determine which party to meet first. In early caucuses, the mediator usually meets first with either the initiator of the dispute or the party that called for the caucus. Caucuses held later in negotiations follow a different rule. "If neither side has indicated any flexibility in their bargaining position, the first caucus should be held with the party appearing most inflexible. In such situations, some movement is necessary if negotiations are to proceed along fruitful lines" (Maggiolo, 1972, p. 53). If, however, the mediator perceives that one of the parties is extremely upset or is exhibiting emotional distance from or hostility toward the mediator, the intervenor may choose to caucus with that party first.

There is no general rule for duration of a caucus. Some mediators argue that private meetings should be held for as long as necessary to accomplish a desired purpose (Maggiolo, 1972), while other intervenors argue for brief time-specific meetings. Common practice and courtesy dictate that if a caucus is to take more than an hour, a formal break should be called in negotiations so that the party with whom the caucus is not being held is not kept waiting.

Regardless of how long a caucus with one party lasts, the mediator should confer with the other party before reconvening joint sessions. Meeting with the other party demonstrates equitable and impartial behavior and may also be an occasion to test options that have developed in the first caucus. Meeting with the other party can alleviate his or her curiosity about what has occurred in caucus, maintains the trust relationship between the intervenor and the parties, and helps educate disputants about what will transpire when they return to joint session.

Unless specified otherwise, conversations held between the mediator and disputants in caucus are considered confidential. Confidentiality generally encourages parties to be more candid in conversations with the mediator and enables them to explore options that entail more risk.

Mediators can play stronger roles as allies to parties in caucus and can be more supportive than is acceptable in joint session. This often enables parties to progress and to find acceptable options that they resisted in joint session. Care must be taken, however, not to form so close a relationship with the party that neutrality is lost or that the mediator cannot separate from the party and assume responsibility for the joint session.

Mediators can also be more firm with parties in caucus than they can in joint session. Mediators can perform reality testing, propose hypothetical options, and question a party's judgment in caucus, which they cannot do in joint session. The mediator in caucus can protect the negotiator's integrity while asking firm questions and creating doubt about the viability of adhering to hard-line positions.

Information shared with mediators in caucus is often crucial to reaching agreement with other disputants. The confidentiality barrier often inhibits this information from being used with other parties to affect agreement. The mediator can pursue several strategies to use the information. First, he or she may directly obtain the party's permission to use the information with the other party by explaining how it will be used and what benefits could result.

Second, the mediator may explain that he or she would like to talk with the other party about information discussed in the caucus and ask, "Is there anything that we have talked about that you would not like me to disclose?" This process allows the party to specifically identify what he or she wishes to remain confidential and gives the mediator the authority to disclose other information as he or she sees fit.

Third, the mediator may take an idea generated with one disputant and claim it as his or her own when talking with another disputant. This conceals the proposal's connection with the other party—making it perhaps more acceptable—and enables the mediator to test a possible settlement without committing any of the parties to it. If both parties agree to a solution but do not realize that the other is in agreement, the mediator must then decide who is to propose the solution, and how it is to be framed.

It is crucial that the party who proposes a solution developed in caucus owns it as his or her own and is not presenting it to do a favor for the mediator. The party must own and be able to defend the offer if he or she is to present it in joint session. This is true whether or not the mediator knows that the proposal is acceptable to the other side. The mediator may otherwise be accused of forcing his or her own preferences on the disputants.

During caucuses with the parties, the mediator should determine how the parties will be brought together again in joint session. Factors to consider include how to (1) explain the purpose and results of the caucus, (2) determine which party speaks first after the caucus, and (3) decide how offers will be made after the caucus. Many of these strategic questions must be answered while the caucuses are in session so that the mediator can prepare the parties for their next moves.

While there are no firm rules for mediator and negotiator activities that result from a caucus, there are some general guidelines. Parties with greater power are able to make the first move after a caucus without losing integrity or advantage. Parties with offers contingent on another party's offer should speak only after the first offer has been made. Simultaneous offers or incremental alternating offers are often in order. Mediators should take care to sequence speakers to ensure that the order of presentation does not prejudice a party's interests or so that they do not inadvertently offer any premature concessions due to a mistimed offer.

Caucuses and Manipulation. Although the caucus is one of the most common and effective contingent strategies, it is not without problems. Caucuses provide mediators with the greatest opportunity to manipulate parties into an agreement because disputants do not have the advantage of face-to-face communication to test the accuracy of information exchanged.

Keltner (1965, pp. 74–75) notes that "in separating the parties during negotiations the mediator establishes himself as the main channel of communication between the parties. For example, in a separate session with the company the mediator expresses doubts that the offer which he is asked to carry to the union will be accepted, thereby *minimizing* the possibility of acceptance. Shortly thereafter he will meet the union and will *maximize* the desirability of acceptance of the proposal. This control and manipulation of the channel of communication and the introduction into it, thereby, of evaluative material provides him with some strength in bringing the parties closer together toward an area of agreement."

The ability to control, manipulate, suppress, or enhance data, or to initiate entirely new information, gives the mediator an inordinate level of influence over the parties. The ethics of such control and the proper role of the intermediary are hotly debated topics among mediators (Stevens, 1963). Young (1972, p. 57) observes that "it is difficult for an intermediary to engage in such manipulative activities without exhibiting some degree of partiality among the original players, either explicitly or implicitly. This raises a variety of problems concerning the acceptability of partial behavior on the part of intermediaries. And it may generate additional tactical rigidities in the interactions among the original players if they become concerned with actual or perceived partiality on the part of an intermediary."

An additional problem with caucuses arises with tensions pushing toward disclosure of information and confidentiality. The majority of mediators treat communications in the caucus as confidential. Parties occasionally reveal information to the mediator that may place him or her in a potentially compromising position. For example, a husband may tell a mediator that he has a hidden bank account that his wife does not know about and that he does not want to include in the financial settlement, or a party may acknowledge to a mediator that he or she has lied or made a false claim in the joint session that will adversely affect the outcome for the other party. These examples illustrate how the mediator, by using a caucus and ensuring confidentiality, places himself or herself in an ethical bind. Should confidentiality be the mediator's highest value or should full disclosure of information relative to a fair settlement of the dispute have primacy? There is probably not one right answer to this question, but because of problems created by the intervenor's commitment to confidentiality, many mediators take great care when using the caucus. Some mediators inform the parties what they are willing or not willing to hear and where the limits of confidentiality end. For example, several ethical codes or model standards require that the mediator disclose the limits of confidentiality at the beginning of the mediation session and carefully describe when confidentiality will be broken. Lack of full financial disclosure, child abuse, or imminent physical danger, for example, are limits to confidentiality defined in the "Model Standards of the Association of Family and Conciliation Courts" (1984).

Other mediators refuse to ensure confidentiality in caucuses and use them merely to discuss issues without the tension induced by the physical presence of the other party. While this procedure is an exception, not the rule, it does protect the mediator from being placed in a bind between confidentiality and revelation of information that was requested to be held in confidence.

Regardless of its susceptibility to confidentiality problems and manipulation, the caucus remains one of the major contingent mediator strategies. In many disputes, settlement would be impossible if separate meetings were not conducted.

Mediator Power and Influence

Ideally, all disputes should be resolved by rational dialogue and goodwill. However, mistrust and power imbalances prevent this in a significant number of conflicts. Parties often resort to the exercise of power to determine the outcome of negotiations. Mediators, too, use various means of influence to change the dynamics of bargaining. For mediators to be effective, they must know how to manage the means of influence and power the parties exercise and know how to exercise pressure themselves.

Power or *influence* is the capability of a person or group to modify the outcome, benefits, or costs of another in the context of a relationship (Thibaut and Kelly, 1959). The capacity to enhance the outcome for another party depends on the exercise of various means of influence that either discourage or encourage the possibility of various options. Mediators, although neutral in relationship to the parties and generally impartial toward the substantive outcome, are directly involved in influence activities designed to move disputants toward settlement. In this section I will examine two topics related to the mediator's exercise of power or influence. First, I will identify the forms that mediator influence takes, and second, I will explore how this influence may be exercised when parties have (1) equal or (2) unequal power.

Influence is usually designed to change the viewpoint or condition of another. Means of influence can be placed on a continuum that indicates the amount of leverage or pressure that is being applied to encourage change and the degree of directiveness of the initiator. Usually directiveness and pressure are directly proportional to each other. Thus on one end of the continuum the means of influence may exert low pressure to change, and the person using the leverage is not very directive. On the other end, the pressure may be intense, and the initiator is extremely directive. It is possible to identify here a continuum of forms of influence, how much leverage they apply to another person, and how directive the initiative is.

Mediators generally use twelve forms of influence to incline parties toward agreement. I will examine each of these means and explore how they fit on a continuum of pressure to change attitudes or actions of parties.

Management of the Negotiation Process. This means of influence refers to the intervenor's control over the sequence of negotiation steps, problem-solving steps, and the process of managing specific agenda items. The mediator should choose, based on the situation, parties, and issues in dispute, whether to have limited influence and make few procedural suggestions (either general or specific); to be moderately influential and provide some structure; or to be highly influential with much directiveness and a highly detailed procedure over which parties have a low degree of control. Kolb (1983) notes this continuum in her description of labor-management mediators who were "orchestrating," those mediators who made less directive procedural interventions in comparison with the "deal-makers," those who were highly directive and controlled the process. A similar continuum regarding directiveness is also common in family disputes. Coogler (1978) illustrates the more directive end of the continuum, and Stulberg (1981a) is probably at the other end.

Communication Between and Within Parties. The mediator can manage both communication behavior and structure in negotiations. Communication behavior can be managed by using active listening and reframing techniques as clarification and problem definition tools. The structure of communication may be modified by asking the parties to meet together, to talk directly to each other, to talk only to the mediator in each other's presence, or to caucus and communicate only through the intervenor. In caucus, the mediator has extensive control over what will or will not be communicated and can frame information exchange so that it will most likely be accepted. The mediator can be highly influential by being very directive about communicative behavior or structure, or may play a much less directive role.

Physical Setting and Negotiations. Mediators may modify the physical setting to encourage parties to settle. Seating arrangements, table shape, room size, availability of caucusing space, and physically removing negotiations from the scene of conflict can all affect outcome. Highly directive intervenors may use one or many of the above activities to influence settlement.

Timing in Negotiations. Timing refers to when negotiations are started, duration of sessions, the imposition or removal of deadlines for settlement, and timing of specific communications and offers. Mediators can be directive or nondirective in their control of timing depending on their assessment of the parties and the situation.

Information Exchanged Between Parties. Negotiation involves a constant flow of information among the parties and the mediator. The content and form in which information is given, however, varies depending on the situation. Fisher (1978, pp. 141-142) developed an "asking ladder" that arranges how information is given or received based on the initiator's degree of directiveness. The ladder ranges from requests for information to general suggestions, specific suggestions, concrete proposals, and demands in a sequence of directive information exchange. Mediators usually make less directive moves about information and usually ask questions and make suggestions rather than make demands or force parties toward specific substantive conclusions. Mediators may, however, play more directive roles in assisting parties to identify what information is needed for exchange, in what form it should be, and how it will best be heard or received by other parties. Mediators may also occasionally refer parties to sources of needed information.

Associates of the Parties. Associational influence refers to people who are colleagues or friends of disputants who by their opinions or actions can influence the attitudes or behavior of the parties. Mediators inherently exercise associational influence on parties because disputants would not accept association with them if they did not trust or expect to be influenced by them. The degree of mediator associational influence depends on a variety of factors—personality, credibility, experience, ability to present a logical argument, and receptivity of the parties to such influence. Mediators should decide how much they want to exercise their associational influence by how much they voice their opinions on topics of concern to parties.

Associates also include friends, family members, other members of a disputing group, constituents, colleagues, and others who can influence parties' opinions. Mediators should assess when these associates should be included or excluded from the negotiations in order to induce settlement. The trusted words of a professional colleague or the involvement of a stepparent or grandparent in family negotiations may be all that is needed to change the dynamics of the dispute and incline the parties toward settlement. The mediator can often engineer the form and effect of associational influence.

Expert Influence. Mediators can often direct the use of people with particular expertise or areas of knowledge and influence the parties to settle. Mediators can play either directive or nondirective roles in identifying the need for substantive, procedural, or psychological experts; encouraging their use; and proposing procedures for selecting them.

Authority Influence over Parties. Authority refers to a widely recognized right or legitimate power to exercise influence or make a decision. Authority can be vested either in an institution or in a person's formal role. Mediators may exercise some authority when they enter a dispute as a result of their affiliation with a mediation agency or, occasionally, a governmental body. Mediators who work for the Federal Mediation and Conciliation Service or those who are connected with a court or district attorney's office, for example, may be able to exercise more influence than the independent mediator without institutional affiliation because of the prestige of their institutional connections. Parties may defer to the mediator on procedural and sometimes substantive issues because they acknowledge his or her skill, knowledge, and legitimate authority to be involved in a dispute.

Mediators may also call on other authorities to influence negotiators. They may appeal to a party's constituencies, superiors, judges, creditors, custody evaluators, or others to exert pressure on parties to settle. When a mediator obtains outside authorities, he or she is highly directive. Although the mediator's goal may be gentle persuasion of a difficult party, an external authority's pressure is almost tantamount to coercion. Mediators should take extreme care when involving authority figures directly in negotiations.

Habits of Disputants. Many people in conflict have long-standing relationships in which patterns of behavior have been established. Business colleagues, lawyers, teachers, students, and spouses all develop routines that, for better or worse, are accepted as normal.

Mediators can often appeal to personal habits to reach settlement. Agreements to continue to follow a common business practice for accounting or to allow a mother to continue buying clothes for her child after she and the father have divorced may influence parties to agree. Agreement to ratify some element of the status quo is often the first decision that parties may reach.

Parties' Doubt and Unintended Consequences. Probably no negotiated agreement is ever reached without some doubt on the part of the parties that a better settlement might have been obtained if they had been firmer, had bargained longer, or had pursued another means of dispute resolution. Doubt, however, was their rationale for pursuing a negotiated settlement. If they had been certain that they could have reached a more satisfactory agreement by negotiating in a different way or pursuing another approach to dispute resolution, they probably would have done so.

Mediators often use doubt to influence parties toward settlement. Doubt about the viability of a position or settlement option can be raised or explored in joint session, where both parties must bear the potential negative consequences, but more often the mediator raises doubt in one or more parties in a caucus. By raising questions about potential outcomes that the party may not prefer, the mediator can often moderate a party's position and incline them toward mutually acceptable settlement possibilities. For example, a mediator might ask:

- Do you think you can win in court (or other public setting such as before a commission or in the legislature)?

- How certain are you? 90 percent? 75 percent? 50 percent?
- What risk are you willing to take?
- What if you lose?
- What will your life be like then?
- What impact do you think your victory in court (or other arena) will have on your ongoing relationship with the other party?
- Will you ever be able to work together again?
- Who else might be affected?
- What would they think of your position?
- Would you be proud to publicly announce this stance?
- Would others whom you respect feel it is reasonable?
- If you were in the other party's place and this proposal were made to you, would you accept it?
- Could you accept it over the long run?

Through careful questioning that may vary in degree of directiveness, the mediator may begin to create doubt in a party's mind about the feasability of his or her adherence to an option. If misused, this technique obviously approaches manipulation. This means of influence raises questions about the ethics of mediator influence.

Rewards or Benefits. Mediators usually only indirectly influence the rewards that a party receives as a result of negotiation. The other party or parties to the dispute are usually the grantor of those benefits. The major exception to this rule is in international disputes in which the mediator is a representative of a powerful interest or nation and has resources at his or her command to bestow benefits such as foreign aid, military assistance, or recognition if the parties settle.

Mediators do, however, have some indirect rewards to offer the parties as settlement inducements. The mediator's friendship, respect for a person or point of view, interest in a party's personal well-being, or affirmation of how a point was settled can all induce a disputant to agree. The mediator's relationship with the parties is often the only positive reward that he or she can offer in negotiations. If the disputants value this, they may initiate activities that will encourage the mediator to continue his or her positive response.

Another indirect means of rewarding a party is to identify the benefits that the disputant could receive as a result of a settlement and to help him or her visualize what it would be like to have that settlement. Mediators can verbally project what it would mean to have the conflict settled and the tangible benefits from the settlement. If the disputants perceive the mediator's vision as adequate reward for settlement, they may move forward to agreement.

Coercive Influence. Coercive influence refers to the use of force to change another's opinion or behavior against his or her will. Coercive influence depends on decreasing a party's choices for settlement and then increasing the damage that the party will incur if he or she does not accept the designated outcome. Influence in this case is usually extremely directive toward a negotiator's desired behavior. Because mediation is voluntary and the mediator serves the parties, he or she usually has few direct coercive techniques available to influence disputants. Exceptions include some court-related mediators who are empowered by statute to make recommendations to the judge if the parties cannot settle; intervenors practicing med-arb, a mediation-arbitration hybrid in which the parties agree to allow the intervenor to mediate until an impasse occurs, at which time the mediator becomes an arbiter and decides the conflict's outcome; and international mediators with powerful superiors that can damage recalcitrant parties.

There are, however, several indirect coercive techniques that may incline the parties toward settlement. The mediator's display of impatience or displeasure, as indicated by nonverbal communication or verbal statements, may "coerce" a party to move toward agreement. This may be especially true when a party wants the intervenor's respect or wants to maintain the respect of his or her group and when this respect may be eroded by continuing an unpopular course of action. Mediator or peer approval or withdrawal of approval can be very important in moderating hard-line positions.

The mediator's most direct and coercive recourse to influence parties is to threaten to or to actually withdraw from negotiations. This is the ultimate act of disapproval and denial of service to the parties. In one case, a mediator believed that the

parties were not negotiating in good faith and were delaying settlement. The mediator announced that he wanted to terminate
his participation because the parties did not seem to be making
progress. He offered the parties his business card, told them to
call him when they were ready to talk, and walked toward the
door. He never reached it. The parties called him back and settled immediately.

Threats of withdrawal or actual withdrawal are risky for
the mediator and the parties. They may precede a breakdown
in negotiations. Threats to withdraw succeed only if the parties
consider the mediator unexpendable, and only if they believe
the threat. If this is not the case, they may even welcome the
mediator's departure. Mediators should exercise care in using
this technique because it can backfire and leave the intervenor
out of the negotiations or may, even if it works, create resent-
ment or later resistance from the parties.

*Exercise of Power and Influence and Mediator Interven-
tion.* Parties exercise the same twelve forms of influence or
power. However, they are usually much more overt, directive,
and coercive in their means of influencing each other than the
intervenor and have specific substantive gains that they wish to
achieve. Exercising power, however, may or may not achieve
desired results.

Power is not a characteristic of an organization or person
but is an attribute of a relationship. A party's power is directly
related to the power of an opponent. Power relations generally
occur in two forms: *symmetric,* or equal, and *asymmetric,* or
unequal, levels of influence (Bagozzi and Dholakia, 1977).

Symmetrical Power Relations. Practical experience and
social psychological experimentation indicate that when negotiators have an equal or symmetrical power relationship they behave more cooperatively, function more effectively, and behave
in a less exploitive or manipulative manner than when there is
an asymmetrical power relationship (Rubin and Brown, 1975).
Disputes in which parties have roughly equal power facilitate
the use of mediation techniques to achieve settlement.

Mediators, working with parties with equal power, usually attempt to improve the cooperative behavior of the parties,
enhance the perception of equal power in the relationship,

and limit the expression of coercive power in negotiations. The most common influence problems that disputants with equal power have are (1) perceptual difficulties between the parties about symmetry and (2) the negative residue of emotions resulting from past exercise of coercive power within the relationship.

Perception of power symmetry is usually dependent on the ability to measure or project the potential outcome of a dispute if one or more parties decide to exercise their power. For example, if two people contest a piece of property, and both have unlimited funds, equally qualified lawyers, and case law to back up their argument, the perception of each other's power may be relatively easy to determine. This is true because the variables by which power is measured—capital, personnel, and case law—are the same.

However, what if the sources of power are different so that the quantities of power and even the standards of measurement are not the same? For example, in some labor-management negotiations, labor must assess management's ability to carry on production with the prospect of a strike, management's staffing capabilities, product stockpiles, and public demand for the product. The employer must assess the number of employees who are willing to strike, the assets available to the union and its allies to sustain a strike, the climate of public opinion that might support the strikers, and so forth. In this instance, the basis of power for the parties is different as are the variables used to measure the power of the parties.

When parties have different bases of influence, a power assessment problem often develops. This often results in a breakdown in negotiations. Parties return to negotiations only after they have exercised and tested their power and have developed a more accurate assessment of the power of the other parties. For example, many divorcing spouses attempt to negotiate issues in dispute, fail, and hire lawyers. A large proportion of these cases settle before the case actually opens. The act of testing the strength and will of an opponent to go to court may be an important step in developing an accurate perception of another disputant's power.

Unfortunately, testing power often involves the exercise

of coercive power and tends to produce negative effects on the ability of the parties to negotiate. Even in symmetrical relations, exercise of power—especially coercive power—may lead to increased resistance to settle or an irreversible breakdown of negotiations.

Mediators in disputes in which parties have equal power relationships, but symmetry is hard to determine because of different power bases or measures, should attempt to change the perceptions of each party toward the other's power without encouraging the parties to resort to coercion.

Changing a perception about power, especially when the parties have symmetrical relationships, is usually accomplished by developing an accurate power assessment mechanism or changing conditions so that power is irrelevant. In the first case mediators can privately encourage a party to list his or her own sources or bases of power and then identify the costs and benefits of exercising it (Fisher, 1969; Bellows and Moulton, 1981). The same procedure should then be followed for assessing the opponent's power. The process may be repeated, if necessary, with the other side. A cross-reference of costs and potential outcomes will usually incline parties toward a mutual recognition of symmetrical power relations.

The second technique requires parties to shift their focus from power relationships to interests. By calling attention to the process of how needs can be satisfied, the mediator can persuade the parties to avoid emphasis on how they can force the opposing party into submission.

Asymmetrical Power Relations. Although symmetrical power relations seem to be the optimal relationship for effective bargaining, this type of relationship is not the norm for many disputes. Parties differ in the form or amount of power or influence they possess in relation to one another.

Mediators in disputes in which parties have asymmetrical or unequal power relationships face two kinds of problems: (1) perceptual problems—situations in which the stronger party believes that the weaker party has equal power, or situations in which the weaker party has in inflated view of his or her strength; and (2) extremely asymmetrical relationships—situations in which a party is in a much weaker position, and both parties know it.

Mediators work with both weaker and stronger parties to minimize the negative effects of unequal power. When a mediator encounters a situation in which the balance of power is unequal, the weaker party bluffs about his or her power, and the stronger party accepts the bluff, the mediator should usually meet with the bluffing party to educate him or her about the potential costs of being found out or called on to carry out the bluff. The other party's discovery of the deception can lead to a deterioration in relationships and may lead to retaliation if the victim of the bluff is the stronger party.

If the intervenor is successful in convincing the party that the costs of bluffing are too high, the mediator and the party should jointly search for a way to retreat from the bluff or minimize the importance of power dynamics in the context of the negotiations. Retreating from a bluff or minimizing the effects of bluff can often be achieved by ceasing to make threatening statements or false promises and obscuring the explicitness of statements describing the consequences of disagreement.

In power situations in which parties appear to have an asymmetrical relationship and the bases of power are different, the mediator may attempt to obscure the strength of influence of both parties. Mediators can pursue this strategy to create doubt about the actual power of the parties by questioning the accuracy of data, the credibility of experts, the capability of mobilizing coercive power, or the degree of support from authority figures. These techniques will prevent the parties from ascertaining the balance of power. If a party cannot determine absolutely that he or she has more power than another, he or she usually does not feel free to manipulate or exploit an opponent without restraint.

By far the most difficult problem mediators face regarding power relationships is the instance in which the discrepancy between the strength of means of influence is extremely great. The mediator, because of his or her commitment to neutrality and impartiality, is ethically barred from direct advocacy for the weaker party, yet is also ethically obligated to assist the parties in reaching an acceptable agreement.

Wall (1981) argues that the mediator's primary task is to manage the power relationship of the disputants. In unequal power relationships the mediator may attempt to balance power. "To strike the balance, the mediator provides the necessary power underpinnings to the weaker negotiator—information, advice, friendship—or reduces those of the stronger" (p. 164).

If this strategy is adopted, the mediator should initiate moves to assist the weaker party in mobilizing the power he or she possesses. The mediator should not, however, directly act as an organizer to mobilize or develop new power for the weaker disputant unless the mediator has gained the stronger party's approval. To act as a secret advocate puts the mediator's impartiality and effectiveness as a process intervenor at risk.

Empowering moves may include assisting the weaker party in obtaining, organizing, and analyzing data and identifying and mobilizing his or her means of influence; assisting and educating the party in planning an effective negotiation strategy; aiding the party to develop financial resources so that the party can continue to participate in negotiations; referring a party to a lawyer or other resource person; and encouraging the party to make realistic concessions.

Wall (1981) notes that stronger parties often welcome a mediator's involvement in power balancing. The mediator can assist a weaker party who is unorganized and unable to negotiate in preparing to engage in a productive exchange that will benefit both parties. This role of the mediator as organizer has been practiced in husband-wife disputes (Haynes, 1981), labor-management conflicts (Perez, 1959), community disputes (Lincoln, 1976), large-scale environmental contests (Dembart and Kwartler, 1980), and interracial disputes (Kwartler, 1980).

Multiperson Negotiation Teams

When negotiations are between more than two disputants, interpersonal dynamics become exponentially more complex. This section will detail one format for additional negotiators: the formation of a team. The next section of the chapter will deal with an extension or expansion of the team and will describe mediator moves designed to assist negotiators in multi-party disputes.

A negotiation team is a group composed of two or more people who share similar experiences, interests, likes, dislikes, or sentiments. In negotiations, teams composed of several people try to gain the best advantage for their collective group.

Basis for Team Formation and Mediator Moves. People form teams to negotiate issues of concern for a variety of reasons. A team may be a coalition of weaker parties who are trying to increase their influence. A team may also be a group of people who want to verbally represent a broader viewpoint or include more diversity of opinion or expertise than a sole negotiator. Teams may also be selected for negotiation because the team members do not trust one person to negotiate for their interests. Negotiation teams are also formed to provide a more efficient representative body for wider constituencies such as community groups or labor unions.

By the time a mediator is asked to assist in a dispute, the parties have usually already formed teams. When this occurs, the mediator must work with the people whom the parties have selected. Occasionally, however, a mediator may enter a dispute before team formation has occurred. When this occurs, a mediator may significantly assist disputants in forming negotiation teams.

Although the mediator cannot and should not select the negotiating team's members, he or she may suggest criteria for selecting team members. A team member should understand the various issues in the dispute, be able to identify and articulate his or her own interests and those of other team members, and represent the concerns of a broader constituency if one exists. Other team members and the wider constituency should have confidence in each team member so that agreements reached at the negotiating table will be credible and acceptable to those represented by the team (McSurely, 1967). Rapport, credibility, and ability to deal with people who are on an opposing team are also possible criteria. A team that selects people who cannot negotiate or who will be unacceptable to the other side is useless. It makes no sense for negotiations to break down over a question of personnel if competing interests are the principal issues that divide people.

In addition to suggesting general criteria for the selection of team members, the mediator may also initiate a process of team formation. In initiating negotiations between black and white student groups in a highly polarized and volatile school desegregation dispute, Lincoln (1976) dared each group to select representatives and see if they could achieve desired results. Fear that their groups would not be good enough negotiators to reach a settlement and would embarrass them spurred the youths to select representative teams and negotiate with the other students.

Although most mediators do not play this extreme catalytic role, they can make some significant procedural suggestions. Mediators can often suggest the number of representatives appropriate to the dispute, the type of expertise that would be beneficial, and a decision-making process for selecting team members. One mediator of a complex housing dispute reported that she found scores of disgruntled renters ready to meet with their landlord. The mediator determined that an undifferentiated group would not be able to bargain effectively with the landlord. She also saw that the disorganized state and raucous manner of the tenants might even provoke more resistance from the landlord. The mediator, who had been called by the tenants and accepted by the landlord, refused to mediate the case until the tenants organized themselves and selected a bargaining team. After suggesting possible criteria for team membership, including some listed above, the mediator suggested a specific number of representatives and a manner of deciding whom to appoint.

Team Dynamics and Mediation Strategies. Once the disputants have selected a team, the mediator should carefully analyze and assess the group's crucial dynamics, individual and group interests, personal behavior patterns of team members and how they interact with people on their side or with the opposing team, internal team power relationships, and team decision-making structure.

A negotiating team, when viewed by an opponent, may appear monolithic, unified, and unshakable in its commitment to a stated position or alternative. Usually, however, this is not the case. Negotiation teams are composed of distinct people, and each has different interests and may vary in strength of commitment to his or her own needs, those of other team members, or group interests as a whole. Mediators should carefully assess the spectrum of interests within a team to determine the potential for noncompetitive interests both within each team and between the teams.

Negotiation styles of team members are closely related to their interests (Frost and Wilmot, 1978; Rubin and Brown, 1975). Mediators should assess the degree of collaborative behavior against the degree of competitive behavior within the team. Colosi and Berkeley (1980) identify three types of team members: stabilizers, nonstabilizers, and quasi-mediators. Stabilizers are those committed to negotiations and a settlement, often at any cost. Nonstabilizers may not be committed to negotiations, may be disruptive, and may be unwilling to settle regardless of the offer. The quasi-mediator wants to build a realistic and workable settlement that meets as many needs as possible for all the parties. The quasi-mediator is the mediator's ally and will work to forge an agreement. The allies may alternately support each other to bolster their respective proposals or activities.

Mediators should find quasi-mediators with moderate interests and collaborative styles within a team, because the intervenor will need assistance in moving the team toward agreement.

Negotiating team members also have diverse means of influence or power that they bring to the negotiation table. Mediators should assess the influence relationships that exist between team members in an effort to understand internal team dynamics. Mediators should use the power-analysis techniques discussed earlier—formal positions and reputational and decision-making models—to determine who has influence within a group.

The group's decision-making methods are closely related to the power relationships within the team. In general, negotiation teams tend to make decisions by (1) *fiat* or *hierarchical decision making* and (2) *consensus.* The two procedures often reflect the organizational structure of the team and also reflect power relationships between team members.

Hierarchical decision making occurs when one or more team members make a decision that is accepted or deferred to by team members on the basis of the decision maker's legitimate authority, coercion, or ability to grant benefits to other team members. This decision-making model is characteristic of hierarchically organized institutions such as government agencies, businesses, or bureaucratically organized groups. This decision-making process succeeds only when adherence of team members to the decision maker's choices can be ensured by the means of influence listed above. If allegiances cannot be ensured, the team's cohesion will suffer greatly under the stress of joint sessions.

The second method of decision making within a team is consensus. Consensus involves the synthesis of ideas and interests of all team members to form a broad, general agreement on issues in question. Consensus may be used because team members hold a philosophical commitment to the process, or it may be the only functional way that the group can reach agreement. In negotiations in which team members are representatives of independent groups, or in which one group is neither dominant in terms of power nor recognized as the central decision maker, consensus may be the only way a group can develop a coalition with a common purpose.

 Voting is not an effective procedure for decision making within teams. A vote taken within a team may cause irreparable divisions that may result in decreased team cooperation in joint sessions, direct collaboration with an opponent, or rejection of the negotiation process itself. Divisions caused by voting and majority rule can only be avoided if the team makes decisions by consensus or one party has either legitimate authority or coercive power to make binding decisions for the team.

Negotiators are often not familiar with appropriate internal decision-making procedures. Mediators may be called on to be process advisers to in-team negotiations, and may even mediate a dispute within a dispute. The inability of a negotiation team to manage internal conflict and make group decisions can be as detrimental to successful negotiations as an impasse in joint session.

The mediator's role in aiding negotiation teams in making decisions may vary significantly—from that of an educator who informs the parties about the types of appropriate decision-making procedures for in-team negotiations, to a process observer who makes an occasional procedural suggestion to assist parties in bargaining more effectively, and an actual facilitator of team meetings (Kolb, 1983). The role of the mediator in in-team meetings may vary considerably and often depends on the team's knowledge of and sophistication in internal negotiation processes, the amount of commonality between interests of team members, and the facilitative skills of the team members. In community disputes in which negotiators are appointed informally, have little experience working together, and may have little or no experience in either in-team or joint session negotiations, the mediator may play a significant role in internal team bargaining. He or she may both educate the team members about how to negotiate and facilitate meetings (Doyle and Straus, 1976; Coover, Deacon, Esser, and Moore, 1977).

Types of Team Negotiations. The addition of negotiators to a dispute not only increases the complexity of in-team negotiation, but also increases the range of possible interactions between people on two or more opposing teams. In two-person negotiations, the two central actors are the primary channels through which communications occur. Additional participants not only increase the amount and complexity of the communications between two or more opposing sides, but also raise the problem of coordinating communication. Lincoln identifies three types of negotiation that occur at meetings of disputants in which each party has multiple representation (Lincoln, n.d.).

Bilateral bargaining occurs when there are two sides and communication occurs primarily between the spokespeople of the two groups. Bilateral bargaining is often considered "official" communication between the teams, as it is most likely to express either the consensus of the teams or the team position as expressed by the hierarchical decision maker.

Alongside the official communications that pass between the teams may be two types of unilateral bargaining. *Unilateral conciliatory bargaining* usually occurs between the quasi-mediators on negotiating teams or between members of opposing teams that have some common interest or bond. Conciliatory bargaining is usually conducted either publicly or privately with the negotiating team's explicit or implicit consent. The goal of conciliatory bargaining is to find a formula or alternative that will satisfy both parties. The conciliatory bargainer is not primarily motivated by personal gain.

In contrast to conciliatory bargaining, *unilateral vested-interest bargaining,* or under-the-table bargaining, is almost always motivated by a particular negotiator's drive for personal gain. This objective may even be sought at the expense of the interests of fellow team members. Vested-interest bargaining is almost always conducted covertly, although occasionally there may be a public sellout by one member of a team.

Mediators can play an important role in facilitating bilateral bargaining as well as conciliatory bargaining and inhibiting unilateral vested-interest bargaining. Mediators can influence effective bilateral negotiations by assisting and supporting the major spokespersons for each side. Kolb (1983) notes that in disputes in which the spokespersons are skilled in negotiation, the mediator need only affirm and support the spokesperson in the activities that he or she is pursuing. In doing so, the mediator informs the team that their leader is on the right track. In cases in which the spokesperson is not an expert negotiator, the mediator may have to coach the spokesperson on how to carry out his or her role as the central negotiator. This coaching may include process suggestions, education about specific tactics, and questions to help clarify interests and goals.

Mediators also help team members communicate to the other team more clearly. By using some of the communication skills mentioned in earlier chapters the mediator can help promote more effective dialogue. Mediators can also assist teams in conducting conciliatory bargaining by encouraging and aiding quasi-mediators to develop consensus within teams. Quasi-mediators may also be encouraged to communicate messages to the other team that promote positive relationships as well as moderate proposals that meet the interests of all parties. Mediators can often work directly with quasi-mediators to create bargaining ranges or sets of acceptable alternatives.

Teams with Constituents

Members of negotiating teams often do not make the final decision in a dispute. Teams are frequently responsible to other parties who have not been present at negotiations. Individuals or groups that have final authority to ratify a decision reached through negotiations are usually (1) a bureaucratic constituency or (2) a horizontal constituency.

A *bureaucratic constituency* consists of a hierarchy of decision makers who may or may not be present at negotiations and who must sign or signify final approval of a settlement before it is considered valid. Bureaucratic constituencies are most common when one party is a governmental agency, a hierarchically organized company or industry, or a bureaucratically organized institution such as a hospital or social service agency.

Final approval of a settlement by persons not present may be an organization's genuine procedural requirement, or may be a negotiating tactic a team employs to weaken an opponent's direct influence (Cohen, 1980; Stevens, 1963). A negotiator's argument that he or she is not empowered to make the final decision may provide that team with additional power based on the claim that a higher authority does not approve of the settlement, or may provide additional time necessary for bureaucratic review or approval that can be used to bolster a negotiating position. The need to consult a bureaucracy can be either a help or a hindrance depending on the negotiator's perspective. It may alleviate pressure on a negotiator for final decision making, or it may hinder the development of trust with another team.

The second type of constituent approval is *horizontal constituent approval.* This form of decision making exists when a negotiator is responsible to a wider constituency that is not organized in a bureaucratic manner. Relatives, co-workers, public interest groups, tenants' unions, prisoners, and even industry associations may be organized in this manner. Negotiating teams that are responsible to horizontally organized groups usually must gain approval of a settlement reached through negotiations through a form of ratification. Voting is probably the most common procedure horizontally organized constituent groups use, although consensus may also be used. For voting or consensus to work, however, the constituent groups must all accept it as the process for settlement approval. Failure of an acceptable ratification and commitment-ensuring procedure for approving negotiated settlements is one of the principal causes of a breakdown in negotiations in which one of the teams is both horizontally organized and responsible to a horizontally organized constituency.

The lack of procedure for constituent approval can end in disaster. One of the many reasons why negotiations between inmates at Attica Prison and New York State failed in the late 1960s was the lack of procedures on the part of inmates to ratify any agreements that were reached (*Attica, The Official Report . . . ,* 1972; Wicker, 1975). This is common among public interest groups either when they do not have institutional means for ratifying negotiated settlements or when ratification does not bind and commit all members to adhere to an agreement. Constituency ratification problems, however, are not confined to public interest groups. In mediated negotiations over information exchange and stipulations pertaining to oil and gas drilling in federal Wilderness Study Areas, environmentalists challenged Rocky Mountain Oil and Gas Association and Independent Petroleum Association of the Mountain States, the two industry associations involved, to explain how they would gain individual company ratification and commitment to any agreement. Both organizations, although maintaining a hierarchically organized staff, had horizontally organized constituent companies. Neither organization had a formal constituencywide means for approving or gaining commitment to negotiated settlements. Ironically, the environmental groups had decision-making structures that were similar and had the same problems as the industry organizations.

The mediator's primary role is not to work with the constituents of a negotiator or negotiating team. However, some efforts in this area may be necessary to attain a settlement's approval.

First, mediators may assist negotiating teams in identifying and organizing their constituents. Mediators may aid teams in defining to whom they are responsible and who should ultimately be involved in final ratification and decision making (Straus, Clark, and Suskind, n.d.). This task may be relatively easy when teams are hierarchically organized or responsible to a bureaucratic constituency, or extremely difficult when the team and constituency are horizontally organized. The task may be especially complex when a negotiating organization has elements of both models. This type of ratification process occurs in some unions when agreements reached in negotiation must be approved by the executive committee, the union president, and the union members at large.

Second, mediators may assist the parties in explicating to each other constraints imposed on the negotiators by their various bureaucratic or horizontal constituencies and the ratification procedures that they will use to reach accord. Early notification of both the procedure to be used for approval of a settlement and the time necessary to do so can reduce unnecessary conflicts that may arise from false procedural expectations.

Third, mediators may work with negotiators or negotiating teams to develop specific procedures for notifying constituent groups about developments in negotiations. Constituent groups often expect their representatives or negotiation teams to bring back for their approval a settlement that resembles the team's opening position. This is usually an unrealistic expectation. Constituencies, like negotiators, must be educated about the composition of a realistic and probable settlement. Constituent education must occur throughout the negotiation process so that the final proposed settlement that reaches the constituency is not a surprise and so that the constituency has had an opportunity to contribute during bargaining. For the constituency to reach substantive, procedural, and psychological closure on any given issue or package of issues, the constituency must believe that it is the best substantive deal that could have been negotiated given the options available, the power constellations of the parties, and external social forces. The constituency must feel that its negotiators used the best process at their disposal and that the constituency had adequate opportunity for contributing to the negotiations. The constituency must also trust its representatives and believe that they have bargained in good faith to obtain the best solution possible.

In some disputes, the negotiators take full and adequate responsibility for educating and obtaining input from their constituency. In other conflicts, the lack of negotiating experience, failure to understand the importance of the educational process, poor procedures, or constraints on negotiation privacy result in distance between negotiators and constituents. This distance may have serious effects on the likelihood of ratification of an agreement when the final terms of the settlement are disclosed and the constituency is not prepared for the gap between its expectations and the actual outcome of negotiations.

Mediators can occasionally intervene between negotiators and their constituencies before and after the announcement of the terms of settlement to avoid settlement rejection. Mediators can suggest educational procedures to negotiators that will keep constituencies informed of progress during negotiation. Mediators may also attempt to convince negotiators that a potential option for settlement is acceptable to their constituency (Stevens, 1963), and may assist in developing procedures to promote constituent input to the negotiation team.

Fourth, the mediator may assist the negotiator or negotiating team in convincing a recalcitrant constituency that the negotiator or team has worked as much as possible to promote the interests of constituents (Kerr, 1954). This may entail discussing the merits of the substantive proposals and contrasting them to what the opponent originally offered, demonstrating the benefits of a proposal to the constituents, discussing the effectiveness of negotiation, and verifying the integrity and commitment of a constituency's negotiators.

So far I have discussed what a mediator does to assist a negotiator in working with his or her constituency. The mediator may also work with a constituency to modify the behavior of a negotiator or negotiating team. A mediator, through either public or private statements, may indicate to a constituency that a negotiator is being too firm and may suggest that the constituents encourage the negotiator to abandon a hard-line position (Shapiro, 1970). The mediator may also appeal directly to the constituents for concessions that will advance negotiations (Douglas, 1962).

Mediation Services Funding

Mediation services, like most other intervention activities (therapy, legal assistance, or arbitration), must often be purchased. Arrangement for payment may be an important part of early mediator strategy. Funding for mediation services tends to come from three sources: (1) joint payment by disputants, (2) payment by a single party, or (3) payment by an independent source.

In labor-management disputes, the mediator's fee may be borne equally by the labor union and the company involved, or may be covered by public revenues. In community and interpersonal disputes, joint payment, at least in equal shares, is not always possible. An early mediator strategy may be to start negotiations with a discussion of how to pay the mediator's fee rather than on a substantive issue. An approach of this type has two advantages.

First, parties have the opportunity to bargain with each other on an issue that is not as emotion-laden as the substantive issues in dispute. "Practice" negotiations on the issue of the mediation fee allow the parties to learn about each other's negotiating style, test for possibilities of agreement, evaluate perceptions, and demonstrate good faith.

A second strategic advantage to negotiating the mediation fee early in the entry phase and reaching an agreement on how the financial burden is to be borne is that it increases the commitment of the parties to the process. If the parties have agreed to make a financial or in-kind contribution to fund the mediation or have agreed to engage in joint fund raising, they are more likely to commit themselves to negotiate their differences. Therapists have long used this approach to increase commitment to the therapeutic process, as have lawyers in the form of retainers (Norton and Mayer, 1981).

In many disputes, especially in the community sector, the financial disparity between the parties may be extreme. Community groups—racial or ethnic minorities, senior citizen organizations, environmental groups, or spouses in traditional marriages—may not have access to funds to directly pay for mediation. Some alternative to shared funding needs to be established before starting mediation. One option is for the party with superior financial resources to pay for the mediation services, but this approach may raise questions about whether the mediator has been "bought" and whether impartial behavior can be expected if only one side has contributed. Although one-party payment may have a negative psychological effect on the other party and may foster distrust of the mediator, such a model of financing can also have positive effects. The party with weaker financial resources may see the financial commitment of the other party as a genuine act of good faith and an assurance that the other party wishes to settle.

If disputants opt for the single-party payment model, the mediator needs to ascertain that the party with fewer resources agrees that this is an acceptable means of payment for intervention services and that the disputants believe that the source of funding will have no effect on the mediator's neutral behavior. It may be important for the party to commit in writing. In other cases, a verbal agreement may be all that is possible because a written statement may damage a party's credibility with its constituents.

The final means of funding mediation services is to secure funding from a third party. Sources used in the past to fund mediation include the general operating budget of the mediation organization, trade associations, sympathetic foundations, governmental revenues, and grants.

Third-party funding may be imperative if mediation in-

volves parties with low incomes, is to be conducted over an extended period of time, involves multiple parties and complex
issues, or requires outside research and data collection to resolve
issues in question. Outside funding has the advantage of providing "neutral" financial backing for the services of the impartial
intervenor, but it may have the disadvantage of decreased commitment to settlement if the parties have no financial investment. Several third-party models have been successfully used
to fund mediation services.

Some states, counties, and cities have funded mediation
projects. Many states have long supported labor-management
mediation, and several are now establishing offices to specifically provide intermediaries in other arenas. New Jersey,
Alaska, Wisconsin, and Massachusetts, with the financial assistance of the National Institute of Dispute Resolution, have re-
cently established state programs in community or environmental arenas. An innovative state funding model has been in effect
for several years in Texas. By state law, counties are allowed to
charge an additional small fee to parties filing court cases. These
fees are used to support alternative dispute resolution services.
Several mediation organizations in Dallas and Houston use this
model. Cities and counties have also funded mediation services
by supporting independent projects such as nonprofit landlord-
tenant mediation services, or by attaching mediation to current
programs such as the consumers affairs section of a district attorney's office.

Courts have also funded mediation services (McIsaac,
1983; Salius, 1983; and Vorenberg, 1982). Judges who have
been overwhelmed with civil caseloads have established programs to resolve those cases more rapidly and efficiently.

Grants from governmental agencies and private foundations have also been used to fund mediation activities. Law Enforcement Assistance Administration grants from the U.S. Justice Department provided establishment funds for several neighborhood justice centers, and the U.S. Health and Human Services Department has supported projects and research on child
custody and divorce and the mediation of treatment plans for
families of abused children. Several federal land management

agencies have also paid for mediation services. Private foundations have also supported mediation projects or interventions.
The Ford and Hewlett Foundations and the National Institute
for Dispute Resolution have been national leaders in this effort.
Many local foundations have also made significant contributions
toward funding mediation activities.

Funding the Parties Themselves

The parties must often be funded for them to participate
in negotiations or mediation. In interpersonal disputes, divorcing spouses may need temporary funding to support themselves
while negotiating a final financial settlement. In community disputes, citizen's groups may need financial assistance to participate in bargaining or to equalize access to data or resource
people.

Questions of how to fund negotiating parties have not
been explored in any depth in mediation literature. Development of procedural models for negotiator financing has been
accomplished in divorce and child custody disputes (Coogler,
1978). Few data are available on financing of community disputes (Baldwin, 1978). Exceptions include the National Coal
Policy Project negotiations of 1976-1980, in which industry
provided money for environmental groups to hire researchers
(Murray, 1978), and the Metropolitan Water Roundtable, in
which the mediation organization and one of the parties assisted citizen interest groups in obtaining funds for their participation in negotiations over meeting Denver's water needs.

Conclusion

Conflict is an omnipresent phenomenon in human interaction. Conflicts can lead to productive and positive changes or growth or to the destruction and degradation of relationships. A crucial variable in dispute outcome is the means that the participants use to resolve their differences. Now, more than ever before, there is a need for dispute resolution procedures that assist parties in meeting their needs, satisfying their interests, and minimizing physical and psychological harm. Mediation is one process that can make an important contribution to peaceful dispute resolution.

For mediation to achieve widespread application as a means of dispute resolution, several changes need to occur. First, the public needs to be educated about the viability of mediation. People need to be aware of mediation and must believe that it can help them before they will be willing to try it. Mediation is currently underutilized not because of its lack of applicability but because participants in disputes are not aware of mediation's benefits. Public education about the process should become a priority among mediators and others interested in peaceful dispute resolution.

Second, more research needs to be conducted on mediation formats, procedures, strategies, and tactics, and more information is needed about what mediators do that enables parties to manage intense emotional multiparty conflicts, imbalances of power, and communications problems.

Third, participants in conflicts, mediators, and other pro-

297

fessionals need to search for new types of conflicts in which mediation can be applied. We need to develop a Gandhian approach that involves experimentation to discover new applications for mediation. Although mediation is not a panacea and does not guarantee perfect settlements in all conflicts, it is an approach that has wider application than is currently recognized.

Finally, mediation must become institutionalized. Mediation has for too long been conducted on an ad hoc basis. Enough is now known to formalize the instruction of prospective mediators and to increase the number of organizations that can offer the service regularly. Students need to be introduced to mediation principles and procedures early in their education so that they can apply them in their lives. Additional formal courses of instruction need to be developed for secondary, undergraduate, graduate, and professional schools. Additional educational seminars need to be available to the public to train people in mediation.

In addition to education, funding must be developed that will promote the development of mediation organizations and agencies in the private and public sectors. Funding must come from governmental agencies, the private sector, foundations, and individuals who will utilize mediation on a fee-for-service basis. Only through funded institutionalization will mediation become readily accessible to a broader public and be applied to the range of conflicts that exist in society today.

Resource A

Code of Professional Conduct

Preamble

Mediation is an approach to conflict resolution in which an impartial third party intervenes in a dispute, with the consent of the parties, to aid and assist them in reaching a mutually satisfactory settlement to issues in dispute.

Mediation is a profession with ethical responsibilities and duties. Those who engage in the practice of mediation must be dedicated to the principle that all disputants have a right to negotiate and to attempt to determine the outcomes of their own conflicts. Mediators must be aware that their duties and obligations relate to the parties who engage their services, to the mediation process, to other mediators, to the agencies that administer the practice of mediation, and to the general public.

Mediators are often professionals (attorneys, therapists, and social workers) who have obligations under other codes of ethics. This code is not to be construed as a competitive code of behavior but as an additional guideline for professionals performing mediation. When mediating, professionals will be bound by the ethical guidelines of this code.

Note: Drafted by Christopher W. Moore, Partner, Center for Dispute Resolution, and adopted by the Colorado Council of Mediation Organizations, January 1982.

This code is not designed to override or supercede any laws or government regulations that prescribe responsibilities of mediators and others in the helping professions. It is a personal code of conduct for the individual mediator and is intended to establish principles applicable to all professional mediators employed by private, city, state, or federal agencies.

1. The Responsibility of the Mediator to the Parties

The primary responsibility for the resolution of a dispute rests on the parties themselves. The mediator should recognize at all times that the agreements reached in negotiations are voluntarily made by the parties. It is the mediator's responsibility to assist the disputants in reaching a settlement. At no time should a mediator coerce a party into agreement. The mediator should not attempt to make a substantive decision for the parties. Parties may, however, agree to solicit a recommendation for settlement from the mediator.

It is desirable that agreement be reached by negotiations without a mediator's assistance. Intervention by a mediator can be initiated by the parties themselves or by a mediator. The decision to accept mediation rests with the parties, except when mediation is mandated by legislation, court order, or contract.

Mediators will inform all parties of the cost of mediation services before intervention. Parties should be able to estimate the cost of the service in relation to that of other dispute resolution procedures.

Ideally, when costs are involved, the mediator should attempt to have parties agree to bear the costs of mediation equitably. When this is not possible, all parties should reach agreement as to payment.

2. Responsibility of the Mediator to the Mediation Process

Negotiation is an established procedure in our society as a means of resolving disputes. The process of mediation involves a third-party intervention into negotiations to assist in the development of alternative solutions that parties will voluntarily ac-

cept as a basis for settlement. Pressures that jeopardize voluntary action and agreement by the parties should not be a part of
mediation.

The Mediation Process. Mediation is a participatory process. A mediator is obliged to educate the parties and to involve
them in the mediation process. A mediator should consider that
such education and involvement are important not only to resolve a current dispute but also to prepare the parties to handle
future conflicts in a more creative and productive manner.

Appropriateness of Mediation. Mediation is not a panacea
for all types of conflicts. Mediators should be aware of all procedures for dispute resolution and the conditions under which
each is most effective. Mediators are obliged to educate participants as to their procedural options and to help them choose
wisely the most appropriate procedures. The procedures should
clearly match the type of outcome that is desired by the parties.

Mediator's Role. The mediator must not limit his or her
role to keeping the peace or regulating conflict at the bargaining
table. The mediator's role should be that of an active resource
person whom the parties may draw on and, when appropriate,
the mediator should be prepared to provide both procedural
and substantive suggestions and alternatives that will assist the
parties in successful negotiations.

Since the status, experience, and ability of the mediator
lend weight to his or her suggestions and recommendations, the
mediator should evaluate carefully the effect of interventions or
proposals and accept full responsibility for their honesty and
merit.

Since mediation is a voluntary process, the acceptability
of the mediator to the parties as a person of integrity, objectivity, and fairness is absolutely essential for the effective performance of mediation procedures. The manner in which the mediator carries out professional duties and responsibilities will be
a measure of his or her usefulness as a mediator. The quality of
character as well as intellectual, emotional, social, and technical
attributes will reveal themselves in the conduct of the mediator
and in his or her oral and written communications with the parties, other mediators, and the public.

Publicity and Advertising. A mediator should not make any false, misleading, or unfair statement or claim as to the mediation process, its costs and benefits, or his or her role, skills, or qualifications.

Neutrality. A mediator should determine and reveal all monetary, psychological, emotional, associational, or authoritative affiliations that he or she has with any of the parties to a dispute that might cause a conflict of interest or affect the perceived or actual neutrality of the professional in the performance of duties. If the mediator or any one of the major parties feels that the mediator's background will have or has had a potential to bias his or her performance, the mediator should disqualify himself or herself from performing the mediation service.

Impartiality. The mediator is obligated during the performance of professional services to maintain a posture of impartiality toward all involved parties. *Impartiality* is freedom from bias or favoritism either in word or action. Impartiality implies a commitment to aid all parties, as opposed to a single party, in reaching a mutually satisfactory agreement. Impartiality means that a mediator will not play an adversarial role in the process of dispute resolution.

Confidentiality. Information received by a mediator in confidence, private session, caucus, or joint session with the disputants is confidential and should not be revealed to parties outside the negotiations. Information received in caucus is not to be revealed in joint session without receiving prior permission from the party or person from whom the information was received.

The following exceptions shall be applied to the confidentiality rule: In the event of child abuse by one or more disputants or in a case in which a mediator discovers that a probable crime will be committed that may result in serious psychological or physical harm to another person, the mediator is obligated to report these actions to the appropriate agencies.

Use of Information. Because information revealed in mediation is confidential and the success of the process may depend on this confidentiality, mediators should inform and gain consent from participants that information divulged in the process of mediation will not be used by the parties in any future adversarial proceedings.

The mediator is also obligated to resist disclosure of confidential information in an adversarial process. He or she will refuse to testify voluntarily in any subsequent court proceedings and shall resist to the best of his or her ability the subpoena of either his or her notes or person. This provision may be waived by the consent of all parties involved.

Empowerment. In the event that a party needs either additional information or assistance in order for the negotiations to proceed in a fair and orderly manner or for an agreement to be reached that is fair, equitable, and has the capacity to hold over time, the mediator is obligated to refer the party to resources—either data or persons—who may facilitate the process.

Psychological Well-Being. If a mediator discovers before or during mediation that a party needs psychological help, the mediator shall make appropriate referrals. Mediators recognize that mediation is not an appropriate substitute for therapy and shall refer parties to the appropriate procedure. Mediation shall not be conducted with parties who are either intoxicated or who have major psychological disorders that seriously impair their judgment.

The Law. Mediators are not lawyers. At no time shall a mediator offer legal advice to parties in dispute. Mediators shall refer parties to appropriate attorneys for legal advice. This same code of conduct applies to mediators who are themselves trained in the law. The role of an impartial mediator should not be confused with that of an attorney who is an advocate for a client.

The Settlement. The goal of negotiation and mediation is a settlement that is seen as fair and equitable by all parties. The mediator's responsibility to the parties is to help them reach this kind of settlement.

Whenever possible, a mediator should develop a written statement that documents the agreements reached in mediation.

A mediator's satisfaction with the agreement is secondary to that of the parties.

In the event that an agreement is reached that a mediator

feels (1) is illegal, (2) is grossly inequitable to one or more parties, (3) is the result of false information, (4) is the result of bargaining in bad faith, (5) is impossible to enforce, or (6) may not
hold over time, the mediator may pursue any or all of the following alternatives:

1. Inform the parties of the difficulties that the mediator sees
   in the agreement.
2. Inform the parties of the difficulties and make suggestions
   that would remedy the problems.
3. Withdraw as mediator without disclosing to either party the
   particular reasons for the withdrawal.
4. Withdraw as mediator but disclose in writing to both parties the reasons for such action.
5. Withdraw as mediator and reveal publicly the general reason for taking such action (bargaining in bad faith, unreasonable settlement, illegality, and so forth).

Termination of Mediation. In the event that the parties
cannot reach an agreement even with the assistance of a mediator, it is the responsibility of the mediator to make the parties
aware of the deadlock and suggest that negotiations be terminated. A mediator is obligated to inform the parties when a
final impasse has occurred and to refer them to other means of
dispute resolution. A mediator should not prolong unproductive
discussions that result in increased time and emotional and
monetary costs for the parties.

3. The Responsibility of the Mediator to Other Mediators

A mediator should not enter any dispute that is being mediated by another mediator or mediators without first confer-
ring with the person or persons conducting such mediation. The
mediator should not intercede in a dispute merely because another mediator may also be participating. Conversely, it should
not be assumed that the lack of mediation participation by one
mediator indicates a need for participation by another mediator.

In those situations in which more than one mediator are

participating in a particular case, each mediator has a responsibility to keep the others informed of developments essential to a cooperative effort and should extend every possible courtesy to co-mediators.

During mediation, the mediator should carefully avoid any appearance of disagreement with or criticism of co-mediators. Discussions as to what positions and actions mediators should take in particular cases should not violate principles of confidentiality.

4. The Responsibility of the Mediator to His or Her Agency and Profession

Mediators frequently work for agencies that are responsible for providing mediation assistance to parties in dispute. The mediator must recognize that as an employee of such agencies, the mediator is their representative, and that he or she will not be judged solely on an individual basis but also as a representative of an organization. Any improper conduct or professional shortcoming, therefore, reflects not only on the individual mediator but also on the employer, and in so doing, it jeopardizes the effectiveness of the agency, other agencies, and the acceptability of the mediation process itself.

The mediator should not use his or her position for personal gain or advantage or engage in any employment, activity, or enterprise that will conflict with his or her work as a mediator.

Mediators should not accept any money or item of value for the performance of services other than a regular salary or mutually established fee, or incur obligations to any party that might interfere with the impartial performance of his or her duties.

Training and Education. Mediators learn their trade through a variety of avenues—formal education, training programs, workshops, practical experience, and supervision. Mediators have the responsibility to constantly upgrade their skills and theoretical grounding and shall endeavor to better themselves and the profession by seeking some form of further education in the negotiation and mediation process during each year in practice.

A mediator should promote the profession and make contributions to the field by encouraging and participating in research, publishing, or other forms of professional and public education.

Expertise. Mediators should perform their services only in those areas of mediation in which they are qualified either by experience or by training. Mediators should not attempt to mediate in an unfamiliar field or when there is risk of psychological, financial, legal, or physical damage to one of the parties due to the mediator's lack of experience.

A mediator is obligated to seek a co-mediator trained in the necessary discipline or refer cases to other mediators who are trained in the required field of expertise when he or she does not possess the required skills.

Voluntary Services. A mediator is obligated to perform some voluntary service during each year of practice to provide assistance to those who cannot afford to pay for mediation and to promote the field. It is left to the individual mediator to determine the amount and kind of service to be rendered for the good of the profession and of society.

Mediators should cooperate with their own and other agencies in establishing and maintaining the quality, qualifications, and standards of the profession. Mediators should participate in individual and agency evaluations and should be supervised either by an agency, a mutually established peer, or the professional organization's board of ethics. Mediators involved in any breach of this code of conduct should notify their agency of the breach. Mediators hearing of violations of this code of ethics should also report this information to their agency or the board of ethics.

5. Responsibility of the Mediator to the Public and Other Unrepresented Parties

Negotiation is in essence a private, voluntary process. The primary purpose of mediation is to assist the parties in achieving a settlement. Such assistance does not abrogate the rights of the parties to resort to economic, social, psychological, and legal sanctions. However, the mediation process may include a responsibility of the mediator to assert the interest of the public or other unrepresented parties in order that a particular dispute be settled, that costs or damages be alleviated, and that normal life be resumed. Mediators should question agreements that are not in the interest of the public or other unrepresented parties whose interests and needs should be and are not being considered. Mediators should question whether other parties' interests or the parties themselves should be present at negotiations. It is understood, however, that the mediator does not regulate or control any of the content of a negotiated agreement.

A mediator shall not use publicity to enhance his or her own position. When two or more mediators are mediating a dispute, public information should be managed by a mutually agreeable procedure.

Resource B

Sample Contact Letter

Center for Dispute Resolution
1900 Wazee Street
Denver, Colorado 80202
(303) 295-2244

Dear Mr. Brown:

We have been contacted by Ms. Jones to determine if the Center for Dispute Resolution can be of assistance to both of you in resolving your disagreements. The Center provides mediation services for people who want to resolve their own conflicts without having to go to court. A mediator is a trained third party who assists people in negotiating their own settlements in an informal, private, and cooperative manner. The mediator will not make a decision for you but will provide a problem-solving structure and process that many people have found helpful.

A written agreement is reached in nearly 80 percent of the cases mediated, and we find that most participants feel that their concerns have been dealt with fairly and much more rapidly than if they had pursued a judicial decision. Mediated agreements also appear to be more satisfactory and more durable because they have been developed by the participants themselves and have been agreed on voluntarily. Before reaching a final settlement, the agreement may be reviewed by your lawyer to ensure that your legal rights have been protected.

Please see the attached brochure for additional information on the Center for Dispute Resolution. Also enclosed is a fee schedule for our services.

A mediator from the center will call you within the next week to discuss the possibility of using our services. Our staff member will be glad to answer any questions you have about the process. If you have any questions before that time, please feel free to call me at (303) 295-2244.

Truly yours,

Cynthia Smith
Office Administrator

Resource C

Sample Waiver and Consent Form

The purpose of this waiver and consent form is to ensure that you, our client, understand the nature of our service and the responsibilities you have to maintain the confidentiality of the mediation process.

Your Initials

_____ I understand that the Center for Dispute Resolution offers neither legal advice nor legal counsel.

_____ I agree that I will not, at any time (before, during, or after mediation of this dispute), call the mediator as an adversarial witness in any legal or administrative proceeding concerning this dispute.

_____ I agree that I will not subpoena or call for the production of any records, notes, or work product of the mediator in any legal or administrative proceeding that arises before, during, or after the mediation of this dispute. However, any agreement resulting from mediation that is intended by the parties to have legal effect and to be legally enforceable may be subpoenaed, called for, or produced in any proceedings to which it is relevant, unless the agreement specifically provides otherwise.

I have read the above and have no further questions regarding the confidentiality of this process.

_____
Signature

_____
Date

Resource D

Sample Agreements

Sample Memorandum of Understanding

This is a memorandum of understanding regarding the revision of the contract of employment between Dr. Richard Singson, director of and representative for the Fairview Medical Clinic, 3504 Arizona Avenue, Smithville, Colorado, and Dr. Andrew Whittamore, a physician working at the same clinic.

Because of personal difficulties between Dr. Andrew Whittamore and his wife, Dr. Janelle Whittamore, who also works at Fairview Medical Clinic, it is agreed by Dr. Singson and Dr. Andrew Whittamore that the latter should continue to practice medicine for the Fairview Medical Clinic, but that his principal office should not be at the clinic's address listed above. This arrangement will allow the Whittamores the physical separation that they both desire.

The following points detail the agreements reached by Dr. Andrew Whittamore and the clinic regarding establishment of a separate office.

1. Dr. Andrew Whittamore will remain an employee of the Fairview Medical Clinic for the next two-and-a-half years, although his practice will not be at the clinic's address listed above.
2. Dr. Andrew Whittamore will find new office space on his own time. The time frame for the search is left up to Dr. Whittamore.

312

3. Dr. Andrew Whittamore's current desk and office furniture will be moved from the clinic to his new office.
4. Dr. Andrew Whittamore will pay one-half of the cost for all new equipment purchased for his new office. The cost of the equipment will be prorated and deducted from his salary on a monthly basis over the next two-and-a-half years. The furniture will remain the property of the clinic.
5. Moving expenses will be equally borne by the clinic and Dr. Andrew Whittamore.
6. The clinic will continue to provide Dr. Whittamore with a full-time nurse-receptionist.
7. Dr. Whittamore will continue to have full access to the laboratory, staff, and facilities of the clinic.
8. All billing from Dr. Whittamore's practice will be managed by the bookkeeper for the clinic.
9. Dr. Whittamore will duplicate at his own expense all new patient records developed through his separate practice and file records in the central file of the clinic. Duplicate reports on patient care should be submitted to the clinic by the end of each month.

Both doctors agree to comply fully with this agreement and expect that the arrangement will be mutually beneficial. Should problems arise in the implementation of the agreement, both doctors agree to return to mediation before pursuing another course of dispute resolution.

It is the understanding of Drs. Whittamore and Singson that this agreement will be reviewed by their respective lawyers before it becomes effective.

_____   _____
Richard Singson, M.D.   Andrew Whittamore, M.D.
(for Fairview Medical Clinic)

_____   _____
Date   Date

Sample Settlement Agreement

This agreement is made between Roger Larkin, who resides at 102 Juniper Avenue, Boulder, Colorado, and Mary Larkin, who resides at 980 Sumac Street, Boulder, Colorado. Mary and Roger were married on October 8, 1968, and were separated on November 8, 1983. They have two children, Brad (eight) and Kirsten (six).

Because of disputes and irreconcilable differences, Roger and Mary have decided to live separately and to obtain a legal divorce. In view of their desire to live apart for the rest of their lives, Mary and Roger have decided to divide their property and possessions and to agree on the arrangements for custody and support of their children.

Roger and Mary agree to the following points:

I. Child Custody

Mary and Roger are both dedicated parents who, although separating, want their children to have a meaningful and positive relationship with their mother and their father. In light of their common concern for Brad and Kirsten, both parents agree to joint legal custody of the children. The meaning of *joint custody* is detailed below.

A.   *Residence and Visits*
  1.   The children will rotate their place of residence every three weeks so that they will spend equal time living with each of their parents. This arrangement will be tried for six months from the date of signing this agreement. If this system is satisfactory, it will be continued. Otherwise, a new system of one-month rotations will be tried for the next six months. At the end of one year from the date of signing, a final agreement will be reached between Roger and Mary on the length of residential rotations for the children. A mediator or arbitrator will be used if necessary.
  2.   Each parent shall have the children visit and stay with

him or her for two weekends of each month, regardless of where the children are residing the rest of the time.
   a. A weekend consists of Friday afternoon (beginning 3:00–3:30 P.M.) through Sunday evening (ending 7:30–8:00 P.M.). The parent picking up the child for the visit is responsible for either the Friday or the Sunday supper.
3. One night each week the parent with whom the children are not living shall have an overnight visit with Brad and Kirsten. This night will be arranged by mutual agreement of the parents in consultation with the children. The preferred night for these visits is Wednesday.
   a. These evening visits begin before supper (5:30–6:00 P.M.) and end after breakfast (8:30–9:00 A.M.) the following day.
4. One night each week the parent with whom the children are not living may have one child for an overnight visit. This is a special one-to-one time for the parent and child.
   a. Each child will have a designated night to visit the parent with whom they are not living. This opportunity will occur every three weeks. The preferred night for one-to-one visits is Thursday.
   b. The same time provisions apply for this evening as for Wednesday nights.
5. When a child reaches ten years of age, the parents, in consultation with the child, may decide to have the child reside with one or the other parent for periods longer than the established rotation. This agreement will be initiated if the child desires to have an extended period of residence with a particular parent, or if both parents deem extended residence beneficial for the emotional health of the child.
B. *Holidays*
   1. The children will spend the following holidays in 1983 with the parent designated below:
      • Christmas Eve—Roger

- Christmas Day—Mary
- Thanksgiving—Roger
- Father's Day—Roger
- Easter—Mary
- Mother's Day—Mary

The schedules for Christmas Eve, Christmas Day, Thanksgiving, and Easter will be alternated in each subsequent year.

2. Parents have the option of having the children visit them on the parent's birthday.

3. On the children's birthdays:

    a. The parents will alternate holding birthday parties for each child.

    b. The parent who holds the party will cover the expenses for the celebration. The nonhost parent is responsible only for his or her own present(s) for the child.

    c. The parent who is not hosting the party has the right to attend the birthday celebration.

    d. The children's birthdays are special days in themselves and do not count as visitation days.

C. *Vacations*

1. Each parent may have two weeks of vacation per year with both of the children. *Vacation* means an uninterrupted time with the children.

    a. Vacations should be taken with both children.

    b. The location of the vacation is at the discretion of the vacationing parent.

    c. If the vacation time of a parent falls in the middle of a rotation period when the children are residing with the other parent, the children will be able to spend the two weeks with the vacationing parent. However, on their return, they will complete the time remaining in the three-week rotation with the parent with whom they were living before the vacation.

    d. The children's expenses on a vacation are the responsibility of the vacationing parent. The nonvacationing parent will, however, provide each child with $10 spending money for the two-week period.

e. During vacation, communication should be encouraged, if possible, between the children and the nonvacationing parent. This communication may be as infrequent as one phone call. Communication with the nonvacationing parent is, however, up to the discretion of the vacationing parent.

D. *Grandparents' Visits*

1. Grandparents should visit their grandchildren when the children are residing with Mary or with Roger; that is, Mary's parents will see the children when they are with Mary, and Roger's parents will see the the children when they are with Roger.

2. In the event of either Roger's or Mary's death, the grandparents of the deceased will have visitation rights with their grandchildren.

a. This visitation will consist of one visit per month, which may last up to one weekend in duration. A weekend is Friday afternoon through Sunday evening.

E. *Medical and Health Care*

1. If a child needs medical care, it is the responsibility of the parent with whom the child is residing to take the child to the doctor.

2. Major medical decisions about the health care of both the children will be made jointly by Roger and Mary.

3. The children will be kept on the health maintenance plan that currently covers Roger. Each parent agrees to use this plan for the children.

a. If a change in health plans is anticipated, the revision of this agreement will be made through consultations between Mary and Roger.

4. If a dental health plan is secured by Roger, both parents agree to use it.

F. *Education*

1. Mary and Roger agree to continue using the same care-

taker and day-care system that they currently have and will consult with each other if new child-care arrangements are needed.

2. The children will remain in public school in either Mary's or Roger's school district.

    a. A change in schools will be made by joint consultation between the parents.

G. *Death of a Parent*

1. In the event of either Roger's or Mary's death, the remaining parent will become the sole custodian of the children, and the children shall reside with him or her.

2. In the event that both parents should die, Mary's parents will become legal custodians of the children.

H. *Moving*

1. In the event that one of the parents moves outside of the Denver metropolitan area (five counties), he or she will forfeit the right of physical custody of the children to the parent who remains in the five-county area.

2. When a child reaches ten years of age, the parents, in consultation with the child, may decide with whom the child will reside. This decision may result in the child moving away from the Denver area.

    a. If a joint decision on the living situation of the child cannot be reached by the parents, Roger and Mary agree to use either mediation or arbitration to make a decision.

    b. If a change in a child's residence is required, this change will occur between school years if possible.

II. Child Support

A. *Day-to-Day Expenses*

1. Mary and Roger agree to pay the necessary housing and food expenses for the children when the children are living with them.

2. The parents will equitably share the cost of toys and clothing for each child.

B.   *Medical*
   1.   Roger agrees to assume the cost of any and all medical health plans or insurance that covers the children.
   2.   Roger will cover the cost of braces on Brad's teeth.
C.   *Education*
   1.   Roger will assume the cost of day care for the children until the time when such supervision is no longer necessary.
   2.   Discontinuation of day care for the children will be a joint decision of Mary and Roger.
   3.   Roger and Mary agree to establish a higher education fund for the children.
      a.   Each parent will contribute 1 percent of his or her income to this fund beginning in fiscal year 1984. The contribution of each parent will increase to 2 percent in 1987.
      b.   If either parent stops working, he or she will continue to contribute to this fund at a rate of 1 percent of his or her income for the last working year.

III. Property Division

A.   Roger and Mary affirm that the income and property listed in Appendix A of this agreement are a total disclosure of their individual and joint assets and liabilities.

---------------------------------   ---------------------------------
Roger Larkin   Mary Larkin

B.   The assets listed above shall be divided as follows:
   1.   Roger will give Mary $9,000 in cash before or at the time of the signing of this settlement. This is an equal division of their savings fund and checking accounts.
   2.   Roger owes Mary an additional $12,000 as her equity in the home. It will be paid according to the following schedule:

     a.   Roger will pay $500 per month for two years. The first payment will be made on June 1, 1984.

     Mary and Roger Larkin affirm that all the information in this agreement is true, and they further affirm that they will act in good faith to carry out the terms of this agreement.

_____   _____
Roger Larkin   Mary Larkin

_____   _____
Date   Date

_____   _____
Witness/Mediator   Witness/Mediator

_____   _____
Date   Date

References

"AAA Designs ADR Insurance Procedures." *Dispute Resolution,* 1984, *13,* 12.

Aiken, M., and Mott, P. "Locating Centers of Power." In M. Aiken and P. Mott (eds.), *The Structure of Community Power.* New York: Random House, 1970.

American Arbitration Association. "An Overview of Mediation." New York: American Arbitration Association, n.d.

Antoun, R. *Arab Village.* Bloomington: Indiana University Press, 1972.

Argyris, C. *Intervention Theory and Method: A Behavioral Science View.* Reading, Mass.: Addison-Wesley, 1970.

Attica: The Official Report of the New York State Special Commission on Attica. New York: Praeger, 1972.

Aubert, V. "Competition and Dissensus: Two Types of Conflict and Conflict Resolution." *Journal of Conflict Resolution,* 1963, *7* (1), 26-42.

Auerbach, J. *Justice Without Law: Resolving Disputes Without Lawyers.* New York: Oxford University Press, 1983.

Bach, G., and Goldberg, H. *Creative Aggression: The Art of Assertive Living.* New York: Doubleday, 1974.

Bagozzi, R., and Dholakia, R. "Mediational Mechanisms in Interorganizational Conflict." In D. Druckman (ed.), *Negotiations: Social Psychological Perspectives.* Beverly Hills, Calif.: Sage, 1977.

Baldwin, P. (ed.). *Environmental Mediation: An Effective Alternative?* Palo Alto, Calif.: RESOLVE, Center for Environmental Conflict Resolution, 1978.

Bazerman, M., and Lewicki, R. (eds.). *Negotiating in Organizations.* Beverly Hills, Calif.: Sage, 1983.

Behn, R., and Vaupel, J. *Quick Analysis for Busy Decision Makers.* New York: Basic Books, 1982.

Bellman, H. "Mediation as an Approach to Resolving Environmental Disputes." *Proceedings of the Environmental Conflict Management Practitioners Workshop.* Florissant, Colo., Oct. 1982.

Bellows, G., and Moulton, B. "Assessment: Framing the Choices." In G. Bellows and B. Moulton (eds.), *The Lawyering Process.* Mineola, N.Y.: Foundation Press, 1981.

Berger, P., and Luckmann, T. *The Social Construction of Reality: A Treatise on the Sociology of Knowledge.* Garden City, N.Y.: Doubleday, 1967.

Berkowitz, L. "Stimulus/Response: The Case for Bottling Up Rage." *Psychology Today,* 1973, 7 (2), 24–31.

Bernard, S., Folger, J., Weingarten, H., and Zumeta, Z. "The Neutral Mediator: Value Dilemmas in Divorce Mediation." In J. A. Lemmon (ed.), *Ethics, Standards, and Professional Challenges.* Mediation Quarterly, no. 4. San Francisco: Jossey-Bass, 1984.

Bethel, C., and Singer, L. "Mediation: A New Remedy for Cases of Domestic Violence." In H. Davidson and others (eds.), *Alternative Means of Family Dispute Resolution.* Washington, D.C.: American Bar Association, 1982.

Bianchi, H. "Returning Conflict to the Community: The Alternative of Privatization." Unpublished manuscript, Amsterdam, Netherlands, 1978.

Biddle, A., and others. *Corporate Dispute Management 1982.* New York: Bender, 1982.

Bingham, G. "Does Negotiation Hold a Promise for Regulatory Reform?" *Resolve,* Fall 1981, pp. 1–8.

Bingham, G. *Resolving Environmental Disputes: A Decade of Experience.* Washington, D.C.: Conservation Foundation, 1984.

Blake, R., and Mouton, J. S. "Union Management Relations: From Conflict to Collaboration." *Personnel,* 1961, *38,* 38-51.

Blake, R., and Mouton, J. S. *Solving Costly Organizational Conflicts: Achieving Intergroup Trust, Cooperation, and Teamwork.* San Francisco: Jossey-Bass, 1984.

Blake, R., Mouton, J., and Sloma, R. "The Union-Management Intergroup Laboratory: Strategy for Resolving Intergroup Conflict." In W. Bennis and others (eds.), *The Planning of Change.* New York: Holt, Rinehart & Winston, 1961.

Blake, R., Shepard, H., and Mouton, J. *Managing Intergroup Conflict in Industry.* Houston, Tex.: Gulf, 1964.

Blake, R., and others. "The Union-Management Intergroup Laboratory." *Journal of Applied Behavioral Science,* 1965, *1,* 25-27.

Bonner, M. *Group Dynamics.* New York: Ronald Press, 1959.

Boulding, K. *Conflict and Defense.* New York: Harper & Row, 1962.

Brett, J., and Goldberg, S. "Mediator Advisors: A New Third Party Role." In M. Bazerman and R. Lewicki (eds.), *Negotiating in Organizations.* Beverly Hills, Calif.: Sage, 1983.

Bronstein, R. "Mediation and the Colorado Lawyer." *Colorado Lawyer,* 1982, *11* (9), 2315-2323.

Brookmire, D., and Sistrunk, F. "The Effects of Perceived Ability and Impartiality of Mediators and Time Pressure on Negotiation." *Journal of Conflict Resolution,* 1980, *24* (2), 311-327.

Brown, B. "Face Saving and Face Restoration in Negotiation." In D. Druckman (ed.), *Negotiations: Social Psychological Perspectives.* Beverly Hills, Calif.: Sage, 1977.

Brown, D. "Divorce and Family Mediation: History, Review, Future Directions." *Conciliation Courts Review,* 1982, *20* (2), 1-37.

Brown, L. D. *Managing Conflict of Organizational Interfaces.* Reading, Mass.: Addison-Wesley, 1983.

Brown, L. M. *How to Negotiate a Successful Contract.* Englewood Cliffs, N.J.: Prentice-Hall, 1955.

Burgess, H. "The Foothills Water Treatment Project: A Case Study in Environmental Mediation." Cambridge: Environmental Negotiation Project, Laboratory of Architecture and Planning, Massachusetts Institute of Technology, 1980.

Burton, J. *Conflict and Communication: The Use of Controlled Communication in International Relations.* London: Macmillan, 1969.

Carpenter, S., and Kennedy, J. "Information Sharing and Conciliation: Tools for Environmental Conflict Management." *Environmental Comment,* May 1977.

Carpenter, S., and Kennedy, J. "Conflict Anticipation: A Site Specific Approach for Managing Environmental Conflict." Paper presented at fall meeting of the Society of Mining Engineers of AIME, Tucson, Ariz., Oct. 1979.

Carpenter, S., and Kennedy, J. "Environmental Conflict Management." *Environemntal Professional,* 1980, *2* (1), 67–74.

Chalmers, E., and Cormick, G. *Racial Conflict and Negotiating.* Ann Arbor, Mich.: Institute of Labor and Industrial Relations, 1971.

Chandler, J. P. (ed.). *Teachings of Mahatma Gandhi.* Lahore, India: Indian Printing Works, 1945.

Clark, P., and Cummings, F. "Selecting an Environmental Conflict Management Strategy." In P. Marcus and W. Emrich (eds.), *Working Papers in Conflict Management.* New York: American Arbitration Association, 1981.

Clark-McGlennon Associates. *Patuxent-River Cleanup Agreement.* Boston: Clark-McGlennon Associates, 1982.

Cohen, A., and Smith, R. "The Critical-Incident Approach to Leadership Intervention in Training Groups." In W. Dyer (ed.), *Modern Theory and Method in Group Training.* New York: Van Nostrand Reinhold, 1972.

Cohen, H. *You Can Negotiate Anything.* Secaucus, N.J.: Lyle Stuart, 1980.

Colosi, T., and Berkeley, A. "The Negotiating Table: Bridging Troubled Waters." Unpublished manuscript, American Arbitration Association, Washington, D.C., 1980.

Comeau, E. "Procedural Controls in Public Sector Domestic Relations Mediation." In H. Davidson and others (eds.), *Alternative Means of Family Dispute Resolution.* Washington, D.C.: American Bar Association, 1982.

Coogler, O. J. *Structured Mediation in Divorce Settlement.* Lexington, Mass.: Lexington Books, 1978.

Cook, J., Rochl, J., and Shepard, D. *Executive Summary Final Report.* Washington, D.C.: Neighborhood Justice Field Institute, U.S. Department of Justice, 1980.

Coover, V., Deacon, E., Esser, C., and Moore, C. W. *Resource Manual for a Living Revolution.* Philadelphia, Pa.: New Society Press, 1977.

Cormick, G. "Mediating Environmental Controversies: Perspectives and First Experience." *Earth Law Journal,* 1976, 2.

Cormick, G. "Intervention and Self-Determination in Environmental Disputes: A Mediator's Perspective." *Resolve,* Winter 1982, pp. 1-7.

Coser, L. *The Functions of Social Conflict.* Glencoe, Ill.: Free Press, 1956.

Coser, L. *Continuities in the Study of Social Conflict.* New York: Free Press, 1967.

Creighton, J. *Communications.* Tulsa, Okla: Synergy, 1972.

Cross, J. *The Economics of Bargaining.* New York: Basic Books, 1969.

Cross, J. "Negotiation as a Learning Process." *Journal of Conflict Resolution,* 1977, 21 (4), 581-606.

Crowfoot, J. "Negotiations: An Effective Tool for Citizen Organizations?" *The NRAG Papers,* 1980, 3 (4).

Curle, A. *Making Peace.* London: Tavistock, 1971.

Dahl, R. *Who Governs? Democracy and Power in an American City.* New Haven, Conn.: Yale University Press, 1961.

D'Antonio, W., Loomis, C., Form, W., and Erickson, E. "Institutional and Occupational Representations in Eleven Community Influence Systems." *American Sociological Review,* 1961, 26 (3), 440-446.

Davis, R., Tichane, M., and Grayson, D. "The Effects of Alternative Forms of Dispute Resolution on Recidivism in Felony Offenses Between Acquaintances." Unpublished manuscript, Brooklyn Dispute Resolution Center, 1980.

Delbecq, A., Vandeven, A., and Gustafson, D. *Group Techniques for Program Planning.* Glenview, Ill.: Scott, Foresman, 1975.

Dembart, L., and Kwartler, R. "The Snoqualmie River Conflict:

Bringing Mediation into Environmental Disputes." In R. Goldmann (ed.), *Roundtable Justice: Case Studies in Conflict Resolution.* Boulder, Colo.: Westview Press, 1980.

Deutsch, M. "Trust and Suspicion." *Journal of Conflict Resolution,* 1958, *2* (4), 265-279.

Deutsch, M. "The Effect of Motivational Correlation upon Trust and Suspicion." *Human Relations,* 1960, *13* (2), 125-139.

Deutsch, M. "Conflicts: Productive and Destructive." *Journal of Social Issues,* 1969, *25* (1), 7-41.

Deutsch, M. *Resolution of Conflict.* New Haven, Conn.: Yale University Press, 1974.

Douglas, A. *Industrial Peacemaking.* New York: Columbia University Press, 1962.

Downing, T. "Strategy and Tactics at the Bargaining Table." *Personnel,* 1960, *37* (1), 58-63.

Doyle, M., and Straus, D. *How to Make Meetings Work.* Chicago: Playboy Press, 1976.

Dubois, R., and Mew Soong Li. *The Art of Group Conversation.* New York: Association Press, 1963.

Eckhoff, T. "The Mediator, the Judge, and the Administrator in Conflict Resolution." *Acta Sociologica: Scandinavian Review of Sociology,* 1966-67, *10,* 148-172.

Epstein, A. "Dispute Settlement Among the Tolai." *Oceana,* 1971, *41* (4), 157-170.

Felsteiner, W., and Williams, L. "Mediation as an Alternative to Criminal Prosecution." *Law and Human Behavior,* 1978, *2* (3), 223-244.

Filley, A. *Interpersonal Conflict Resolution.* Glenview, Ill.: Scott, Foresman, 1975.

Fisch, R., Weakland, J., and Segal, L. *The Tactics of Change: Doing Therapy Briefly.* San Francisco: Jossey-Bass, 1982.

Fisher, R. "Fractionating Conflict." In R. Fisher (ed.), *International Conflict and Behavioral Sciences: The Craigville Papers.* New York: Basic Books, 1964.

Fisher, R. *International Conflict for Beginners.* New York: Harper & Row, 1969.

Fisher, R. *International Mediation: A Working Guide.* New York: International Peace Academy, 1978.

Fisher, R., and Ury, W. *Getting to Yes: Negotiating Agreement Without Giving In.* Boston: Houghton Mifflin, 1981.

Fisher, R. J. "Third Party Consultation: A Method for the Study and Resolution of Conflict." *Journal of Conflict Resolution,* 1982, *16* (1), 67–94.

Folberg, J. "Divorce Mediation: A Workable Alternative." In H. Davidson and others (eds.), *Alternative Means of Family Dispute Resolution.* Washington, D.C.: American Bar Association, 1982.

Folberg, J., and Taylor, A. *Mediation: A Comprehensive Guide to Resolving Conflicts Without Litigation.* San Francisco: Jossey-Bass, 1984.

Freedman, L., Haile, C., and Bookstaff, H. *Confidentiality in Mediation: A Practitioner's Guide.* Washington, D.C.: American Bar Association, 1985.

Freire, P. *Pedagogy of the Oppressed.* New York: Herder and Herder, 1970.

Freud, S. *A General Introduction to Psycho-Analysis.* Garden City, N.Y.: Garden City Publishing, 1943. (Originally published 1920.)

Frost, J., and Wilmot, W. *Interpersonal Conflict.* Dubuque, Iowa: Brown, 1978.

Galper, M. *Joint Custody and Co-Parenting: Sharing Your Child Equally. A Sourcebook for the Separated or Divorced Family.* Philadelphia, Pa.: Running Press, 1980.

Galtung, J. "Is Peaceful Research Possible? On the Methodology of Peaceful Research." In J. Galtung (ed.), *Peace: Research-Education-Action.* Copenhagen, Denmark: Ejlers, 1975a.

Galtung, J. "On the Meaning of Nonviolence." In J. Galtung (ed.), *Peace: Research-Education-Action.* Copenhagen, Denmark: Ejlers, 1975b.

Ginsberg, R. B. "American Bar Association Delegation Visits the People's Republic of China." *American Bar Association Journal,* 1978, *64*, 1516–1525.

Goffman, E. *The Presentation of Self in Everyday Life.* Garden City, N.Y.: Doubleday, 1959.

Goffman, E. *Strategic Interaction.* Philadelphia: University of Pennsylvania Press, 1969.

Gordon, T. *Leadership Effectiveness Training.* New York: Wyden, 1978.

Gulliver, P. H. *Neighbors and Networks.* Berkeley: University of California Press, 1971.

Gulliver, P. H. *Disputes and Negotiations.* New York: Academic Press, 1979.

Hall, E. T. *The Hidden Dimension.* Garden City, N.Y.: Doubleday, 1966.

Hamilton, P. "Counseling and the Legal Profession." *American Bar Association Journal,* 1972, *58,* 39-42.

Harter, P. "Regulatory Negotiation: The Experience So Far." *Resolve,* Winter 1984, pp. 1-10.

Haynes, J. *Divorce Mediation: A Practical Guide for Therapists and Counselors.* New York: Springer, 1981.

Henley, N. *Body Politics—Power, Sex, and Nonverbal Communication.* Englewood Cliffs, N.J.: Prentice-Hall, 1977.

Hinde, R. (ed.). *Nonverbal Communication.* Cambridge, England: Cambridge University Press, 1972.

Hokanson, J. "Psychophysiological Evaluations of the Catharsis Hypothesis." In J. Hokanson and E. Megargee (eds.), *The Dynamics of Aggression.* New York: Harper & Row, 1970.

Hunter, F. *Community Power Structure: A Study of Decision Makers.* Chapel Hill: University of North Carolina Press, 1953.

Irving, H. *Divorce Mediation: A Rational Alternative to the Adversary System.* New York: Universe Books, 1980.

Jackins, H. *The Human Side of Human Beings.* Seattle, Wash.: Rational Island Press, 1978.

Jennings, M. K. *Community Influentials: The Elites of Atlanta.* New York: Free Press, 1964.

Kelly, H. "A Classroom Study of the Dilemmas in Interpersonal Negotiations." In K. Archibald (ed.), *Strategic Interaction and Conflict: Original Papers and Discussion.* Berkeley, Calif.: Institute of International Studies, 1966.

Keltner, J. "Communications and the Labor-Management Mediation Process: Some Aspects and Hypotheses." *Journal of Communication,* 1965, *15* (2), 64-80.

Kerr, C. "Industrial Conflict and Its Mediation." *American Journal of Sociology,* 1954, *60,* 230-245.

Kessler, S. *Creative Conflict Resolution: Mediation.* Atlanta, Ga.: Society of Professionals, 1978.

Kochan, T., and Jick, T. "The Public Sector Mediation Process, a Theory and Empirical Examination." *Journal of Conflict Resolution,* 1978, *22* (2), 209–237.

Kochman, T. *Black and White Styles in Conflict.* Chicago: University of Chicago Press, 1981.

Kolb, D. *The Mediators.* Cambridge, Mass.: MIT Press, 1983.

Kraybill, R. "Institutionalizing Mediation as an Alternative Dispute Settlement Mechanism: An Ethical Critique." In R. Kraybill and L. Buzzard (eds.), *Christian Conciliation Sourcebook.* Oak Park, Ill.: Christian Legal Society, 1979.

Kriesberg, L. *The Sociology of Social Conflicts.* Englewood Cliffs, N.J.: Prentice-Hall, 1973.

Kwartler, R. "This Land Is Our Land: The Mohawk Indians v. the State of New York." In R. Goldmann (ed.), *Roundtable Justice: Case Studies in Conflict Resolution.* Boulder, Colo.: Westview Press, 1980.

Labor-Management Relations Act. Taft-Hartley Act, 1947, Section 203(b).

Lake, L. *Environmental Mediation: The Search for Consensus.* Boulder, Colo.: Westview Press, 1980.

Landsberger, H. "Final Report on a Research Project in Mediation." *Labor Law Journal,* 1956, *7* (8).

Lansford, H. "The Metropolitan Water Roundtable: A Case Study in Environmental Conflict Management." Boulder, Colo.: ACCORD Associates, 1983.

Laue, J., and Cormick, G. "The Ethics of Intervention in Community Disputes." In G. Bermont and others (eds.), *The Ethics of Social Intervention.* New York: Wiley, 1978.

Lederach, J. P. "La regulacion del conflito: interpersonal y de grupos redudidos" [The regulation of conflict: Interpersonal and small groups]. Unpublished manuscript, University of Colorado, 1984.

Levinson, D. "The Intergroup Relations Workshop: Its Psychological Aims and Effects." *Journal of Psychology,* 1954, *38,* 103–126.

Levinson, D., and Sohermerhorn, R. "Emotional Attitudinal Effects of an Intergroup Relations Workshop on Its Members." *Journal of Psychology,* 1951, *31,* 243-256.

Li, V. *Law Without Lawyers: A Comparative View of Law in China and the United States.* Boulder, Colo.: Westview Press, 1978.

Lincoln, W. F. "Presenting Initial Positions." Unpublished manuscript, National Center for Collaborative Planning and Community Services, Watertown, Mass., 1981.

Lincoln, W. F. *Mediation: A Transferable Process for the Prevention and Resolution of Racial Conflict in Public Secondary Schools.* New York: American Arbitration Association, 1976.

Lincoln, W. F. "Types of Negotiations." Unpublished manuscript, National Center for Collaborative Planning and Community Services, Watertown, Mass., n.d.

Lovell, H. "The Pressure Lever in Mediation." *Industrial and Labor Relations Review,* 1952, *6* (1), 20-29.

McCarthy, J. (ed.). *Resolving Conflict in Higher Education.* New Directions for Higher Education, no. 32. San Francisco: Jossey-Bass, 1980.

McCarthy, J., and others. *Managing Faculty Disputes: A Guide to Issues, Procedures, and Practices.* San Francisco: Jossey-Bass, 1984.

McIsaac, H. "Manditory Conciliation Custody/Visitation Matters: California's Bold Stroke." *Conciliation Courts Review,* 1983, *19* (2), 51-73.

McSurely, A. *How to Negotiate.* Louisville, Ky.: Southern Conference Educational Fund, 1967.

McWhinney, R., and Metcalf, K. Conversation between the author and these Canadian mediators from Toronto at the annual meeting of the Association of Family and Conciliation Courts, Denver, Colo., May 1984.

Maggiolo, W. *Techniques of Mediation in Labor Disputes.* Dobbs Ferry, N.Y.: Oceana, 1972.

Maier, N., and Hoffman, L. "Quality of First and Second Solutions in Group Problem Solving." *Journal of Applied Psychology,* 1960, *44,* 278-283.

Maslow, A. *Toward a Psychology of Being.* New York: D. Van Nostrand, 1968.

Mayer, B. S. "Conflict Resolution in Child Protection and

Adoption." In J. A. Lemmon (ed.), *Mediating Between Family Members.* Mediation Quarterly, no. 7. San Francisco: Jossey-Bass, 1985.

Mernitz, S. *Mediation of Environmental Disputes: A Sourcebook.* New York: Praeger, 1980.

Milne, A. "Family Self-Determination: An Alternative to the Adversarial System in Custody Disputes." Paper presented at the winter meeting of the Association of Family and Conciliation Courts, Fort Lauderdale, Fla., Dec. 3, 1981.

"Model Standards of the Association of Family and Conciliation Courts." Portland, Oreg.: Association of Family and Conciliation Courts, 1984.

Moore, C. W. "Mediator Checklist." Denver, Colo.: Center for Dispute Resolution, 1981.

Moore, C. W. *Code of Professional Conduct.* Denver, Colo.: Colorado Council of Mediation Organizations and the Center for Dispute Resolution, 1982a.

Moore, C. W. *Natural Resources Conflict Management.* Boulder, Colo.: ACCORD Associates, 1982b.

Moore, C. W. "Obstacles to Effective Divorce Mediation." In J. Folberg and A. Milne (eds.), *Divorce Mediation.* New York: Guilford Press, forthcoming.

"Municipal Human Relations Commissions: Organizations and Programs." *Report No. 270.* Chicago: International City Managers' Association, 1966.

Murray, F. (ed.). *Where We Agree: Report of the National Coal Policy Project.* Boulder, Colo.: Westview Press, 1978.

Nader, L. "Styles of Court Procedure: To Make the Balance." In L. Nader (ed.), *Law in Culture and Society.* Chicago: Aldine, 1969.

Norton, P., and Mayer, S. "Involving Clinicians in Fee Collections: Implications for Improving Clinical Practice and Increasing Fee Income in a Community Mental Health Center." *Community Mental Health Journal,* 1981, *17* (3).

O'Hare, M., Bacow, L., and Sanderson, D. *Facility Siting and Public Opposition.* New York: Van Nostrand Reinhold, 1983.

Orenstein, S. G. "The Role of Mediation in Domestic Violence Cases." In H. Davidson and others (eds.), *Alternative Means of Family Dispute Resolution.* Washington, D.C.: American Bar Association, 1982.

Pearson, J. "Divorce Mediation: Strengths and Weaknesses over Time." In H. Davidson and others (eds.), *Alternative Means of Family Dispute Resolution.* Washington, D.C.: American Bar Association, 1982.

Pearson, J. "Denver Child Custody Project Final Report to the Piton Foundation and Colorado Bar Association." Denver, Colo.: Center for Policy Research, 1984.

Perez, F. A. "Evaluation of Mediation Techniques." *Labor Law Journal,* 1959, *10* (10), 716-720.

Peters, E. *Strategy and Tactics in Labor Negotiations.* New London, Conn.: National Foreman's Institute, 1955.

Phear, W. P. A conversation with the author at a meeting of the Association of Family and Conciliation Courts, Ethics Working Group, Keystone, Colo., Mar. 10-11, 1984.

Polsby, N. "How to Study Community Power." *Journal of Politics,* 1960, *22,* 474-484.

Pruitt, D. *Negotiation Behavior.* New York: Academic Press, 1981.

Pruitt, D., and Lewis, S. "The Psychology of Integrative Bargaining." In D. Druckman (ed.), *Negotiations: A Social Psychological Perspective.* Beverly Hills, Calif.: Sage, 1977.

Rapoport, A., and Chammah, A. M. "Sex Differences in Factors Contributing to the Level of Cooperation in the Prisoner's Dilemma Game." *Journal of Personality and Social Psychology,* 1965, *2,* 831-838.

Ray, L., and Smolover, D. *Consumer Dispute Resolution: Exploring the Alternatives.* Washington, D.C.: American Bar Association and U.S. Department of Consumer Affairs, 1983.

Reynolds, W., and Tonry, M. "Professional Mediation Services for Prisoner's Complaints." *American Bar Association Journal,* 1981, *67,* 294-297.

Ricci, I. *Mom's House, Dad's House.* New York: Collier Books, 1980.

Richardson, J., and Margulis, J. *The Magic of Rapport: The Business of Negotiation.* New York: Avon Books, 1984.

Richardson, S., Dohrenwend, B. S., and Klein, D. *Interviewing: Its Forms and Functions.* New York: Basic Books, 1965.

Riskin, L. "Mediation and Lawyers." *Ohio State Law Journal,* 1982, *43,* 29-60.

Rogers, C. "The Non-Directive Method as a Technique of Social Research." *American Journal of Sociology,* 1945, *50* (4), 279–283.

Rubin, J. (ed.). *Dynamics of Third Party Intervention: Kissinger in the Middle East.* New York: Praeger, 1981.

Rubin, J., and Brown, B. *Social Psychology of Bargaining and Negotiation.* New York: Academic Press, 1975.

Salem, R. "Mediating Political and Social Conflicts: The Skokie-Nazi Dispute." In J. A. Lemmon (ed.), *Community Mediation.* Mediation Quarterly, no. 5. San Francisco: Jossey-Bass, 1984.

Salius, A. J. (ed.). "Program Description: Services Provided in Minor Criminal Cases in the Geographical Area Courts." Unpublished manuscript, Family Division, Superior Court, State of Connecticut, 1983.

Saposnek, D. T. *Mediating Child Custody Disputes: A Systematic Guide for Family Therapists, Court Counselors, Attorneys, and Judges.* San Francisco: Jossey-Bass, 1983.

Saposnek, D. T. "What Is Fair in Child Custody Mediation." In J. A. Lemmon (ed.), *Making Ethical Decisions.* Mediation Quarterly, no. 8. San Francisco: Jossey-Bass, 1985.

Sawyer, J., and Guetzkow, H. "Bargaining and Negotiating in International Relations." In H. Kelman (ed.), *International Behavior: A Social Psychological Analysis.* New York: Holt, Rinehart & Winston, 1965.

Schein, E. *Process Consultation: Its Role in Organization Development.* Reading, Mass.: Addison-Wesley, 1969.

Schelling, T. "An Essay on Bargaining." *American Economic Review,* 1956, *46* (3), 281–306.

Schelling, T. *The Strategy of Conflict.* Cambridge, Mass.: Harvard University Press, 1960.

Schreiber, F. B. *Domestic Disturbances: Officer Safety and Calming Techniques.* St. Cloud, Minn.: Center for Studies in Criminal Justice, St. Cloud University, 1971.

Shallert, E. "Settlement of Civil Litigation in Federal Courts: The Judge's Role." Unpublished paper, Cambridge, Mass., 1982.

Shanahan, J., and others. *Negotiated Investment Strategy.* Dayton, Ohio: Kettering Foundation, 1982.

Shapiro, F. "Profiles: Mediator." *New Yorker,* 1970, *46,* 36–58.

Sharp, G. *Politics of Nonviolent Action.* Boston: Porter Sargent, 1973.

Shaw, M. "Mediating Between Parents and Children." In H. Davidson and others (eds.), *Alternative Means of Family Dispute Resolution.* Washington, D.C.: American Bar Association, 1982.

Sherif, M., and others. *Intergroup Conflict and Cooperation: The Robbers Cave Experiment.* Norman: University of Oklahoma Book Exchange, 1961.

Shonholtz, R. "Neighborhood Justice Systems: Work, Structure, and Guiding Principles." In J. A. Lemmon (ed.), *Community Mediation.* Mediation Quarterly, no. 5. San Francisco: Jossey-Bass, 1984.

Simkin, W. *Mediation and the Dynamics of Collective Bargaining.* Washington, D.C.: Bureau of National Affairs, 1971.

Simmel, G. *Conflict and the Web of Intergroup Affiliations.* New York: Free Press, 1955.

Simokaitis, M. *Preparing for Negotiations.* St. Louis, Mo.: Washington University Community Crisis Intervention Project, n.d.

Sommer, R. "Further Studies of Small Group Ecology." *Sociometry,* 1965, *28,* 337–348.

Sommer, R. *Personal Space: The Behavioral Basis of Design.* Englewood Cliffs, N.J.: Prentice-Hall, 1969.

Steinmetz, S., and Straus, M. *Violence in the Family.* New York: Harper & Row, 1974.

Stevens, C. *Strategy in Collective Bargaining Negotiations.* New York: McGraw-Hill, 1963.

Stewart, C., and Cash, W. *Interviewing: Principles and Practices.* Dubuque, Iowa: Brown, 1974.

Straus, D. "Managing Environmental Complexity: A New Look at Environmental Mediation." *Environment Science and Technology,* 1979, *13* (6), 661–665.

Straus, D., Clark, P., and Suskind, L. *Guidelines to Identify, Manage and Resolve Environmental Disputes.* New York: Research Institute, American Arbitration Association, n.d.

Straus, M. "A Sociological Perspective on the Prevention and Treatment of Wifebeatings." In M. Roy (ed.), *Battered Women.* New York: Van Nostrand Reinhold, 1977.

Stulberg, J. *Citizen Dispute Settlement: A Mediator's Manual.* Tallahassee, Fla.: Supreme Court of Florida, 1981a.

Stulberg, J. "The Theory and Practice of Mediation: A Reply to Professor Suskind." *Vermont Law Review,* 1981b, *6* (1), 85–117.

Survey Research Center. *Interviewer's Manual.* Ann Arbor: Survey Research Center, Institute for Social Research, University of Michigan, 1969.

Suskind, L. "Environmental Mediation and the Accountability Problem." *Vermont Law Review,* 1981, *6* (1), 1–47.

Talbot, A. *Settling Things: Six Case Studies in Environmental Mediation.* Washington, D.C.: Conservation Foundation, 1983.

Thibaut, J., and Kelly, H. *The Social Psychology of Groups.* New York: Wiley, 1959.

Thomas, K. "Conflict and Conflict Management." In M. Dunnette (ed.), *Handbook of Industrial and Organizational Psychology.* Chicago: Rand McNally, 1976.

Title X, Civil Rights Act, 1964, U.S. Code, *42,* Sec. 2000.

Van Zandt, H. "How to Negotiate in Japan." *Harvard Business Review,* Nov.–Dec. 1970, pp. 45–56.

Vorenberg, E. W. "State of the Art Survey of Dispute Resolution Programs Involving Juveniles." Dispute Resolution Papers, Section 1, American Bar Association, Special Committee on Alternative Means of Dispute Resolution (Division of Public Service Activities), July 1982.

Wall, J. "Mediation: An Analysis Review and Proposed Research." *Journal of Conflict Resolution,* 1981, *25* (1), 157–180.

Walton, J. "Substance and Artifact: The Current Research on Community Power Structure." *American Journal of Sociology,* 1966, *71* (4), 430–438.

Walton, R. *Interpersonal Peacemaking: Confrontations and Third Party Consultation.* Reading, Mass.: Addison-Wesley, 1969.

Walton, R., and McKersie, R. *A Behavioral Theory of Labor Negotiations.* New York: McGraw-Hill, 1965.

Warren, C. "The Hopeful Future of Mediation: Resolving Environmental Disputes Outside the Courts." In P. Baldwin (ed.), *Environmental Mediation: An Effective Alternative?* Palo Alto, Calif.: RESOLVE, Center for Environmental Conflict Resolution, 1978.

Watzlawick, P. *The Language of Change.* New York: Basic Books, 1978.

Wehr, P. *Conflict Regulation.* Boulder, Colo.: Westview Press, 1979.

Werner, L. *International Politics: Foundations of the System.* Minneapolis: University of Minnesota Press, 1974.

Wheeler, M. Lecture in Divorce Mediation Seminar, Boulder, Colo., Spring 1982.

Wicker, T. *A Time to Die.* New York: Quadrangle/New York Times, 1975.

Wildau, S. T. *Guidelines for Mediating Domestic Violence Cases.* Denver, Colo.: Center for Dispute Resolution, 1984.

Williams, G. *Legal Negotiation and Settlement.* St. Paul, Minn.: West, 1983.

Wixted, S. "The Children's Hearings Project: A Mediation Program for Children and Families." In H. Davidson and others (eds.), *Alternative Means of Family Dispute Resolution.* Washington, D.C.: American Bar Association, 1982.

Young, O. "Intermediaries: Additional Thoughts on Third Parties." *Journal of Conflict Resolution,* 1972, *16* (1), 51-65.

Zartman, I. W., and Berman, M. *The Practical Negotiator.* New Haven, Conn.: Yale University Press, 1982.

Index

A

Accommodation, strategy of, 68, 69-70
ACCORD Associates, xiv
Active listening, for responding to emotions, 128-129
Administrative dispute resolution, for conflicts, 5, 7
Africa, mediation in, 20
Agenda: approaches to setting, 182-185; mediator assistance with, 185-186; planning tentative, 120-122
Aiken, M., 83, 321
Air Quality Dialogues, 259
Alaska, state funding in, 295
Alternation: for agenda setting, 183; for options, 210
American Arbitration Association, 18, 21, 24, 53, 321
Antoun, R., 20, 321
Approaches and arenas for mediation: analysis of selecting, 61-77; background on, 61-62; commitment to, 74-75; conflict strategies for, 67-72; coordination of, 75-77; cost of, 72; criteria for selecting, 72-74; and disputant relationship, 73; general move categories in, 63-77; interest identification for, 63-64; and internal dynamics, 73; mediator-disputant relationship in, 62-63; and outcomes, 64-67; and power, 74; time of, 72-73
Arbitration, of conflicts, 5, 7
Argyris, C., 14, 73, 75, 104, 154, 321
Attica Prison, 290, 321
Aubert, V., 174, 178, 231, 321
Auerbach, J., 21, 321
Authority: and influence, 274-275; of mediator, 17, 156-157
Avoidance: for conflict management, 4, 5; of issues, 179; strategy of, 68, 69

B

Bach, G., 129, 321
Bacow, L., 235, 331
Bagozzi, R., 278, 322
Baldwin, P., 260, 296, 322

337

Bargaining stage, final: analysis of, 227-247; arbitrary procedures for, 237; and deadlines, 239-247; and incremental convergence, 228-231; issues postponed or abandoned in, 237-238; and leap to agreement, 231-233; mediator role in, 231, 232, 233-235; positional or interest-based, 35-39; and principled agreements, 233-235; procedural means for, 235-238; procedural timeline for, 236; situations in, 227-228; and third-party decision makers, 236-237
Bazerman, M., 215, 322
Begin, M., 230
Beginning stage: analysis of, 153-171; choosing an opening for, 167-168; communication facilitated in, 168-170; emotional climate positive in, 170-171; mediator tasks during, 153; opening negotiations in, 162-167; opening statements for, 154-162; turned over to disputants, 168
Behavioral guidelines: in beginning stage, 161-162; planning for, 119-120
Behn, R., 74, 322
Bellman, H., 34, 40, 322
Bellows, G., 74, 280, 322
Berger, P., 175, 322
Berkeley, A., 285, 324
Berkowitz, L., 131, 322
Berman, M., 140, 142-143, 204, 228, 232, 234-235, 336
Bernard, S., 34, 322
Best alternative to a negotiated agreement (BATNA), 226
Bethel, C., 23, 322
Bianchi, H., 19, 322
Biddle, A., 23, 322
Bingham, G., 23, 251, 322-323
Blake, R., 23, 69, 139, 166, 215, 323
Bluffs: and asymmetrical power, 281; on positions and interests, 194-196

Bonner, M., 24, 323
Bookstaff, H., 109, 327
Boulding, K., 175, 323
Brainstorming: for issues, 193; for options, 212-214
Brett, J., 23, 323
Bronstein, R., 107, 323
Brookmire, D., 212, 323
Brown, B., 14, 58, 124, 180, 195, 211-212, 229, 231, 278, 285, 323, 333
Brown, D., 20, 323
Brown, L. D., 23, 323
Brown, L. M., 256, 323
Building-block approach: for agenda setting, 184-185; for option generation, 204-205
Burgess, H., 147, 323-324
Burton, J., 166, 324

C

California: Community Boards in, 110; legitimacy issue in, 137-138; marital conciliation court in, 49-50
Canada, open meetings in, 110
Carpenter, S., xiv, 23, 57, 78n, 259, 324
Carter, J., 215
Cash, W., 81, 91, 334
Catholic Church, mediation by, 19
Caucuses: analysis of strategies for, 263-271; and bluffs, 194; confidentiality of, 267-268, 270; and deadlines, 243; explanation of, 159-160; facilities for, 114; and inflated expectations, 225; for issue identification, 181-182; location of, 265; and manipulation, 269-271; need for, 263-264; nonverbal communication in, 150; protocol for, 265-269; timing of, 264-265; for venting emotions, 129-130
Center for Dispute Resolution, xiv, 52, 308-311
Chalmers, E., 22, 324
Chammah, A. M., 140, 332

Chandler, J. P., 212, 324

Change, reinforcing, and misperceptions, 135-137

China, and mediation, 20, 21

China, People's Republic of, People's Conciliation Committees in, 20

Civil Rights Act of 1964, Title X of, 21-22, 335

Civil rights disputes, mediation for, 21-22

Clark, P., 64-65, 252, 255-256, 258, 259, 291, 324, 334

Clark-McGlennon Associates, 50, 324

Cohen, A., 24, 324

Cohen, H., 145, 242, 289, 324

Colorado: data dispute in, 102; Public Utilities Commission of, 52. See also Denver

Colorado Council of Mediation Organizations, 299n

Colosi, T., 285, 324

Columbus, Ohio, open meetings in, 110

Comeau, E., 50, 160, 324

Commitment: to approaches and arenas, 74-75; in beginning stage, 162; in entry stage, 54-55; to options, reducing, 201-203; and planning, 104, 122; to settlement, 253-255

Communication: in beginning stage, 168-170; and conciliation, 143-147; and degree of formality, 151; with gestures, eye contact, and demeanor, 148-149; and hypothesis building, 28; and issues language, 180-182; managing, 144-147; mediator power over, 272; nonverbal, and conciliation, 147-152; and objects, 151-152; and space, 149-151; techniques for, 169-170; timing of, 146

Community disputes: bargaining in, 235; beginning stage in, 156; entry stage of, 45, 50, 51, 56; funding mediation in, 293, 294, 295, 296; issue defining in, 173, 179;

mediation for, 22; options in, 205; power in, 282; settlement stage in, 252, 259-260, 261; team negotiations in, 284, 287

Community Relations Service (CRS), 21-22

Competition, strategy of, 67-68

Compromise, negotiated, 68, 70

Conciliation: approaches for, 124-152; background on, 124-125; and communication, 143-147; concept of, 124; and legitimacy, 137-140; and misperceptions or stereotypes, 132-137; and nonverbal communication, 147-152; and perception of trust, 140-143; and perceptual problems, 137-140; and strong emotions, 125-132

Confidentiality: in caucuses, 267-268, 270; limits of, 118-119, 160; professional code on, 302; waiver and consent form for, 310-311

Conflict: administrative dispute resolution for, 5, 7; approaches to managing and resolving, 1-12; arbitration of, 5, 7; and avoidance, 4, 5; causes and interventions for, 27; causes of, 101-102; emerging, 16; example of, 1-3; extralegal approaches for, 5, 8-10; informal discussions for, 4, 5; judicial approach for, 5, 7-8; latent, 16; legislative approach for, 5, 8; levels of, 16-17; manifest, 16-17; mediation approach for, 5, 6; negotiation approach to, 5, 6; nonviolent action for, 5, 9; purity of, 64; realistic and unrealistic, 101, 125-127; role of, ix; symbolic termination of, 260-261; violence for, 5, 9-10

Conflict analysis, and data collection, 96

Connecticut, open meetings in, 110

Coogler, O. J., 23, 41, 54, 120, 272, 296, 325

Cook, J., 24, 45-46, 48, 251, 254, 325
Cooperation, affirmation of, 155. *See also* Conciliation
Coordination: of approaches and arenas, 75-77; options for, 76-77
Coover, V., xiv, 97, 287, 325
Cormick, G., 22, 23, 34, 49, 57, 324, 325, 329
Coser, L., 16, 101, 125, 248, 260, 325
Credibility: building, in entry stage, 50-52; in interviewing, 86-87
Creighton, J., 128, 142, 198, 325
Criminal justice system: and deadlines, 239; and mediation, 22-23
Cross, J., 187, 239, 325
Crowfoot, J., 57, 73, 325
Cummings, F., 64-65, 324
Curle, A., 16, 124, 132, 325

                        D

Dahl, R., 84, 325
D'Antonio, W., 83, 325
Data collection: approaches to, 78-102; background on, 78-79; and conflict analysis, 96; decision-making approach to, 84; by direct observation, 80; entry for, 56-57; factors in, 79; framework for analysis of, 79-80; and information integration, 97-100; and interpreting data, 100-102; by interviews, 81-82, 84-95; methods of, 80-82; on people, 97, 98; persons appropriate for, 82; positional approach to, 83; purposes for, 78-79; on relationships and dynamics, 97, 99; and reporting, 96; reputational approach to, 83-84; from secondary sources, 80; strategy selection for, 83-87; on substantive issues, 99-100; and verifying data, 100
Davis, R., 46, 325
Deacon, E., xiv, 97, 287, 325
Deadlines: in bargaining, 239-242; characteristics of, 240-242; dangers of, 245-246; mediator management of, 242-246; usefulness of, 246-247
Delbecq, A., 214, 325
Dembart, L., 49, 50, 282, 325-326
Denver: funding in, 296; mediation rejection rates in, 46; options generation in, 206; timing and setting issues in, 146-147
Denver Water Board, 147
Deutsch, M., 140, 143-144, 229, 326
Dholakia, R., 278, 322
Discussion groups, for options, 214
Disputants: beginning stage turned over to, 168; capability of, 31, 34; funding for, 296; hidden interests of, 187-198; mediator relationship with, 62-63; planning for, 105-110; power equality between, 34-35; psychological conditions of, 116-119, 166-167; teams of, 282-293
Dohrenwend, B. S., 93, 332
Douglas A., 59, 125, 130, 293, 326
Downing, T., 45, 326
Doyle, M., 287, 326
Dubois, R., 166, 326

                        E

Eckhoff, T., 17, 326
Education on mediation: in entry stage, 53-54; planning for, 122
Egypt: and first offer, 230; and negotiating document, 215
Emotions: active listening for, 128-129; in beginning stage, 170-171; and conciliation, 125-132; legitimacy of, 139-140; manifestations of, 127; negative transference of, 126; realistic and unrealistic, 125-127; recognizing, 155; responding to, 127-129; restimulation of, 126; suppressing, 131-132; venting, 129-131
Entry: analysis of, 44-60; by appointment, 49-50; contact letter for, 308-309; for data collection, 56-57; by direct invitation, 44-

47; implementing, 55-56; initiated by mediator, 48-49; means of, 44-50; mediator tasks in, 50-55; and problem-solving timing, 57-60; by referral from secondary parties, 47-48; timing of, 56-60

Environmental Protection Agency, 147

Epstein, A., 20, 326

Erickson, E., 83, 325

Esser, C., xiv, 97, 287, 325

Europe, mediation in, 19-20

F

Family disputes: bargaining in, 235, 244; beginning stage in, 167; conciliation stage in, 134, 141; and confidentiality of caucus, 270; data collection in, 82; entry stage in, 46, 49-50; funding in, 296; hidden interests in, 188; issue defining in, 175-176; mediation for, 23; and mediator power, 272, 282; mediator's role in, 40, 41; options in, 203, 210-211, 215; participants in, 105, 138; power in, 279; sample settlement of, 314-320; settlement stage of, 249, 252, 258, 261; strategies in, 64, 69

Federal Mediation and Conciliation Service, 21, 40, 274

Felsteiner, W., 22, 326

Filley, A., 113, 181, 212, 326

Fisch, R., 186, 326

Fisher, R., 35, 109, 123, 130, 136, 139, 142, 143, 166, 183, 192, 204, 212, 215, 216-217, 219, 225, 226, 228, 232, 254, 262, 273, 280, 326-327

Fisher, R. W., 166, 327

Fixed-sum negotiations, outcomes possible in, 219-220

Florida, executive action in, 259

Folberg, J., 24, 54, 108, 109, 118, 160, 327

Folger, J., 34, 322

Ford Foundation, 296

Form, W., 83, 325

Freedman, L., 109, 327

Freire, P., 191, 327

Freud, S., 126, 327

Frost, J., 285, 327

G

Galper, M., 215, 327

Galtung, J., 24, 327

Gandhi, M., 298

Gary, Indiana, open meetings in, 110

Ginsberg, R. B., 20, 327

Goffman, E., 24, 133, 327

Goldberg, H., 129, 321

Goldberg, S., 23, 323

Golten, M. M., xiv

Gordon, T., 93, 128, 139, 328

Grayson, D., 46, 325

Green, E., xv

Grey, R., xv

Guetzkow, H., 175, 333

Gulliver, P. H., 4, 6, 20, 182-183, 227-228, 328

Gustafson, D., 214, 325

H

Haile, C., 109, 327

Hall, E. T., 149-150, 328

Hamilton, P., 62, 328

Harter, P., 23, 328

Haynes, J., 23, 34, 41, 109, 176, 282, 328

Henley, N., 147-148, 150, 328

Hewlett Foundation, 296

Hinde, R., 148, 328

Hoffman, L., 212, 330

Hokanson, J., 131, 328

Hunter, F., 83, 328

Hypothesis building, and interventions, 26-29

Hypothetical modeling: of interests, 192; for options, 214

I

Impartiality: and asymmetrical power, 281-282; concept of, 15-16; professional code on, 302; statement of, 157-158

Implementation: and compliance criteria, 250-251; concept of, 248; of entry stage, 55-56; factors in, 250; grievance procedures for, 253; monitoring, 251-253; of settlement, 248-250

Independent Petroleum Association of the Mountain States, 290

Influence or power: and approaches and arenas, 74; assessment of, 280; associational, 273-274; asymmetrical, 280-282; and authority, 274-275; coercive, 277-278; concept of, 271; equality of, 34-35; forms of, 272-278; of mediators, 271-282; in options, 211; symmetrical, 278-280; of team members, 285-286

Informal discussions, for conflict management, 4, 5

Interests: acceptance and agreement for, 196-198; analysis of uncovering, 187-198; for approaches and arenas, 63-64; as bargaining base, 35-39; bluffs on, 194-196; concept of, 37-38; difficulties in identifying, 187-189; direct moves for discovering, 192-193; indirect moves for discovering, 191-192; in integrative options, 210-211; as issue base, 174, 176-178; legitimacy of, 139; opening focus on, 164; in options generation, 208-212; and positions equated, 189; procedures for identifying, 189-190; productive attitudes toward, 190-191; strategy of, 68, 71; substantive, 37; testing of, 192

Interpersonal disputes: deadlines in, 246-247; funding mediation of, 293; issue reframing in, 177-178; nonverbal communication in, 148-149; options in, 203, 209-211; power in, 279; settlement stage of, 249, 252

Intervention: concept of, 14; focus of, 43; level of, 42; target of, 42-43

Interviews: appropriate approach for, 87-90; data collection type of, 81-82; format of, 89-90; questioning and listening in, 90-95; rapport and credibility in, 86-87; recording information in, 94-95; sequence of, 84-85; structure of, 88-89; timing of, 85-86

Irving, H., 23, 328

Isolation, as avoidance, 69

Israel: and first offer, 230; and legitimacy issue, 138; and negotiating document, 215

Issues: analysis of defining, 172-186; avoidance of, 179; in bargaining, postponed or abandoned, 237-238; complexity of, 39; consensual or dissensual types of, 174; fractionation of, 204-205; identifying and framing, 175-176; interest-based, 174, 176-178; language and syntax for, 180-182; legitimacy of, 139; opening focus on, 164; reframing variables for, 176-179; and superordinate goals, 179; timing for reframing of, 180; and topic areas, 173-175; unnecessary, 174-175, 238; value-based, 174, 178-179; variables in defining, 172-173

J

Jackins, H., 126, 129, 328

Japan: mediation in, 20; performance bonds in, 260

Jennings, M. K., 83, 328

Jesus, 19

Jewish rabbis, as mediators, 19-20, 21

Jick, T., 25, 329

Jordan, mediation in, 20

Judicial approach: for conflict resolution, 5, 7-8; for settlement supervision, 258

Juniper Street Collective, xv
Jusdon, S., xv
Justice, types of, 235

K

Kakwirakeron, 53
Kelly, H., 140, 271, 328, 335
Keltner, J., 269, 328
Kennedy, W. J. D., xiv, 23, 57, 78n, 259, 324
Kerr, C., 57, 292, 328
Kessler, S., 125, 329
Kettering Foundation, 23, 61, 110
Kheel, T., 45, 246
Klein, D., 93, 332
Kochan, T., 25, 329
Kochman, T., 149, 329
Kolb, D., 34, 40, 41, 116, 244, 272, 287, 288, 329
Kraybill, R., 15, 329
Kriesberg, L., 64, 329
Kwartler, R., 22, 49, 50, 53, 282, 325-326, 329

L

Labor-management disputes: and deadlines, 239, 246; entry stage in, 45, 49, 50; funding mediation for, 293, 295; issue reframing in, 177; legitimacy in, 137-138; mediation for, 21; and mediator power, 272, 282; mediator's role in, 40; options in, 209, 215; physical setting for, 113-114; power in, 279; settlement stage in, 258; timing in, 146
Labor-Management Relations Act of 1947, 21, 329
Lake, L., 23, 240, 329
Lakey, B., xiv
Landlord-tenant disputes: issue reframing in, 181; mediation of, 24; participants in, 106
Landsberger, H., 50, 130, 329
Lansford, H., 47, 50, 110, 329
Latin America, mediation in, 20
Laue, J., 34, 329

Law Enforcement Assistance Administration, 295
Lawyers, as participants, 107-108
Lederach, J. P., 20, 329
Legislative approach: for conflict resolution, 5, 8; for settlements, 258-259
Legitimacy: concept of, 137-138; and conciliation, 137-140; of emotions, 139-140; of issues and interests, 139; of person or party, 138-139
Levinson, D., 166, 329-330
Lewicki, R., 215, 322
Lewis, S., 192, 209, 332
Li, V., 20, 330
Lincoln, W. F., 22, 48, 163-164, 165-166, 282, 284, 287, 330
Listening, active, and emotions, 128-129
Logistics, described in beginning stage, 160-161
Logrolling, for options, 209-210
Loomis, C., 83, 325
Lovell, H., 34, 330
Luckmann, T., 175, 322

M

McCarthy, J., 22, 49, 330
McIsaac, H., 295, 330
McKersie, R., 35, 133, 135-136, 212, 225, 228, 335
McSurely, A., 283, 330
McWhinney, R., 110, 330
Maggiolo, W., 145, 262, 266, 267, 330
Maier, N., 212, 330
Margulis, J., 94, 332
Maslow, A., 154, 330
Massachusetts, state funding in, 295
Mayer, B. S., xiv, xv, 23, 258, 330-331
Mayer, J., xv
Mayer, P., xv
Mayer, S., xv, 331
Mayer, T., xv
Media, planning for, 109-110
Mediation: agenda setting stage of,

182-185; analysis of process of, 1-43; arenas of, 19-24; assessing options stage of, 218-226; barriers to study of, x-xi; beginning stage of, 153-171; code of professional conduct for, 299-307; concept of, 6, 13-19, 118; conciliation in, 124-152; conclusion on, 297-298; conditions for, 11-12; conducting, 153-217; for conflict resolution, 5, 6; data collection and analysis for, 78-102; defined, 155-157; elements in, 13-19; entry stage of, 44-60; final bargaining stage of, 227-247; formal settlement stage of, 248-261; funding of, 293-296; future of, 297-298; goal of, 38; groundwork for, 44-152; hidden interests in, 187-198; history of, 19-21; hypothesis building and interventions in, 26-29; issue definition stage of, 172-186; moves and interventions in, 24-26; negotiation related to, 6, 14; options generating stage of, 199-217; planning for, 103-123; procedures for, 13-43, 158-159; refusal of, 46; selecting strategy for, 61-77; special situations in, 262-296; stages of, 29-30, 32-33; termination of, 304; variables influencing strategies and moves in, 30-43; as voluntary, 19

Mediators: acceptability of, 14-15; agenda setting role of, 185-186; authority of, 17, 156-157; bargaining role of, 231, 232, 233-235; beginning stage tasks of, 153; caucus roles of, 267; deadline management by, 242-246; disputant relationship with, 62-63; entry initiated by, 48-49; entry tasks of, 50-55; functions of, 17-18; goal of, 17; introduction of, 154-155; issue-defining tasks of, 172; and negotiation teams, 287, 288-289, 291-293; power and influence of, 271-282;

procedural orientation for, 40; professional responsibilities of, 300-307; rewards controlled by, 276-277; role definition for, 39-43, 155-157; substantive orientation for, 41; training and education of, 305-306

Melanesia, mediation in, 20
Mernitz, S., 23, 331
Metcalf, K., 110, 330
Metropolitan Water Roundtable, 206, 296
Mew Soong Li, 166, 326
Mexico, mediation in, 20
Milne, A., 167, 331
Misperceptions or stereotypes: and association or disassociation, 135; and common association, 135; and conciliation, 132-137; and mask-mirage analogy, 132-133; and reinforcing change, 135-137; and similar attitudes, 133-135

Moore, B., xv
Moore, B., xv
Moore, C. W., xiv, 23, 36, 65-71, 74, 97, 118, 120-122, 163-166, 287, 299n, 325, 331
Mott, P., 83, 321
Moulton, B., 74, 280, 322
Mouton, J., 23, 69, 139, 166, 215, 323
Movement for a New Society, Training Affinity Group of, xiv
Moves: in approaches and arenas, 63-77; concept of, 24; contingent, 25-26; for interest discovering, 191-193; noncontingent, 25; variables influencing, 30-43
Murray, F., 259, 296, 331

N

Nader, L., 20, 331
National Coal Policy Project, 259, 296
National Institute of Dispute Resolution, 295, 296
Negative transference: of emotions, 126; and offers, 230

Negotiated compromise, strategy of, 68, 70

Negotiated Investment Strategy, 23, 61, 110

Negotiating document, single-text, for options, 215

Negotiation: concept of, 6; conditions for, 10-11; for conflict resolution, 5, 6; mediation related to, 6, 14; location of, 110-112; opening, 162-167; planning for, 105-110, 115; and strategies, 35-39

Neighborhood Justice Centers (NJCs), 22

Neutrality: and asymmetrical power, 281-282; as avoidance, 69; concept of, 15-16; professional code on, 302; statement of, 157-158

New Jersey, state funding in, 295

New York: rapport in, 53; team negotiation in, 290

Nominal group process, for options, 214

Nonviolent action, for conflict resolution, 5, 9

Norton, P., 294, 331

O

Offers, in final bargaining, 229-231

O'Hare, M., 235, 331

Oppenheimer, M., xiv

Options: analysis of generating, 199-217; assessing, 218-226; awareness of need for, 200-204; commitment to, reducing, 201-203; interests in, 208-212; and positional bargaining and counterproposals, 207-208; procedures for generating, 206-216; strategies for generating, 204-206; strong and weak types of, 216-217

Orenstein, S. G., 23, 331

Organizational disputes: data collection in, 83; entry stage in, 56; interests in, 196-197; issue re-

framing in, 178; mediation for, 23; options in, 202; settlement stage in, 252, 255

Outcomes: and approaches and arenas, 64-67; compromise, 65, 66; impasse, 65, 66; win-lose, 65-66, 67-68; win-win, 65, 67

P

Palestine Liberation Organization, 138

Parker, S., xiv

Participants. See Disputants

Pearson, J., 46, 57, 58, 251, 332

Perez, F. A., 34, 59-60, 282, 332

Persuasion, and bluffs, 195

Peters, E., 332

Phear, W. P., 40, 332

Physical arrangements, planning for, 112-114

Planning stage: agenda setting in, 120-122; approaches to designing, 103-123; background on, 103-105; and behavioral guidelines, 119-120; concept of, 103; for education, 122; for issues, interests, and settlement options, 115-116; issues of, 104-105; for location of negotiations, 110-112; and media, 109-110; for negotiation, 115; for participants in negotiations, 105-110; for physical arrangements, 112-114; and psychological condition of participants, 116-119; and special problems, 123

Polsby, N., 84, 332

Positions: as bargaining basis, 35-39; bluffs on, 194-196; as data collection approach, 83; interests equated with, 189; offers inhibited in bargaining from, 229-231; opening focus on, 164; and options, 207-208

Power. See Influence or power

Principles: in agenda setting, 183-184; and bargaining agreements, 233-235; to options generation, 205-206

Procedure, opening focus on, 165-166

Pruitt, D., 142, 192, 209, 332

Psychological conditions of disputants: and planning, 116-119; opening focus on, 166-167

Public policy disputes: beginning stage in, 166-167; conciliation stage in, 133-134; data collection in, 82, 101-102; deadlines in, 240; entry stage in, 48, 49, 52, 53; funding mediation in, 295, 296; hidden interests in, 193, 195-196; issue reframing in, 179; mediation for, 23; mediator's role in, 40, 41; options in, 203, 206; participants in, 109-110; power in, 282; settlement stage in, 259; strategies in, 61, 70; team negotiations in, 290-291; timing and setting in, 147

Q

Questions, interview types of, 91-94

R

Rapoport, A., 140, 332

Rapport: establishing, in entry stage, 52-53; in interviewing, 86-87

Rationalization, and bluffs, 195

Ray, L., 24, 332

Reframing, of issues variables, 176-179

Resistance points, and settlement range, 220

Resource persons: outside, for options, 215-216; as participants, 107-109

Resources, expansion of, for options, 209

Reynolds, W., 23, 332

Ricci, I., 54, 125, 176, 215, 332

Richardson, J., 94, 332

Richardson, S., 93, 332

Riskin, L., 107, 332

Rochl, J., 24, 45-46, 48, 251, 254, 325

Rocky Mountain Oil and Gas Association, 290

Rogers, C., 128, 333

Rowley, 53

Rubin, J., 14, 47, 58, 124, 180, 211-212, 229, 278, 285, 333

S

Sadat, A., 230

St. Paul, Minnesota, open meetings in, 110

Salem, R., 22, 333

Salius, A. J., 295, 333

Sanderson, D., 235, 331

Saposnek, D., 23, 40, 41, 189, 256, 333

Sawyer, J., 175, 333

Schein, E., 54, 333

Schelling, T., 107, 250, 333

Schreiber, F. B., 114, 333

Secondary parties, as participants, 107

Segal, L., 186, 326

Settlement: acceptable field of, 223-224; achieving formal, 248-261; analysis of reaching, 218-296; assessing options for, 218-226; balance in, 257; clarity and detail of, 256-257; commitment to, 253-255; externally executed, 254-260; final bargaining for, 227-247; formalizing, 253-261; implementing, 248-250; and indemnification agreement, 259-260; judicial supervision of, 258; as legal contracts, 255-260; legislative action from, 258-259; and monitoring performance agreement, 251-253; options for, 199-217; and performance bonds, 260; positive view in, 257-258; professional code on, 303-304; range in, 219-226; samples of, 312-320; self-executing, 249, 253-254; and symbolic termination activities, 260-261

Settlement range: approaches to, 219-223; and bargaining range, 219-221; and cooperative problem solving, 222-223; and inflated expectations, 224-226; negative, 221-222, 226; positive, 220-221; recognizing, 223-226

Shallert, E., 239, 333

Shanahan, J., 23, 61, 333

Shapiro, F., 45, 146, 240, 246, 293, 333

Sharp, G., 9, 334

Shaw, M., 23, 334

Shepard, D., 24, 45-46, 48, 251, 254, 325

Shepard, H., 69, 323

Sherif, M., 179, 334

Shonholtz, R., 22, 110, 334

Simkin, W., 21, 57, 334

Simmel, G., 266, 334

Simokaitis, M., 74, 334

Singer, L., 23, 322

Singson-Whittamore dispute: background of, 1-3; conflict management approaches in, 4, 6, 7, 8, 9, 10-12; negotiation procedures for, 35, 36, 37-38; sample settlement for, 312-313

Sistrunk F., 212, 323

Skokie, Illinois, mediation in, 22

Sloma, R., 139, 323

Smith, R., 24, 324

Smolover, D., 24, 332

Sohermerhorn, R., 166, 329-330

Sommer, R., 113, 334

Spain, water court in, 20

Steinmetz, S., 131, 334

Stevens, C., 136, 168, 194, 195, 207, 212, 239, 269, 289, 292, 334

Stewart, C., 81, 91, 334

Strategies: for approaches and arenas, 67-72; and complexity of issues, 39; and conflict development and timing of entry, 31; for data collection, 83-87; and definitions of mediator's role, 39-43; and disputant capability, 31, 34; and negotiation procedures, 35-39; and power equality, 34-35; selection of, 61-77; variables influencing, 30-43

Straus, D., 109, 252, 255-256, 258, 259, 287, 291, 326, 334

Straus, M., 131, 334

Stulberg, J., 19, 34, 40, 90, 107, 114, 117, 175, 181, 272, 335

Substance: data collection on, 99-100; in interests, 37; as mediator orientation, 41; opening focus on, 163-164

Survey Research Center, 86, 335

Suskind, L., 34, 41, 252, 255-256, 258, 259, 291, 334, 335

T

Talbot, A., 23, 335

Target point, and settlement range, 219-220

Taylor, A., 24, 54, 109, 118, 160, 327

Tchozewski, C., xv

Teams, negotiating: analysis of, 282-293; with constituents, 289-293; for data collection, 82; decision making by, 286-287; dynamics and strategies of, 284-287; forming, 283-284; influence on, 285-286; and mediators, 287, 288-289, 291-293; types of negotiations by, 287-289

Telephone companies dispute: agenda setting in, 183-184; complexity of, 39; planning stage for, 104

Terry, S., xiv

Texas, state funding in, 295

Therapists, as participants, 108-109

Thibaut, J., 271, 335

Thomas, K., 64-65, 335

Tichane, M., 46, 325

Timing: of caucuses, 264-265; of communication, 146; of entry, 56-60; of interviews, 85-86; of issues reframing, 180. See also Deadlines

Timothy, 19

Tone setting, planning for, 116-118
Tonry, M., 23, 332
Trust: base of, 140-142; building, 142-143; perception of, 140-143. *See also* Conciliation

U

U.S. Air Force Academy, 113-114
U.S. Army Corps of Engineers, 259
United States Conciliation Service, 21
U.S. Department of Health and Human Services, 295
U.S. Department of Justice, 21, 295
U.S. Department of Labor, 21
United Farmworkers Union, 137-138
Ury, W., 35, 130, 183, 192, 204, 212, 215, 219, 226, 327

V

Values as issue base, 174, 178-179
Vandeven, A., 214, 325
Van Zandt, H., 149, 335
Vaupel, J., 74, 322
Violence, for conflict resolution, 5, 9-10
Vorenberg, E. W., 110, 295, 335

W

Wall, J., 262, 282, 335

Walton, J., 83, 335
Walton, R., 35, 133, 135-136, 166, 212, 225, 228, 335
Warren, C., 208, 335-336
Washington: executive action in, 259; mediator initiative in, 49
Watzlawick, P., 175, 336
Weakland, J., 186, 326
Wehr, P., xiv, 26, 336
Weingarten, H., 34, 322
Werner, L., 20, 336
Wheeler, M., 15, 336
Wicker, T., 290, 336
Wigington, N., xv
Wildau, S. T., xiv, xv, 23, 336
Williams, G., 108, 336
Williams, L., 22, 326
Wilmot, W., 285, 327
Wilson, N., xiv
Wirth, T., 146-147
Wisconsin, state funding in, 295
Withdrawal, as avoidance, 69
Wixted, S., 23, 336
Woodrow, P., xiv

Y

Young, O., 15, 145, 163, 176-177, 230, 249, 269-270, 336

Z

Zartman, I. W., 140, 142-143, 204, 228, 232, 234-235, 336
Zumeta, Z., 34, 322